WILD JAMS
and
JELLIES

WILD JAMS
and
JELLIES

*Delicious Recipes
Using 75 Wild Edibles*

JOE FREITUS AND SALLI HABERMAN

STACKPOLE
BOOKS

Published by
STACKPOLE BOOKS
5067 Ritter Rd.
Mechanicsburg, PA 17055
www.stackpolebooks.com

Printed in the United States of America

10 9 8 7 6 5 4 3 2 1

This is a significantly revised and updated edition of the book *Wild Preserves: Illus-
trated Recipes for Over 100 Natural Jams and Jellies*, originally published in 1977 by
Stone Wall Press.

Cover design by Wendy A. Reynolds

Cover credits: jar image © John Foxx/Alamy; photo of Viburnum trilobum *© 2005
Steven Foster*

Plant illustrations © Salli Haberman

Library of Congress Cataloguing-in-Publication Data

Freitus, Joe.
   [Wild preserves]
   Wild jams and jellies : delicious recipes using 75 wild edibles / Joe Freitus and Salli
Haberman.
      p. cm.
   Originally published: Wild preserves. Washington, D.C. : Stone Wall Press, 1977.
   ISBN-13: 978-0-8117-3247-5
   ISBN-10: 0-8117-3247-9
   1. Jam. 2. Jelly. 3. Cookery (Wild foods) 4. Wild plants, Edible. I. Haberman, Salli.
II. Freitus, Joe. Wild preserves. III. Title.

TX612.J3F73 2005
641.8'52—dc22
                              2005021507

To Euell Gibbons,
who made the world a better place to live;
whose love of nature and its plentiful bounty
gave us a renewed interest in natural foods;
whose name will be remembered forever

CONTENTS

INTRODUCTION

MANY COOKBOOKS HAVE A SECTION ON HOW TO PREPARE PRE-serves. Others deal specifically with the preparation of jams and jellies. Nonetheless, there are few in-depth guides for the person who wants to focus on wild edibles. For many years we have been preparing jellies and other preserves from wild fruit, and we have experimented with many household and wild-food cookbooks in order to adapt and adopt final recipes.

Our goal in this book is to share our recipes and our practical approach to preserving edible wild fruit, which is an abundant and delicious natural resource. It also has information on plant identification to help you locate wild edibles. The drawings and plant descriptions will serve as a handy reference as you go about the countryside, foraging for ripe fruit.

You will notice that the book's basic recipes occasionally repeat themselves with little or no variation. This is to allow you to continue working without having to flip back and forth in the book. Where the fruit from a particular plant species is similar to other species, we have treated them as one. However, in the case of the Viburnums, we have separated most of them because of differences in quantity, taste, pectin, and so forth.

We hope this book will open up a new gastronomic world for you—a world of tasty and nutritious jellies, jams, preserves, conserves, marmalades, leathers, butters, wines, and dried foods.

How to Prepare
JAMS, JELLIES,
and
OTHER
PRESERVES

JELLIES, JAMS, PRESERVES, CONSERVES, MARMALADES, LEATHERS, and butters can add zest and a touch of color to a meal. Dwell on the thought of homemade blueberry jam on hot toast on a frosty winter morning—a touch of summer splashed against a frigid winter. Jellied fruits have long been the pride of farmwives competing for blue ribbons at country fairs and club shows. The making of jellies, jams, and preserves offers both men and women an opportunity to be highly creative; we greatly enjoy experimenting with fruit combinations, colors, and flavors. And the flavor of a colorful jam is always enhanced by the knowledge that you made it yourself.

Making jellies and jams is also an excellent way to utilize the abundance of wild fruit in your area. Irregularly shaped or bruised fruit can be used despite its outward appearance. Many people hesitate to use such fruit because they are used to eating store-bought foodstuffs. In preservation, however, the fruit is reduced to a common pulp by the cooking process. It all tastes great in the end.

TYPES OF PRESERVES

The recipes in this book are basically alike in that they have acidic fruit being preserved with granulated sugar and cooked in order to provide some degree of gelling. They can be divided up into the following categories:

Jelly

Made from the acidic juice of fruit. When cooked with granulated sugar, the final product is translucent and will hold its shape. Good jelly quivers and can be cut with a knife.

Jam
Made from crushed fruit; often contains the skins of the fruit. When cooked with granulated sugar, it has a jellylike consistency but will not hold its shape.

Preserves
Whole or chopped fruit cooked in a thick sugar syrup. It may or may not gell. Fruit can be preserved by one of several methods: cooking it in a syrup, sugaring the prepared fruit, allowing it to stand in sugar and juice, or pouring a sugar-and-water syrup over the fruit.

Conserve
A blend of more than one fruit, usually prepared like jam. May contain a variety of condiments, such as nuts and raisins.

Marmalade
Generally considered to be a special type of jam. It is usually made with citrus fruits such as oranges, lemons, kumquats, and grapefruits. The entire fruit may be used, excluding the seeds, if there are any.

Leather
Made from a fruit puree that is allowed to dry in a thin layer. It may then be rolled or combined with condiments for extra flavor and visual appeal. Often called the jerky of dried fruit.

Butter
Made from blended or pureed fruits that are cooked for a considerable length of time in order to obtain a very smooth consistency. Often the unused pulp from jelly-making can be made into an excellent butter. Butters frequently rely on the taste of the fruit rather than the sweetness of added sugar.

WORKING WITH WILD EDIBLES
It is unwise to assume that all wild or commercial fruits have all of the properties needed to produce good-quality jellies and jams. There are differences in all food products. The level of acidity is an important

factor in good jelly-making, and wild fruits may or may not be more acidic than commercial varieties. Most recipes in standard cookbooks are based on the predictable ranges of fruit pH, size, pulp content, and quantity of juice found in commercial fruit. These ranges are often dramatically different in wild plants, and attempts to adapt conventional recipes may end in failure. This book contains workable recipes intended specifically for use with edible wild fruits.

There are a few basic rules that one must abide by when working with wild fruit. Remember, however, that they do not necessarily pertain to commercial species, and you may ruin a recipe if they are applied that way.

• Not all edible wild fruits contain natural pectin. Those that do may have varying concentrations.

• Fruit that is underripe usually gells best; fully ripened fruit provides a richer flavor. Therefore, it is wise to use a combination of underripe and fully ripened fruit.

• The highest-quality jellies and jams are made by preparing small batches at a time.

• Use no more than the required amounts of water in the cooking process, as water dilutes color and flavor.

• If you use water that has a high concentration of chemicals such as chlorine, it will flavor your final product. Boil out the chlorine or purchase good demineralized water.

• Do not boil juice, pulp, or fruit longer than necessary—make it quick and short.

• Always use sterile, hot jars in the final steps to keep the bacteria away.

• Always store your completed product someplace cool and dark. Direct sunlight destroys color and often upsets the consistency of the gel.

• Before drying herbs and wild fruits, always wash and clean them very carefully, removing damaged areas.

PECTIN

Most individuals go about the jelly- and jam-making process without any real knowledge of the chemistry of pectin and how it works.

Pectin is the name given to a group of plant substances that under certain conditions will form gels. It serves as binding material for plant cells and is therefore found in practically all types of plant growth, especially fruit.

Chemically, pectin is a mixture of complex carbohydrates, araban, and pectic acid. During the jam-making process, the pectic acid is extracted using alcohol, leaving behind the araban. Because of its stable gelling properties, pectin permits the storage of fruits as jellies, jams, and preserves. It is also of considerable nutritional value.

Many fruits lack pectin in sufficient concentrations to effectively yield a gel. Others, such as apples, grapes, currants, and plums, have high pectin concentrations and yield excellent gels.

Fruits high in natural pectin

Apple, all types	Grape (underripe)
Barberry	Irish Moss
Blackberry (underripe)	Mountain Ash
Carrion Flower	Oregon Grape
Crab Apple	Plum
Cranberry (Bog)	Thornapple
Currant	

Fruits low in natural pectin

Bearberry	Honey Locust
Blackberry (ripe)	Manzanita
Black Gum	Mulberry
Black Haw	Nannyberry
Blueberry	Papaw
Buffalo Berry	Peppermint
Canada Mayflower	Persimmon
Cherry	Raspberry
Crowberry	Rose (hips)
Elderberry	Salal
False Solomon's Seal	Sapphireberry
Ground-cherry	Serviceberry
Hackberry	Snowberry

Strawberry
Sumac
Surinam Cherry

Violet
Wintergreen

Using Natural Pectin

If there is not a suitable concentration of natural pectin in a particular edible wild fruit, it can be combined with another fruit that is rich in pectin. Proper selection will ensure a sufficient concentration of pectin. For example, fully ripened blackberries do not have enough natural pectin. (All fruits contain less pectin when fully ripened.) On the other hand, if 10 to 20 percent of your berries are partially ripened (they will be red in color), there will be enough natural pectin to produce a good gel. The alternative would be to combine the ripened berries with an appropriate amount of apple peel juice, plum juice, or some similar fruit that contains a high concentration of pectin.

How To Test for Natural Pectin

Cook a cupful of the desired fruit juice. Extract one tablespoon of the cooked juice and place it into a small glass dish. Add one tablespoon of alcohol and mix slowly. (Grain alcohol is preferred, as denatured or wood alcohol is highly poisonous. If you use denatured or wood alcohol, *do not taste the mixture*.) The result will indicate how much pectin the fruit contains:

● Juices that contain high concentrations of pectin will form large amounts of jelly matter.

● Juices that contain only moderate concentrations of pectin will form smaller, dispersed amounts of jelly.

● Juices low in pectin will yield very small amounts of flaky jelly.

Another simple test uses Epsom salts; the commercial variety will do just fine. Mix one teaspoon of the salts with one tablespoon of cooked fruit juice in a small glass dish. Mix thoroughly, then allow to stand for 20 minutes. If the cooked fruit juice contains enough pectin, it will form a semisolid or gelled mass.

There are several other methods that can be used in determining specific concentrations of fruit pectin, but these are long and very involved. The methods mentioned above determine general levels but do not give specific concentrations, e.g., milligrams of pectin per liter of fruit juice.

Using Commercial Pectin

Commercial pectin is usually produced from the peels of citrus fruit and apple pomace (that is, the pulp of the apple). It usually has a yellow-white color and comes in one of two forms: a thick liquid (such as Certo) or a powder or granular form. Liquid pectin is added to a boiling mixture of fruit juice and sugar; powdered or granular pectin is mixed with the unheated juice. We prefer the liquid pectin because it handles more easily: you can time the cooking process to produce a cooked product and make it the last step in that process. All recipes in this book that mention commercial pectin refer to liquid for this reason.

Jelly or jam that is made with commercial pectin requires less cooking time and less energy to produce. However, more granulated sugar is required with the use of commercial pectin. The use of natural pectin requires a slightly longer cooking time but needs less sugar per cup of wild fruit juice. The yield of jelly per cup of juice is less than with commercial pectin.

SUGAR

Granulated sugar or honey helps in the gel formation. It sweetens and flavors the jelly or jam and acts as a preserving agent. It also helps to firm up the tissues of the ripened fruit. For the purposes of this book, granulated sugar and beet sugar are actually the same, although they are derived from different sources. Corn syrup can also be used. If you hunt down recipes used during World War II, you will find it was used as a substitute for granulated sugar, which was scarce.

Many individuals have given serious thought to finding a workable alternative to granulated sugar. Health and medical officials cite the role of sugar in tooth decay, coronary diseases, diabetes, and many other serious problems. For these reasons and others, some individuals substitute honey, which contains many vitamins and minerals. There are almost as many opinions on and methods for using honey as there are people who make jellies and jams. Whatever you decide, one thing is certain: it requires a lot more time and energy. The cooking time will be longer and you will need to add commercial pectin.

ACIDS

High acid content in the wild fruit is required in order for the gel to set up and helps to enhance the flavor. Usually, the acid concentration varies between different wild fruits as well as within the same fruit. The acid content is somewhat higher in slightly ripened fruit than in fully ripened fruit. Fruits may well be rich in natural pectin but lack sufficient concentrations of acid to yield a good flavor or gel.

If the fruit or juice used is tart, then there should be a sufficient concentration of acid. If the fruit acids appear to be lacking, then you need to substitute similar acids. Most cooks prefer lemon juice, but apple juice may also be used. Commercial citric acid can also be purchased from your local drugstore as a substitute for lemon juice. It is customary to add ⅛ teaspoon of crystal citric acid in place of each tablespoon of lemon juice.

COOKING EQUIPMENT

A good cook knows that the correct-size kettle, spoon, dish, and so on all help to bring that jelly or jam to the point of perfection. So, before you rush to the cooking area, please select the proper cooking utensils.

A large, heavy saucepan is essential. An 8- or 10-quart pan will allow the fruit mixture to come to a full boil without boiling over. A measuring cup with clearly visible markings is important—you don't want to lose time in trying to figure out each measurement. Additionally, make sure you have a clean wooden spoon (for stirring and tasting), a food or potato masher, food mill, utility or paring knives, ladle, grater (if required), bowls (stainless steel or glass), and an accurate clock or timer. A good candy thermometer can be an aid but is not a necessity.

Last but not least is the jelly bag. This is required for extracting fruit juices for jellies. Commercial jelly bags are available, or you may make one from several layers of cheesecloth or unbleached muslin. We use a bleached and washed white cotton sock. (It does not matter if the heel is reinforced with nylon.) We make up our jellies in 4-pint batches, and the sock is ideal for straining the juices from the fruit pulp. Appalling? Not as long as you use clean, bleached white socks. They are colorful afterwards and not recommended for wearing, as the natural food colors will begin to leach out.

CONTAINERS

The most common method of sealing glass jelly jars has been with paraffin. The problem is that you can only seal your product with paraffin if it is firm; otherwise, it will not provide an even seal. It works well with good jellies and jams but will not provide a good seal for butters, marmalades, preserves, and conserves.

The solution to this problem is to use canning jars with rubberized metal seals. These can be used for almost every form of canning or preserving. They are available as jelly or jam jars with colorful decorations and come in several sizes. The jars are reusable: all that is needed is to renew the seal. They are time-savers in that the time spent handling hot paraffin is eliminated.

The jelly jars should be ready before you start to make your jellies or jams. Check the top edges of the jars for cracks and nicks—anything that impairs a good seal will spoil the jellied product. The jars should be washed in hot soapy water and rinsed well to remove all traces of soap. Never assume that jars are clean; always assume they are laden with bacteria and wash them!

If the jars are to be filled immediately with boiling-hot preserves, scald-rinse them in boiling water and let them stand in the hot rinse water until they are to be used. The jars should be hot when they are filled: cool glassware often cracks when suddenly filled with something very hot. Most cooks prefer to sterilize the clean jars by covering them with water and boiling them for ten minutes or more.

Lids and rim bands of all types should also be kept hot and sterile, but *do not* boil rubber or self-sealing lids with gaskets along with your jars! This will impair their ability to form a proper seal. Instead, put them in a bowl, cover them with boiling water, and let them stand in it until you are ready to use them. If you use a funnel, it should also be sterile.

Think of sterility as the magic ingredient that usually goes unmentioned. It will ensure an enduring product.

A Word about Paraffin

If you do use paraffin to seal jelly or jam jars, it should be poured as soon as possible after the sauce has been poured. About ⅛ inch of hot paraffin will provide a layer sufficient to form a good seal. The hot jar will help seal the paraffin at the edges, but twirl the glass container so that there is an even distribution at the sides of the glass. Once this thin layer has set, pour in a second, somewhat thicker layer to seal the container completely. Paraffin allows you to use jars of various shapes and mouths of different widths. Allow the paraffin on wide-mouthed jars a little more time to thicken than with smaller-mouthed jars.

When melting paraffin blocks, use a double boiler. Pour only clear, hot paraffin. As soon as the paraffin has thickened and the jars have cooled enough to handle, they may be stored in a darkened place until ready to use.

THE COOKING PROCESS

Several methods are used to make jellies and jams. Two of the most basic are the cook-down method and the sugar-juice combination. The cook-down, which is the traditional method, is the practice of cooking the fruit juice until it becomes fairly concentrated. However, prolonged cooking weakens the gelling power of the natural pectin and reduces flavor and color. A minimum of water is used in order to reduce the juice concentration and cooking time.

If you employ the cook-down method, be certain to use fruit that has a good concentration of pectin. A good batch of fruit should contain 20 to 30 percent partially ripened fruit for high pectin concentration, with the rest fully ripened for a good flavor.

A much faster method is to combine the granulated sugar with the fruit juice before cooking. This not only reduces the cooking time but also destroys less pectin. However, this method requires the addition of commercial pectin, as it does not allow sufficient time to extract the natural pectin from the wild fruit.

Making uncooked or raw jam is perhaps the quickest method employed today. As there are no bacteria destroyed this way, these preserves must be kept under constant refrigeration. They should be made in small batches and then stored for only a few weeks at a time. I recommend the uncooked method be used with delicate fruit such as wild strawberries. The cooking process actually destroys their delicate structure and flavor, and it will not yield high-quality jams. They are best preserved as an uncooked jam and used within a short period of time to ensure good flavor.

Wild edible fruits lend themselves to the use of the microwave just as well as any food. The required amount of cooking time with a microwave is less than with a gas or electric stove. There are generally two stages. In stage one, you cook the prepared mixture without the pectin for 3 to 5 minutes or until it's soft. You then remove it from the microwave, thoroughly mix the cooked ingredients, add in the pectin (and lemon juice if needed), and return it to the microwave. In stage two, you cook the mixture for 3 to 4 minutes before you remove it, place it into hot, sterile jars, and seal. For heavier fruit such as apples, the cooking time may be extended one more minute for best results. Sauces take less cooking time, reducing the time by 1 minute.

Whenever you make a jelly or jam product, with or without added pectin, only prepare a small amount. Do not double or triple recipes. It is wise to observe that even experienced cooks, who have prepared jellies and jams for many years, only prepare small batches at a time. (If you have all the proper preparation materials to handle larger amounts of cooked fruit as well as an appropriate recipe, then this advice does not apply.)

The amounts of fruit indicated in each of the recipes is approximate, as the optimal amount will vary with the size and juiciness of a particular fruit. The weight or volume given is needed to yield the amount of juice called for in the recipe.

All fruit should be stemmed—that is, all stems and other debris should be removed. Wash it in cold running water, but do not allow it to stand in water, as this may ruin its firmness. Washing will remove any airborne grime as well as other chemical agents that might be present. If you have gathered your fruit near a busy highway, there exists the possibility of automobile exhaust chemicals coating the skin of the fruit. Some of these may not be water-soluble, but they can be removed by briskly rubbing the fruit under cold, running tap water.

Juice from the fruit can be extracted in a number of different ways. Each recipe will indicate the method best suited to each fruit. Tight-skinned or firm fruit may have to be heated in order to start the flow of juices, and a very small amount of water—called "cooking water"—is usually added. The actual cooking time required to extract the fruit juice may differ depending on the ripeness of the fruit that you are using.

If you are going to make jelly, then you will want to use clear, pulp-free fruit juice. You place the cooked, juicy pulp into a damp jelly bag and allow it to drip freely into a stainless steel or glass container. The clearest jelly is obtained when the juice is allowed to drip without pressure on the jelly bag. The yield will be far less than that which is obtained by pressing and squeezing . . . and you will be tempted to squeeze! However, this will also force pulp through the pores of the bag. A second straining will remove most of the pulp and provide you with a final clarified juice.

The biggest problem in making jelly is telling when it is done. When you use commercial pectin, there is no problem, as the gelling process will quickly follow. It is when you use the cook-down process with natural pectin that you may run into difficulties. In this case, it is important to remove the jelly or jam mixture from the heat before it becomes overcooked. You will certainly know if the jelly or jam has been overcooked: it will exhibit a change in color and it will taste and smell of burnt sugar.

Fortunately, there are three time-proven tests that can aid you in taking your jelly or jam off the heat before it overcooks. They are the sheet test, the temperature test, and the refrigeration test.

Sheet Test

The spoon or sheet test is perhaps the oldest and widest in use, even today. Dip a cool metal teaspoon into the hot jelly as it is cooking. Remove the spoon from the mixture and hold it above the pot, away from the steam. Turn it so that the syrup runs off the side. If the jelly

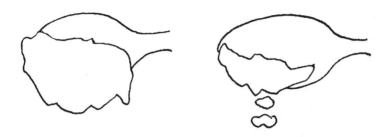

flows off the side of the spoon in a "sheet" (left) consider it done. If it drips off (right), it's not ready yet.

The use of the sheet or spoon test requires some skill and experience, and it is not always dependable. Keep in mind that if you use honey the jelly product will be somewhat softer to begin with.

Temperature Test

A candy thermometer is a handy device for this test, but a deep fat or actual jelly thermometer can be just as useful. Take the temperature of the boiling water before cooking the jelly. Then cook the jelly mixture until it reaches a temperature 8 degrees higher than the temperature of the boiling water. (This of course will vary according to your altitude.)

The concentration of cooked sugar should be such at that point that the mixture will form a satisfactory gel. Be certain that the bulb of your thermometer is covered with jelly in order to obtain a good reading.

Refrigeration Test

Place ½ teaspoon of the boiling jelly on a chilled plate and put it in the freezer compartment of your refrigerator for two minutes. If the mixture gels, then your jelly is ready and can be poured into hot, sterile jars.

FAILURE

There are many possible reasons why you may experience a failure with your final jelly product. There may be one or more contributing factors, especially when you are first adventuring into preserving edible wild fruit, which is not as predictable as commercially grown fruit.

During the cooking process, if you do not constantly stir your preserves, you may find an improper mixture of fruit that floats as the top of the jars. Also be very certain to remove as much of the foam that forms during the boiling process as possible; it consists of air trapped in the hot juices and it can only be removed by skimming the surface using a large spoon.

If jelly or jam jars are improperly sealed, mold may develop, and if yeast gets in, fermentation will result. The taste, consistency, and color will change if preserves are stored for too long a period. Bright red fruits such as strawberries, raspberries, and cranberries fade very easily if left in sunlight.

As stated, it is wise to use only glass or stainless steel cookware. We have done some cooking in aluminum and other types of cookware and found that they tend to give a metallic flavor to jelly or preserves. We prefer stainless steel.

DRYING WILD EDIBLES

The use of dried fruits and herbs has become an enduring part of the culinary history of man. They have been a staple of many societies, especially throughout the winter months. Wild edible fruit can be dried in a variety of ways: naturally, in an oven, with a commercial dehydrator, or through sulfur treatments.

The object of drying wild herbs and fruits is to remove as much moisture as possible. Dehydrating the herbs and fruit prevents the molds, enzymes, yeast, and various hungry bacteria from growing and thereby destroying or spoiling foods. The correct drying process should remove 80 to 90 percent of the water.

The drying process preserves the various oils and flavins found in the fresh plant. The preserving and drying of wild herbs and fruits should always begin with fresh material. Do not crush the harvested leaves and stems, as this will open the glands, releasing the valuable oils and flavins.

Drying Devices

The long-used method for drying herbs and fruit is drying in the sun. Some herbs and fruits cannot tolerate sun-drying and therefore must be dried in warm shade.

Ovens have long been used to dry almost anything, including wet socks. Electric ovens are generally slower than gas-fired ones. Convection ovens are more expensive, but they do an excellent job. (Please note that all oven temperatures given in the following recipes are in degrees Fahrenheit.)

There are several commercial dehydrators that are specially designed for the kitchen and occupy little space. The U.S. Department of Agriculture provides various farm bulletins that have plans for easily made homemade dehydrators.

Vacuum packing is one method of preserving wild fruits or herbs without drying. It removes all the air but maintains the flavor.

Drying Herbs

Select your herbs and harvest them just after the morning dew has left the scene. Spray them with water to remove grime from the leaves, and allow them to dry overnight. The next day, cut the stems to the desired length and make bundles of eight stems, tied at the bottom and hung upside down in a warm, shaded location—a garage will do nicely. Allow the bundle to dry until the leaves are crisp.

Remove the dry leaves and either keep them whole or crush them. Place them into a clean, dry container. Locking plastic bags are great for this type of dry storage; mason jars are also excellent.

Drying Wild Fruits

All wild fruits should be harvested when fully ripe. Once harvested, they should be dried without delay.

Drying in the full sunlight is practiced only when the air is dry, there's plenty of wind, and the day is hot and cloudless. Each wild fruit has a different drying regimen, ranging from two to ten days.

If you are using a drying cabinet equipped with light bulbs, most wild fruit dries in 10 to 12 hours.

The RECIPES

BARBERRY
Berberis spp.

THERE ARE SEVERAL SPECIES OF BARBERRY available throughout the United States. The native shrub *(Berberis canadensis)* can be found growing wild from New England south, along the Appalachian mountains to Georgia, and west to Texas. It attains a height of 1 to 5 feet and thrives in open fields. Oregon grape *(B. aquifolium)* is an evergreen barberry that is native to the west coast of the United States.

In recent years, many species have been imported to the United States by nursery stockmen. European barberry *(B. vulgaris)* and Japanese barberry *(B. thunbergii)* are widely used as hedge shrubs because they tolerate close pruning. Along with *B. canadensis*, they produce yellow flowers that yield scarlet berries later in the summer. They also bear sharp thorns on each branch.

All of the barberries used as ornamentals produce an abundance of fruit that is quite edible. The fruit can be found on the plants throughout the winter months, although it is quite pulpy. It should be picked either in early September or just after the first frost. The berries are tart and you will have to adjust the amount of sugar called for in each of the recipes according to your tastes. Barberries contain natural pectins, so you will not have to add any.

RED BARBERRY JELLY

8 cups ripe fruit
1½ cups granulated sugar per cup juice
1 cup cold water

Wash and stem berries. Place into a saucepan and mash completely. Add 1 cup cold water. Cook over moderate heat until the juice starts to flow (around 10 minutes).

Strain the juice through a jelly bag. For each cup of juice, add 1½ cups of sugar. Pour juice in a deep saucepan, bring mixture to a boil, and hold for 15 minutes or until jelly test is passed. Stir constantly to avoid burning bottom.

Remove mixture, skim off red foam, and pour the jelly into hot, sterile jars. Seal while hot.

BARBERRY JAM

3 lbs. ripe fruit
2 cups cold water
1 cup granulated sugar per cup juice pulp

Place cleaned fruit into a saucepan and add cold water. Cook the mixture over moderate heat until fruit softens. Remove from heat and pass the mixture through a fine sieve or strainer—this will remove seeds and skins.

Measure the juicy mixture, place in a saucepan, and add 1 cup of sugar per cup of pulp. Mix well, bring to boil, and hold for 15 minutes, stirring constantly. Remove foam and pour into hot, sterile jars and seal.

BARBERRY SAUCE

2 cups cold water	1 grated orange rind
2 cups sugar	4 cups ripe berries

Place cold water, grated orange rind, and sugar into a saucepan. Mix well and cook over moderate heat for five minutes. Add washed and stemmed berries. Cook until berries begin to pop (about 5 minutes). When all berries have popped, place the sauce in a bowl and chill. Serve chilled for best results. Makes excellent molds.

SPICED BARBERRY JAM

1 pt. ripe fruit	½ tsp. ground allspice
2 cups sugar	1 tsp. whole cloves
4 cups cider vinegar	1 stick cinnamon

Wash and stem 1 pint of fully ripened berries. Place into a saucepan, and add sugar and cider vinegar. Next, add allspice, whole cloves, and cinnamon. Bring to a boil and hold there until the fruit loses its color. Remove from heat and allow to cool. Strain the mixture. Pour into hot, sterile jars and seal.

PICKLED BARBERRY RELISH

2 lbs. ripe berries	1 tsp. each allspice and
½ pt. diluted cider vinegar	cloves
1½ lbs. sugar	1 cinnamon stick

Wash and stem barberries. Make up a sauce of sugar and cider vinegar. Add spice bag containing allspice, cloves, and cinnamon. Bring the mixture to a boil for 1 full minute, then remove from heat and cool. Add the berries, heating slowly and simmering until they are soft.

Remove from the heat, cover, and place into a refrigerator overnight to cool. The next day, remove spice bag and separate sauce from berries. Pack the barberries into hot, sterile jars. Heat the sauce just to the boiling point, pour it over the berries, and seal. Allow to age for 1 month.

BARBERRY CONSERVE

2 juice oranges	4 cups granulated sugar
3 tbsp. lemon juice	¾ tsp. ground cinnamon
2 qts. ripe fruit	

Slice oranges into very thin sections, removing the seeds. Cook the slices in a little water until tender. Clean and stem ripe berries, and then crush with a masher. Strain the pulp and juice through a strainer or food mill to remove seeds. Add juicy pulp to the cooked oranges and mix well. Add cinnamon, lemon juice, and sugar. Mix well, bring to a boil, then simmer over a low heat until sauce thickens. Remove from heat, pour into sterile jelly jars, and seal.

BARBERRY LEATHER

ripe fruit	2 tsp. lemon juice
½ cup granulated sugar	1 tsp. allspice

Cook enough ripened berries to produce 2 cups fruit pulp. Strain pulp, removing seeds and skin. Add in lemon juice and sugar. You may use honey or corn syrup instead of sugar; for long-term storage, use honey. Mix well. Allow to simmer for a few minutes.

Line a 13- x 15-inch cookie pan with plastic wrap or aluminum foil. Pour mixture evenly into pan. Place in oven and dry at 140 degrees.

Most leathers dry from the outside edge toward the center. While warm, yet dry, roll the leather in plastic wrap and store in freezer. To serve leather, unroll and cover the top surface with a garnish, such as fine sliced coconut, fig spread, a favorite jam or jelly, or mixtures. Best when eaten fresh!

BARBERRY COMPOTE

½ cup honey or sugar	1 tsp. ground ginger
⅓ cup chopped nuts	3 cups ripe fruit
4½ cups cold water	1 tsp. allspice

Combine sugar or honey in a saucepan and stir well, until sugar dissolves. Add in rest of ingredients. Cover and simmer for 10 to 15 minutes. Allow the mixture to cool. Stir well.

Spoon into hot, sterile jars and seal. Store away from sunlight.

BARBERRY JUICE

2 qts. ripe fruit
1 cup water
1 cup lemon juice

Place barberries in a deep saucepan. Add a small amount of water. Cook for 5 to 6 minutes, then crush the fruit completely. Add water and simmer for 5 minutes. Remove the juicy pulp and run it through a few layers of cheesecloth or sock. Collect only the juice. Add lemon juice and mix. Serve chilled. Can also be frozen and used as iced fruit juice.

DRIED BARBERRIES

Select only fully ripened barberries. Wash and stem berries, spread on a cookie tray, and place in a shaded but warm space. Allow to dry until fruit puckers. Remember, seeds are still in place. Drying in an oven at 140 degrees. will hasten the drying process. When properly dry, place in plastic bags or glass jars and seal. Keep out of sunshine. Will keep for three or four months. Can be rehydrated and used for any of the barberry recipes.

BEACH PEA
Lathyrus spp.

BEACH PEAS (*LATHYRUS JAPONI-cus*) are one of the most easily recognized wild edibles, as they resemble their cousin, the common garden pea. The plant attains a length of 1 to 2 feet and generally grows in large patches. It likes gravelly seashores and can often be found growing right down to the tidal edges.

Ranges from Labrador south along the Atlantic Coast of the United States, as well as from Alaska south to Oregon and along the shores of the Great Lakes. The related *L. aleuticus* is found on many of the Aleutian Islands.

The leaves are compound with 3 to 7 pairs of heart-shaped leaflets that are 6 to 9 inches long. The blossoms are bright pink-purple and give way to heavy clusters of small pea pods. The very young pods are sweet and tender enough to be cooked and served as a table vegetable.

Caution: When picking, only remove the pods—do not pull the plant from the ground. This reduces the community of pea plants and is poor ecology!

DRIED BEACH PEAS

Collect enough fresh peas to fill a 5-quart container. Shell the peas and thoroughly wash them. Spread on a cookie sheet and place in a shaded but warm place—a garage will do nicely. It may take 3 to 5 days to dry the peas. Using an oven at 140 degrees drying can be done in a single day. Commercial dryers are more effective. Once the peas are dried, place them in sterile containers; plastic is best. Place in a dark storage area. When ready to use, rehydrate with warm water or cook in water directly. Makes excellent soups and combines well with other vegetables.

BEACH PEA SOUP

2 tbsp. butter	1 carrot
1 medium onion	4 tsp. salt
2 qts. water	pinch parsley
1 lb. dried beach peas	chopped celery

Heat the butter in a soup pan. Add in sliced onion and sauté until lightly browned. Add in boiling water, the peas, and all other remaining ingredients. Cover the pan and reheat to boiling.

Reduce the heat and continue at a simmer for 1½ hours or until peas are very soft. Stir occasionally to prevent sticking to the bottom of the pan.

Serve hot, garnished with paprika. Makes 8 cups of soup.

BEARBERRY
Arctostaphylos spp.

A SMALL, SHRUBBY PLANT THAT is usually found sprawling over the surface of the ground. Bear-berry (*Arctostaphylos uvi-ursi*) is highly branched with a height of 1 to 2 feet, depending on the locale. The leaves are evergreen, smooth, and somewhat leathery. The smaller twigs are generally covered with a fine, hairy fuzz.

The small, white flowers yield a red berry that is smooth and somewhat mealy and bland-tasting. Tannins present in some of the berries account for this acrid taste; cooking destroys the tannins and improves the flavor. The berries appear on the vine in late summer or early fall and remain throughout the cold winter months. They become dried and more pulpy the longer they remain on the vine and therefore should be harvested before any severe frost occurs. The small bushes usually bear a good supply of berries.

This small plant ranges from the Arctic south to Pennsylvania. It thrives in open areas, especially in rock outcroppings and on mountaintops. The alpine bearberry (*A. alpinia*) is found in the Alaskan mountain ranges and bears a blue-black berry.

BEARBERRY JELLY

2 qts. ripe fruit	1 cup sugar per cup juice
1 tbsp. lemon juice	3 oz. liquid pectin

Wash and stem berries. Place into saucepan and cook until fruit pops and the juice flows freely. Remove from heat and squeeze through a jelly bag.

Measure juice, place in saucepan, and add 1 cup of granulated sugar per cup of juice. Add lemon juice and mix thoroughly. Place the mixture over a high heat and boil until sugar dissolves. Stir constantly. Add 3 ounces of liquid pectin and keep the mixture at a hard boil for 1 full minute.

Skim off the deep-red foam. Pour into hot, sterile jelly jars and seal.

BEARBERRY JAM

2 qts. ripe fruit
3 oz. liquid pectin
1 cup sugar per cup juicy pulp

Place washed, ripened fruit into a saucepan and cook over moderate heat for 5 minutes. Remove from heat and mash with a potato masher. Then force the mass through a strainer, food mill, or clean sock in order to remove the skins and seeds. Use as much of the juice and pulp as possible.

Put the juice and pulp combination into a saucepan. Add 1 cup of granulated sugar for each cup of sauce. Mix well and bring to a boil for 1 minute, stirring constantly. Add 3 ounces of liquid pectin, mix well, and boil for 1 full minute. Pour into hot, sterile jelly jars and seal.

BEARBERRY PASTE

2 qts. fresh fruit

Collect, wash, and stem fresh bearberries. Place into a saucepan, add a little water and cook until the berries pop and the juice flows. Remove and pour through a sieve or food mill, removing the seeds. Place the juicy pulp in a large bowl and cover, allowing the mixture to set for 24 hours.

Measure the pulp. Place it in a deep saucepan and add 1 cup of sugar for each cup of pulp. Mix well and boil for 10 minutes, stirring constantly. Pour into hot, sterile jars and seal.

BEARBERRY LEATHER

2 cups ripened fruit
2 tsp. lemon juice
½ cup sugar or honey

Collect, wash, and dice the ripe fruit, then puree using a blender. Add in lemon juice and stir. Add in sugar, corn syrup, or honey. Mix thoroughly.

Line a 13 x 15-inch cookie sheet with plastic wrap. Pour in the fruit puree and spread over sheet. Place in oven at 140 degrees and dry. (Will take 1 to 2 days sun-drying.) While still warm, roll fruit leather and allow to cool. Use a favorite garnish when served.

BEARBERRY RELISH

1 qt. ripe berries	1 medium red pepper
1 medium onion	½ tsp. salt
1 medium green pepper	1½ cups sugar
1½ cups cider vinegar	1 tsp. allspice

Wash and stem fruit and dice. Finely chop the pepper and onion. Combine peppers, onion, and fruit in a large saucepan. Add cider vinegar, granulated sugar, salt, allspice. Mix thoroughly and bring to a boil. Cook at a soft boil for 20 minutes.

Pack the fruit in hot, sterile jars and seal. Store in a cool, dark place.

BEARBERRY SPICY SAUCE

2 cups ripe fruit	2 whole cloves
½ tsp. allspice	1 cup sugar or honey
1 tsp. grated orange rind	1 cup water

Combine sugar or honey and water in a saucepan. Mix and bring to boil for 5 minutes.

Wash and stem fruit, place in a separate saucepan with a little water, and bring to boil for 2 minutes. Remove cooked fruit from heat and force it through a food mill. Obtain as much of the juicy pulp as possible. Combine the pulp and syrup in a saucepan. Add the spices and mix thoroughly. Simmer until thick. This should take 5 to 10 minutes. Add the grated orange rind. Store in hot, sterile jars.

DRIED BEARBERRIES

Gather as many berries as you need. Wash thoroughly, removing stems. Spread on a tray and place in direct sunlight for as many hours as possible. This may take 2 or 3 days of drying in direct sunlight. If need be, place in an oven at 140 degrees for 3 to 4 hours.

Once the fruit is competely dry, place the berries in plastic bags and store in a dry, dark area until ready for use. The dried berries can be eaten raw or rehydrated with warm water.

BEECHNUT
Fagus grandifolia

A TALL TREE WITH SMOOTH, GRAY bark. Height ranges from 80 to 100 feet. Leaves are elliptical or egg-shaped, have coarse-toothed edges, and range in length from 1 to 6 inches. Flowers appear in April and May, and 2 small triangular nuts per flower appear in September and October.

Range is from Nova Scotia south to Florida and west to Texas, then north to Wisconsin. Can be found in some mountains of Mexico and New Mexico. Thrives in dry soils, especially on hills or mountainsides. Young trees can be found bearing fruit in large amounts. Nuts can be harvested when mature, either still on the tree or scattered over the ground. You will have to be diligent when collecting them, though, or the ground feeders will be there before you.

DRIED BEECHNUTS

Remove nutlets from spiny husks and spread them on newspapers in a sunless location—the nuts' thin husks just make drying each nut take that much longer, so be sure to take this step. With a knife, cut each nut in half and remove the meat. It will take 5 to 7 days to dry properly. Drying in a 140-degree oven will take about 6 to 8 hours and gives the nuts a roasted flavor.

Put nuts in a sterile plastic container and store in a dark place. Use as a garnish, especially in fruit leather rolls.

BLACKBERRY
Rubus spp.

THE SPECIES OF BLACKBERRIES ARE numerous and tasty. They range throughout most of North America. Creeping blackberries (*Rubus procumbens*) and highbush blackberries (*R. allegheniensis*) are two of the more common species. Thimbleberries (*R. villosus*) can be found growing from New England west to Michigan and south to Florida.

The high bush blackberry (depicted in the drawing) is a tall plant, growing 3 to 7 feet in height. The canes contain an abundance of large thorns; on the older canes, they are large enough to penetrate heavy clothing.

The fruit is conical in shape, containing numerous small droplets. The berries are pleasant-tasting, though a little tart. When using blackberries as a cooked fruit, it is wise to remove their central pithy substance unless the cooking time is long enough that it will cook away. Barely ripe berries, red in color, are high in natural pectins and gel very well. Fully ripened fruit are ideal for flavor but do not gel easily.

The leaves are compound, with 3 to 5 leaflets, the terminal leaflet being the largest. The undersides are somewhat fuzzy and the edges are small-toothed.

BLACKBERRY JELLY (QUICK METHOD)

2 qts. ripe fruit	2½ cups sugar
juice of 1 lemon	3 oz. liquid pectin

Clean and stem blackberries. Place into a saucepan and crush or run through a food mill. Place the mass into a jelly bag or cheesecloth and allow the juice to drip. (Do not squeeze!) Measure out 2½ cups of the fine juice and place in a saucepan. Add in sugar and mix well. Allow to stand for 10 minutes.

Mix liquid pectin and lemon juice in a separate bowl, then add to the blackberry juice. Stir for 3 minutes. Add the concoction to hot, sterile jelly jars and cover. Allow the jelly to sit at room temperature for 24 hours, then store in a freezer for 4 weeks. Thaw and use when needed.

BLACKBERRY JELLY (COOKED)

2½ qts. blackberries	5 cups sugar
juice of 1 lemon	3 oz. liquid pectin

Clean and wash fruit. Place in a bowl and crush completely, or use a food mill. Heat the mixture until the juice nears boiling. Allow it to simmer over a low heat for 10 minutes. Remove from the heat and pour the mixture into a jelly bag or cheesecloth. Recover 3 cups of juice and pour into a saucepan. Add the lemon juice and stir well. Bring to a boil over a high heat. Stir constantly. Add liquid pectin and boil for 1 full minute more, stirring throughout.

Remove from the heat, skim off the colorful foam (which you can eat on its own—it tastes fine), and pour the juice into hot, sterile jelly glasses and store in a dry, dark place. Makes an excellent addition to fruit leather rolls.

BLACKBERRY-APPLE JELLY

underripe apples	3 cups blackberry juice
3 to 5 tbsp. lemon juice	7 cups granulated sugar

Barely ripened apples contain high concentrations of natural pectin, whereas fully ripened blackberries contain little pectin. By blending the juice of these two fruits, you can produce a delightful natural jelly. To prepare the apples, select any type of cooking or eating apple that is less than 25 percent ripe. Wash well to remove any grime or chemical spray. Slice apples into quarters, and remove the blossoms and stem. Place into a saucepan, cores, skin, and all. Add just enough water to cover the sections, cover, and bring to a boil. Use enough apples to produce 3 cups apple juice. (Add more if you wish to produce a refreshing drink while you work.) Reduce the heat and simmer for about 15 minutes.

Remove the apple sections from the heat and crush them. Return to heat and cook for 5 minutes. Once completely cooked, place the mass into a jelly bag and allow to drip into a bowl. Recover juice.

Clean and wash blackberries while the apples simmer. Place in a container and crush enough fruit to produce 3 cups of juice. Heat juice until it approaches boiling point, then allow it to simmer over a low heat for 10 minutes. Remove from the heat and pour through a jelly bag, collecting juice.

Now blend apple juice and blackberry juice in a deep saucepan. Cook for 5 minutes. Add 7 cups of granulated sugar and 3 to 5 tablespoons of lemon juice if the fruit juice is not tart enough. Next, allow the mixture to boil for 1 full minute. Remove from heat, skim off the foam, and pour the hot juice into hot, sterile jelly jars. Label.

BLACKBERRY JAM

2 qts. blackberries
3 oz. liquid pectin
7 cups sugar or honey

Completely crush fully ripened berries and remove about half the pulp and seeds, using a strainer. Recover 4 cups of juicy pulp and place in a saucepan. Add sugar and mix well. Bring to a boil for 1 full minute.

Add liquid pectin and mix. Bring to a boil and hold for 1 full minute. Stir constantly. Skim off foam and allow to cool for 3 to 5 minutes. Pour into hot, sterile jelly jars, seal, and label.

BLACKBERRY LEATHER

2 cups blackberry puree
2 tsp. lemon juice
$\frac{1}{2}$ cup sugar, honey, or corn syrup

Wash blackberries. Toss into blender and produce a puree. Add in lemon juice and granulated sugar, honey, or corn syrup. Mix thoroughly.

Using plastic wrap, cover a cookie sheet and spread puree across the sheet. Place in bright sunlight. Keep off all insects that may come to dine. Drying time in oven is 6 to 8 hours at 140 degrees. Once dried, roll and store in a locking plastic bag.

BLACKBERRY SAUCE

2 cups cold tap water   1 grated orange rind
2 cups sugar or honey   4 cups ripe berries

Place cold tap water, fresh grated orange rind, and sugar in a saucepan. Mix well and cook over a moderate heat for 5 minutes. Add washed and stemmed blackberries. Cook until berries begin to pop (about 5 minutes). When all berries have popped, pour into hot, sterile jelly jars. You may also place into refrigerator for storage.

SPICY BLACKBERRY SAUCE

4 cups ripe berries	¼ tsp. ground cinnamon
2 cups sugar	2 cups water
1 grated orange rind	pinch ground cloves

Combine orange rind, water, and sugar in a saucepan. Mix and cook over moderate heat for 10 minutes. Add cleaned berries. Cook until the berries pop and the juice runs. Now add cinnamon and cloves. Cook for 5 minutes, stirring frequently. Spoon the hot mixture into hot, sterile jelly jars, seal, and label.

BLACKBERRY CONSERVE

2 qts. ripe fruit	4 cups sugar
3 tbsp. lemon juice	¾ tsp. ground cinnamon
2 juice oranges	

Slice oranges into very thin sections, removing the seeds. Cook the slices in a little water until tender.

Clean and stem ripened blackberries, then crush the fruit. Strain the juicy pulp to remove the seeds. Add the pulp to the cooked oranges and mix well. Add cinnamon, lemon juice, and sugar. Mix well, bring to a boil, then simmer over low heat until the sauce thickens. Remove from heat, pour into hot, sterile jelly jars, seal, and label.

BLACKBERRY WINE

4 qts. berries
6 pts. water
2 cups granulated sugar per quart juice
1 package brewer's yeast

Select fully ripened berries and place them into a large saucepan. Add water. Bring to a gentle boil and hold there for 15 minutes. Remove the juice with a press or jelly bag. To each quart of juice add 2 cups of granulated sugar and mix thoroughly. Next, pour the sweetened juice into a gallon container. Large crocks are preferred, but glass jugs will do nicely as well. Add a cake of live yeast and cover with cotton plugs. Allow to stand for one week. Sterilize more jugs and pour off the fermented juice into them. Cap with wads of sterile cotton, which will keep out the wild yeast and dirt.

Store in a cool, dark place until the brew clears and there is no evidence of further fermentation (no more bubbling). Once all fermentation has ceased, carefully decant or pour off the top portion of the brew, leaving the cloudy residue behind. Pour the clarified liquid into sterile quart wine bottles and cap or cork. Allow to stand for at least 3 to 5 months in order to age.

Makes an excellent though tart red wine. Enjoy!

BLACK GUM
Nyssa sylvatica

A SMALL TREE 20 TO 30 FEET tall, black gum can be found throughout most of the mountainous areas of the eastern United States. It ranges from Maine south to Florida, west to Michigan, and south to Texas. It thrives in wet areas.

The leaves have a dark olive-green color that becomes a spectacular maroon in the fall. The berrylike fruit is ovoid, about ½ inch long and black with a purple sheen. Commonly found in pairs, the fruit usually ripens in early September. It is edible raw, but cooking enhances the flavor. Depending on the birds, it can sometimes still be found on the trees throughout the winter months.

Delightfully colored and flavored jellies have been made for many years from this fruit. It can be cooked into a beautiful blue-colored sauce that is used to enhance the flavor of meat.

The trunk of the tree can also be tapped, much in the same manner of the sugar maple (*Acer saccharum*). The sap flows abundantly in the early spring; it has a rather tart taste, but when allowed to dry, it can be used as a gum for chewing.

BLACK GUM JELLY

2 qts. ripe berries
1 cup sugar per cup juice

½ cup water
3 oz. pectin

Collect black gum berries. They will have a blue-black color when ripe; discard any overripe fruit. Wash and stem, then place in a deep saucepan. Add water and bring to a boil. Reduce the heat and continue to cook until the fruit bursts and the juice runs free.

Next, pour the cooked mixture through a jelly bag or cheesecloth. Measure the juice, pour it into a saucepan, and add 1 cup of granulated sugar for each cup of juice. Bring to a boil and stir until the sugar has dissolved. Add 3 ounces liquid pectin, stir, and boil hard for 1 full minute. Stir constantly to prevent burning. Skim the foam, pour the liquid into hot, sterile jelly jars, seal, and label.

SPICY BLACK GUM JELLY

2 qts. ripe fruit
1 stick cinnamon
½ cup water
3 tbsp. whole cloves

1 cup sugar per cup juice
1 tsp. allspice
3 oz. liquid pectin

Same as the black gum jelly above, with additional spices. After you measure the juice, add the spices and simmer for 10 minutes. Remove the spices and add 1 cup of granulated sugar to each cup of juice. Bring to a boil and continue as above.

BLACK GUM JAM

2 qts. ripe berries
1 cup sugar per cup juice

½ cup water
3 oz. liquid pectin

Clean berries, place them in a deep saucepan, and cook until they are soft and juice flows. With a hand masher, crush fruit completely. Run through a sieve or food mill, removing the skins and seeds. Measure the pulp and place in saucepan. Add 1 cup sugar for each cup of pulp and stir thoroughly. Bring to a boil and hold for 1 minute. Stir constantly. Add liquid pectin and boil for 1 minute. Remove the foam, pour into hot, sterile jelly jars, seal, and label.

SPICY BLACK GUM SAUCE

4 cups berries	¼ tsp. ground cinnamon
2 cups sugar	2 cups water
1 grated orange rind	pinch ground cloves

Combine the orange rind, water, and sugar and cook over moderate heat for 1 minute. Add berries and cook until they pop. Now add cinnamon and cloves and cook for 5 minutes, stirring constantly.

Spoon the mixture into a bowl and place in the refrigerator to chill. Alternatively, spoon hot into hot, sterile jelly jars, seal and label. Serve chilled; often used to flavor meats.

BLACK GUM CONSERVE

4 cups ripe berries	¼ pound chopped seedless raisins
½ cup chopped walnuts	
1½ cups water	8 cups sugar
1 cup finely chopped orange	

Clean berries, dice, and remove seeds. Add to a saucepan with water. Cook until the berries soften, stirring occasionally. Add raisins, walnuts, orange, and sugar. Mix well and cook, stirring constantly. Cook the mixture 20 to 30 minutes, then skim off the foam. Spoon into hot, sterile jelly jars, seal, and label.

DRIED BLACK GUM BERRIES

Harvest as needed or, if you have extra berries after preparing any of the above recipes, wash and stem them thoroughly. Spread the fruit in a flat pan. Place in direct sunlight and allow to dry for 2 or 3 days, or use a drying oven or regular oven set at 140 degrees, which will take much less time.

When dry, place in plastic bags, seal, and place in a dark, dry area for storage. Rehydrate with warm water when ready to use.

BLACK HAW
Viburnum spp.

AN ERECT, WIDELY SPREADING shrub, black haw (*Viburnum prunifolium*) will attain heights of 20 feet or more. It can be found growing in relatively dry soils and has a range from New England south to Georgia. Southern black haw (*V. rufidulum*) is a related species; it grows from Virginia south to Florida and west to Texas.

The leaves are broad, oval in shape and deep green, with sharp-toothed edges. The flowers are white and appear in large clusters that are 2 to 5 inches across. These clusters yield ovoid berries that are dark blue in color. The succulent berries are quite sweet and therefore make excellent jams and jellies; however, they are low in natural pectin. They are generally found ripened from late August to late September, if the birds do not eat them first.

BLACK HAW JELLY

    1 qt. ripened fruit
    1 cup sugar per cup juice
    3 oz. liquid pectin

Wash and stem fruit. Place in a saucepan with a little water and bring to a boil. Reduce heat and cook the fruit until the berries pop. Remove from the heat, run the mixture through a food mill or strainer, and pass the resulting juice through a jelly bag.

Measure the juice and pour into a saucepan. Add 1 cup of granulated sugar for each cup of juice. Bring to a boil and stir constantly until the sugar has dissolved. Add liquid pectin and boil hard for 1 full minute. Skim off foam, pour the mixture into hot, sterile jelly jars, seal, and label.

SPICY BLACK HAW JELLY

1 qt. ripe fruit	1 tbsp. whole cloves
1 stick cinnamon	1 cup sugar per cup juice
1 cup water	1 tsp. ground allspice

Wash and stem fruit. Place it in a saucepan and add 1 cup water. Add the spices in a spice bag and cook the mixture until the fruit pops and the juice runs freely. Remove the spice bag and run the mixture through a jelly bag.

Measure the juice, place into a saucepan, and add 1 cup of sugar for each cup of juice. Mix well and bring to a boil. Add 3 ounces liquid pectin and boil hard for 1 minute. Then skim foam, pour the mixture into hot, sterile jars, seal, and label.

BLACK HAW JAM

1 qt. ripe fruit	1 cup sugar per cup juice
½ cup water	3 oz. pectin

Wash and stem ripe black haws. Place in a saucepan, add water, and cook until fruit pops. Crush the fruit completely with a hand masher. Run the mass through a food mill or strainer. This will remove the skins and seeds.

Measure the pulp and place in saucepan. Add 1 cup of sugar for each cup of juice. Bring to a boil, then add 3 ounces of liquid pectin. Boil and stir for 1 full minute. Remove from heat and skim off foam. Pour into hot, sterile jars, seal, and label

SPICED BLACK HAWS

1 qt. berries	4 to 6 whole cloves
1 stick cinnamon	1½ cups sugar
¼ cup white vinegar	1 tsp. allspice

Make up a spice bag of cinnamon, cloves, and allspice. Wash and stem berries and place in a saucepan. Add white or clear vinegar and sugar. Mix thoroughly. Add the spice bag and allow to simmer over a low heat until mixture thickens.

Remove spice bag and let sit for a few minutes. This will allow the fruit to settle. Spoon the mixture into hot, sterile jelly jars, seal, and label. Allow at least 1 month to season.

BLACK HAW CONSERVE

2 juice oranges	3 cups sugar
3 tbsp. lemon juice	¾ tsp. ground cinnamon
1½ qts. black haws	1 tbsp. brandy

Slice oranges into very thin sections, removing the seeds. Cook in a little water until tender. Clean and stem black haws. Crush the fruit in a pan with a hand masher. (Do not use a blender, as it will pulverize the seeds!) Strain the pulpy mess through a strainer or food mill, removing the seeds. Add the pulp to the cooked oranges and mix well.

Add cinnamon, lemon juice, sugar, and brandy. Mix thoroughly and simmer over a low heat until sauce thickens. Allow to cool a few minutes, then spoon into hot, sterile jelly jars. Seal and label.

BLACK HAW RELISH

2 qts. ripe fruit	1 cup sugar
1 tbsp. ground allspice	$\frac{1}{2}$ tsp. cayenne pepper
3 cups vinegar	6 whole cloves
1 tbsp. ground cinnamon	

Wash and stem black haws and place into a saucepan. Add vinegar and cook until the fruit softens. Remove from the heat and run the mixture through a strainer to remove seeds.

Put the juicy pulp and the skins of the fruit in a saucepan. Add sugar and the spices, and mix thoroughly. Simmer over a low heat until the mixture thickens. Stir occasionally. Pour into hot, sterile jars, seal, and label.

BLACK HAW LEATHER

2 cups black haw puree	$\frac{1}{2}$ cup sugar
2 tsp. lemon juice	shredded coconut

Wash black haws, place in a blender, and puree. Add in lemon juice and mix thoroughly.

Using plastic wrap, cover a cookie sheet. Spread the puree evenly across the sheet. Place in bright sunlight to dry. Cover with a cheesecloth to keep off insects. Drying time in 140-degree oven will be about 6 to 8 hours. Once drying is complete, sprinkle on the shredded coconut and roll. Can be eaten then or stored in a locking plastic bag.

BLACK HAW SAUCE

2 cups water	4 cups ripe berries
2 cups sugar	$\frac{1}{4}$ cup brandy
1 grated orange rind	

Place water, orange rind, and sugar in saucepan. Mix well and cook over moderate heat for 5 minutes. Add washed and stemmed berries. Cook until fruit pops (about 5 minutes). When all berries have popped, run the pulpy mass through a food mill, removing the seeds. Pour liquid into hot, sterile jelly jars, seal, and label. Makes an excellent meat sauce.

DRIED BLACK HAWS

Collect as much fruit as you need, discarding any imperfect or partially eaten fruit. Stem and wash thoroughly. Place the washed berries on a cookie sheet and dry in bright sunshine. This may take 3 to 5 days, depending on heat. Using a 140-degree oven will take 6 to 8 hours. When dry, place the fruit in plastic locking bags and store in a cool, dry place.

Reconstitute with water and use as you would fresh black haws.

BLACK HAW CRÈME DE MENTHE SAUCE

4 cups black haws	1 cup crème de menthe
2 cups sugar	pinch ground cloves
1 grated lemon rind	1 cup water
¼ tsp. ground cinnamon	

Combine the lemon rind, water, and sugar in a saucepan. Mix and cook over moderate heat for 10 minutes. Add berries, and cook until they pop and the juice runs freely. Add cinnamon and cloves. Cook for 5 minutes, stirring frequently.

Remove and run through a food mill or sieve. Add in the crème de menthe and stir. Spoon the mixture into hot, sterile jelly jars, seal, and label.

SWEET AND SOUR BLACK HAW SAUCE

1 cup fruit

1½ tsp. lemon juice

½ cup water

1 tbsp. butter

2 tbsp. sugar

¼ tsp. salt

¾ tsp. cornstarch

Bring fruit and water to boil and cook until fruit pops. Strain through a food mill and save the juicy pulp. Combine cornstarch, sugar, and salt. Stir constantly to dissolve cornstarch. Cook until mixture thickens. Add in lemon juice and butter. Cook for 1 full minute. Remove from heat and pour the sauce into hot, sterile jars, seal, and label.

A good sauce to cook with or to use as a marinade for meats.

BLUEBERRY
Vaccinium spp.

THERE ARE SOME TWENTY OR MORE species of Vaccinium found scattered throughout most of Canada and the United States. They can be found anywhere from mountaintops 2,000 feet high to lowland bogs.

The highbush blueberry (*V. corymbosum*) grows as a shrub to a height of 10 feet or more. The lowbush blueberry (*V. pennsylvanicum*) and the late lowbush blueberry (*V. vacitlans*) usually attain heights of 1 to 2 feet and yield ripe fruit as soon as late June in warmer climates, later in cooler climates. The lowbush blueberry grows best in open, exposed areas and in higher elevations.

The leaves are small (2 to 3 inches long, 1½ inches wide) and bright green, with lighter-green undersides. The leaves alternate on the stems. The flowers appear at about the same time the leaves do; they yield fruit in small but heavy clusters.

The blueberry is certainly one of the finest fruits, if not the finest, that grows in the wild. The small, wild berry has more color and taste than the much larger cultivated varieties, which are not as sweet. When using wild berries, use at least 50 percent partially ripened berries to enhance flavor.

There is always some confusion as to the difference between blueberries and huckleberries. To most individuals, they appear to be the same; to the botanist, there are some fine differences. Both are excellent fare and can be used for jellies, pies, jams, tarts, and just plain eating out of hand.

BLUEBERRY JELLY (WATERLESS)

6 cups blueberries (red and blue)
3 oz. liquid pectin
9 cups sugar

Blueberry jelly is quite expensive to make as well as to buy, if you can find it. Select berries that are slightly underripe, or use at least half red berries, with the rest fully ripe. This will add a superb flavor to your jelly.

Wash and clean blueberries, then either crush them with a masher or use a blender on slow speed. Once mashed, add to a saucepan and gently cook for 10 minutes or until the juice flows. Strain the juicy pulp through a jelly bag. Add sugar. Bring the mixture to a full boil for 1 minute, stirring constantly to prevent bottom burn. Next, add pectin. Hold at a boil for 1 full minute and stir constantly. Skim foam, pour the juice into hot, sterile jelly jars, seal, and label.

BLUEBERRY JELLY (COOKED)

9 cups berries   ½ cup water
¾ cup sugar per cup juice   3 oz. liquid pectin

Wash and clean berries, half red and half ripe. Place in a saucepan and crush. Add water, place over medium heat, and simmer for about 5 minutes. Remove and allow the mix to drip through a jelly bag. Recover the juice and measure.

Now add ¾ cup of granulated sugar for each cup of juice. Mix well in a saucepan. Bring the mixture to a boil. Add 3 ounces of liquid pectin and hold at a boil for 1 full minute, stirring constantly. Drain off the foam, pour the mix into hot, sterile jelly jars, seal, and label.

BLUEBERRY-MINT JELLY

9 cups berries	1½ cups water
3 oz. liquid pectin	¾ cup sugar per cup juice
½ cup mint leaf infusion	

To make your own mint leaf infusion, take ¾ cup of crushed fresh mint leaves. Place in a saucepan, add 1½ cups of water and bring to a boil, remove from the heat, cover, and allow to stand for 10 minutes. Strain the infusion through a layered cheesecloth. Measure out the amount of infusion you need. (Drink the rest for a real treat!)

Wash and clean berries. Crush in a saucepan or in a blender. Combine the blueberries and mint infusion in a saucepan and cook over a moderate heat for 5 minutes. Remove and strain through a jelly bag or sock. Measure the juice and add ¾ cup of sugar for each cup of juice. Mix well and bring to boil. Add liquid pectin, stirring constantly for 1 full minute. Skim foam, pour into hot, sterile jelly jars, seal, and label.

BLUEBERRY-SOUR CHERRY JELLY

1 qt. fully ripe berries	3 oz. liquid pectin
4½ cups sugar	½ cup water
2 lbs. wild red cherries	

Thoroughly crush blueberries in a saucepan or blender. Then add wild red cherries to a separate saucepan and mash. Do not attempt to mash cherries with pits in a blender! Combine the cherries with the mashed blueberries and add water. Place over heat and bring to a boil. Allow to simmer for 10 minutes, keeping the pan covered.

Remove from heat and place in a jelly bag to collect the juice. Recover juices and combine with the sugar; mix well until the sugar is dissolved. Bring to a boil, add liquid pectin, and hold at a boil for 1 full minute, stirring constantly. Skim the foam, pour mix into hot, sterile jelly jars, seal, and label.

BLUEBERRY JAM

9 cups ripe berries
¾ cup sugar per cup sauce
½ cup water

Wash and stem 9 cups of fully ripened berries. Crush in a saucepan, add ½ cup of water, and cook over moderate heat for 5 minutes. Measure the sauce and add ¾ cup of sugar to each cup of sauce. Mix well and bring to boil. Add 3 ounces of liquid pectin and hold at a boil for 1 full minute. Skim foam, pour into hot, sterile jelly jars, seal, and label.

CANNED BLUEBERRIES

ripe fruit
¼ cup sugar per pint of berries

Using regular glass canning jars, wash and stem berries. Place into hot, sterile jars, filling to within ½ inch of top. Add ¼ cup of sugar for each pint of berries. Place the filled jars into a large saucepan and surround with hot water. Bring to boil and cook for 15 minutes.

Cover with hot, sterile lids, seal, and label. Will keep for at least a year.

BLUEBERRY CONSERVE

4 cups ripe berries	1 finely chopped orange
½ cup chopped walnuts	¼ lb. chopped seedless raisins
1½ cups water	8 cups sugar

Wash and stem berries. Add to a saucepan with water. Cook until berries soften, stirring occasionally. Add raisins, walnuts, orange, and sugar. Mix well and stir constantly. Cook the mix 20 to 30 minutes. Then skim the foam, spoon into hot, sterile jars, seal, and label. Great on hot, whole-wheat toast.

BLUEBERRY PRESERVES

2 qts. fruit
½ cup water
6 cups sugar

In a saucepan, add in the fruit and water and cover with sugar. Heat until sugar dissolves. Cook at a boil for 10 minutes, reducing the mixture. Simmer and slow-cook until syrup passes the jelly test. Spoon the mix into hot, sterile glass jars, filling them to within ½ inch from the top; seal and label.

BLUEBERRY LEATHER

2 cups blueberries
2 tsp. lemon juice
½ cup sugar

Wash and stem ripe blueberries. Place in a blender to produce a puree. Add in lemon juice and sugar. Mix thoroughly.

Using plastic wrap, cover a cookie sheet and spread puree across the sheet. Place in bright sunlight and allow to dry for 2 to 3 days. A 140-degree oven is faster: it will dry in 6 to 8 hours. Once the leather is dried, roll it and store in a locking plastic bag. Garnish with coconut shreds, chopped nut meats, or whatever pleases you when you are ready to use it.

DRIED BLUEBERRIES

Pick as many berries as needed. Wash and stem, discarding any imperfect fruit. Place on a cookie sheet and dry in full heat and sunshine, which will take 2 to 3 days or longer. Again, drying in a 140-degree oven takes less time. When the berries are dry, place in a locking plastic bag, seal, and keep in a dark, dry place. Reconstitute when ready with warm water or eat/serve as is. Makes an excellent addition to any homemade gorp or trail mix.

FROZEN BLUEBERRIES

Harvest as many ripe berries as needed. Wash thoroughly and stem. Allow to air-dry for about one hour. Place into locking freezer plastic bags and store in freezer. Be certain to always mark what is in the bag and the date.

BUFFALO BERRY
Shepherdia argentea

AS SHRUB OR SMALL TREE, BUF-
falo berry is somewhat thorny
and will attain heights of 10 to
30 feet. It is a native shrub of
North America and is often used
as an ornamental. It grows in the wild with a range from Alaska south
to California as well as east to New England and south to the
Carolinas.

The shrub has a scraggly appearance; it has light-gray twigs with
thorns and bears simple leaves. The leaves are narrow, oblong, rounded
at the tip, and silver-colored on both surfaces and have entire margins.
The flowers appear in April and yield a dull, red, ovoid fruit about ¼
inch long. The fruit contains a single seed. It is quite acidic but edible,
with a taste similar to that of the wild red currant.

This shrub is a very prolific producer, with branches laden with
fruit. Much of the fruit remains on the shrub throughout the cold
winter months. Cooking greatly improves the acrid taste.

BUFFALO BERRY JELLY

1 qt. ripe berries	1½ cups sugar per cup juice
½ cup cold water	3 oz. liquid pectin

Wash and stem 1 quart of fully ripened berries, place in a saucepan, add ½ cup cold tap water, and bring to a boil. Simmer for 10 minutes. Crush with a masher and simmer again for 5 minutes. Run through a food mill, removing the seeds, then through a jelly bag. Measure the juice, add 1½ cups of granulated sugar to each cup of juice. Mix well and bring to a boil. Add 3 ounces of liquid pectin and bring to a boil for 1 full minute. Stir constantly. Skim the foam, pour liquid into hot, sterile jelly jars, seal, and label.

BUFFALO BERRY CONSERVE

4 cups ripe berries	½ cup chopped nut meats
1½ cups water	1 chopped orange
8 cups sugar	¼ lb. chopped seedless raisins

Wash and clean 4 cups of ripened berries. Add to a saucepan with 1½ cups water. Cook until the berries have softened. Stir occasionally. Add ¼ pound of chopped seedless raisins, ½ cup of chopped nut meats, 1 finely chopped orange, and 8 cups sugar. Mix well and stir. Cook 20 to 30 minutes, then skim foam and pour into hot, sterile jelly jars, seal, and label.

SPICY BUFFALO BERRY SAUCE

4 cups ripe berries	2 cups sugar or honey
2 cups water	¼ tsp. ground cinnamon
1 grated orange rind	pinch ground cloves

Combine the grated rind of a fresh orange, 2 cups of water, and 2 cups of sugar in a saucepan. Mix and cook over moderate heat for 10 minutes. Add 4 cups of cleaned berries. Cook until the berries pop. Now add ¼ teaspoon of ground cinnamon, a pinch of ground cloves and cook for 5 minutes. Stir frequently.

Can be placed in the refrigerator and served chilled; or pour into hot, sterile jelly jars, seal, and label.

DRIED BUFFALO BERRIES

Select as many berries as desired, wash, and stem. Place on a cookie sheets, place in hot, bright sun, and allow to dry. This may take 2 to 3 days. Using a 140-degree oven may take 6 to 8 hours. Once completely dried, place in a dry container (locking plastic bags are great). Store in dark, dry place. Use when needed.

BUFFALO BERRY LEATHER

> 2 cups buffalo berry puree
> 2 tsp. lemon juice
> ½ cup sugar or corn syrup

Wash and stem 2 to 3 cups buffalo berries. Cook over a moderate heat until soft and the juice flows. Remove and place through a food mill to remove the large seeds. Place the juicy pulp in a saucepan, add 1 teaspoons of lemon juice and ½ cup granulated sugar or honey or corn syrup. Mix thoroughly.

Using a plastic wrap, cover a cookie sheet and spread puree across the sheet. Place in bright sunlight. Keep the hungry insects away! Drying time in a 140-degree oven is much faster. Once dried, roll and store in a plastic locking bag.

SWEET AND SOUR BUFFALO BERRY SAUCE

1 cup berries	1½ tsp. lemon juice
½ cup water	1 tbsp. butter
2 tbsp. sugar	½ cup water
¾ tsp. cornstarch	¼ tsp. salt

Cook the berries in ½ cup of water until juices run. Run the hot mixture through a food mill, removing the seeds. Combine the cornstarch, sugar, and salt and pour the hot fruit mix over, stirring constantly. Cook until mess thickens. Add lemon juice and butter; mix well. Cook 1 full minute longer. Pour mixture into a hot, sterile jelly jar, seal, and label. Should yield 1 pint of a good cooking sauce to be used on meats.

BUMELIA
Bumelia lanuginosa

KNOWN BY SEVERAL LOCAL NAMES, such as gum elastic, chittam wood or woolybucket. It can be found growing in wooded areas from Georgia south through Florida and west to Texas, and north to southern Illinois.

A small tree, bumelia grows to a height of 25 feet. Thrives in dry, sandy soils and usually in large, shrubby thickets. Branches are short and brittle and often have small spines. The leaves are oblong, grouped on very short branches, dark green, and over 2 inches in length.

Flowers are small and white. The fruit resembles a large berry; it is fleshy and black and appears singly or in small, loose clusters. Not very tasty when eaten raw, but makes excellent jellies and sauces when ripe and cooked. The trick is to use only fully ripened fruit.

BUMELIA JELLY

1 qt. ripe berries	1½ cups sugar per cup juice
½ cup cold water	3 oz. liquid pectin

Wash and stem 1 quart of fully ripened fruit, place in a saucepan, add in ½ cup water and bring to a boil. Simmer the mess for 10 minutes. Crush with a masher and simmer for 5 minutes. Run the sauce through a food mill to remove seeds and skins. Drain the juice through a jelly bag or old sock. Measure the fruit juice, add 1½ cups sugar to each cups of juice, mix well and bring to a boil for 1 minute. Add 3 ounces of liquid pectin and boil for 1 full minute. Stir constantly. Skim the foam, pour into hot, sterile jelly jars, seal, and label.

Goes well with hot toast.

BUMELIA JAM

1 qt. ripe fruit	1 cup sugar per cup sauce
½ cup water	3 oz. liquid pectin

Wash and stem 1 quart of fully ripened berries. Place in a saucepan, add in ½ cup water and cook until the juices run. With a hand masher crush the fruit completely. Run the mess through a food mill or strainer, removing the skins and seeds.

Measure the juicy pulp and place in a saucepan. Add 1 cup of sugar or honey for each cup of sauce. Bring to a boil, then add 3 ounces of liquid pectin. Boil for 1 full minute. Stir to prevent burning the bottom. Pour into hot, sterile jelly jars, seal, and label. Looks great and tastes great on pancakes!

BUMELIA CONSERVE

1½ qts. ripe fruit	¾ tsp. ground cinnamon
1 juice orange	3 tbsp. lemon juice
8 cups sugar	pinch allspice
¼ lb. seedless raisins	½ cup chopped nut meats
1½ cups water	

Wash and stem 1½ quarts fully ripened berries. Add to a saucepan with 1½ cups water. Cook until the berries soften, stirring occasionally. Add ¼ pound of seedless raisins, ½ cup chopped nut meats, 1 finely chopped orange, seasonings, and 8 cups of sugar. Mix well and cook for 20 to 30 minutes over moderate heat. Skim foam and pour the sauce into hot, sterile jelly jars, seal, and label.

BUMELIA LEATHER

2 cups bumellia puree
2 tsp. lemon juice
$\frac{1}{2}$ cup sugar or corn syrup

Wash and stem enough berries to obtain two cups of puree. Do not use a blender due to seeds. Mash by hand. Add in 2 teaspoons of lemon juice and $\frac{1}{2}$ cup of sugar or corn syrup. Mix thoroughly. Using a plastic wrap, cover a cookie sheet and spread the mix evenly. Place in bright sunshine to dry. May take 1 to 2 days, or use a 140-degree oven and dry in one day. Roll and store in locking plastic bags to keep dry. Garnish and serve. Delightful color and taste!

SPICY BUMELIA SAUCE

4 cups ripe berries
1 grated orange rind
2 cups water

2 cups sugar or corn syrup
$\frac{1}{4}$ tsp. ground cinnamon
pinch ground cloves

Combine the grated rind of 1 orange, 2 cups of water, and 2 cups of sugar or corn syrup in a saucepan. Mix and cook over a moderate heat for 10 minutes. Add 4 cups of cleaned berries. Cook until the fruit pops and the juice flows. Run through a food mill to remove the seeds. Add $\frac{1}{4}$ tsp. ground cinnamon and a pinch of ground cloves. Cook for 5 minutes, stirring frequently.

Spoon the hot mixture into hot, sterile jelly jars, seal, and label.

BUMELIA-GINGER SAUCE

4 cups ripe berries	¼ tsp. ground ginger
¼ cup sugar	⅛ tsp. salt
1 cup boiling water	¼ cup honey

Blend the sugar, honey, ginger, salt in a saucepan. Slowly add in boiling water, stirring constantly. Bring the mix to a boil and cook for 5 minutes.

Remove from the heat and pour the mixture into hot, sterile jelly jars, seal, and label. Goes well on desserts and Asian foods.

DRIED BUMELIA BERRIES

Collect as many berries as needed, wash, and stem. Place on a cookie sheet and then dry in full sunshine and heat, or dry in 140-degree oven. When dried, store in locking plastic bags. To use, rehydrate in warm water until berries plump.

BUTTERNUT
Juglans cinerea

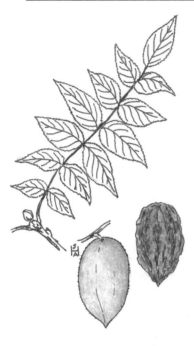

A LARGE TREE THAT MAY REACH heights of 100 feet or more. Leaves are compound, with 11 to 17 leaflets; they are sticky and may range up to 30 inches. Nuts are oblong, 2 inches long, and half as thick. Nut meats are large and heavy.

Ranges from eastern Canada, south along the Appalachian Mountains to Georgia, then west to Arkansas and north to Minnesota. Rarely found growing in pure stands, as trees compete for space. Grows in rich, moist soils, usually on abandoned farm lands, along hedgerows and burned-over areas. Many trees are planted as ornamentals and later found to be a good source of nuts. Many wild trees are harvested for their nuts, which are then sold in the market place.

DRIED BUTTERNUTS

The fruit or nut meat is divided into two sections. Husks should be removed before drying. Use gloves, as the husks contain dyes that stain your skin. Many folks simply put the nuts away somewhere and leave them until they are dry.

Remove the husks and place nuts on a flat surface and allow to dry for several days in a warm but shaded area—the sun will remove too much of the natural oil that flavors the nut meats. The nuts can then be stored in net bags (old onion bags) in a cool, dry place. Spread the nut meats on a cookie sheet and dry in a 140-degree oven for 4 to 5 hours. When the nut meats are dry, place in locking plastic bags, seal, and store.

SALTED BUTTERNUTS

Shell as many nuts as needed and place in an oven until dry. Salt with enough to cover the nut meats. Place in a locking plastic bag and store in a dark, dry place.

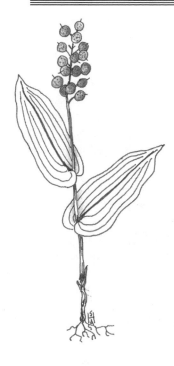

CANADA MAYFLOWER

Maianthemum canadense

THIS LITTLE MEMBER OF THE LILY FAMILY grows in great abundance in pine wood areas. A low ground plant, it grows to a height of 6 to 7 inches in somewhat large, scattered clumps. The single erect stem arises from a slender rootstock. The stem bears 1 to 3 leaves in a zig-zag pattern. This small plant ranges from southern Canada south to the Carolinas and west to Iowa.

The flowers are borne in a terminal cluster. They are fragile, white, and small. They yield greenish-white berries that turn pink, then bright ruby red; some varieties produce pink-red, speckled fruit. The berries appear in late June and ripen in August. The entire plant is edible.

The ripened berries are tart, acidic, and fleshy and have the flavor of cranberries. The fruit contains high concentrations of vitamins A and C.

CANADA MAYFLOWER JELLY

1 qt. ripe berries
1 cup sugar per cup juice
3 oz. pectin

Gather 1 heaping quart of fully ripened berries. Do not use berries that are puckered or dehydrated. Wash and stem. Place in a saucepan, add a little water, cover, and cook over moderate heat until fruit pops. Remove and allow to drip through jelly bag.

Measure the juice and add I cup granulated sugar to each cup of juice. Fruit has a tart taste and therefore you may want to vary the amount of sugar, according to your own taste.

Bring to a boil, add 3 oz. of liquid pectin, and boil for 1 full minute. Sir constantly. Skim the colorful foam, pour into hot, sterile jelly jars, seal, and label.

SPICED CANADA MAYFLOWER JELLY

4 cups ripe fruit	1 tbsp. ground cinnamon
1/3 cup water	1/2 tbsp. ground allspice
3/4 cup vinegar	4 whole cloves
4 cups sugar	3 oz. liquid pectin

Wash and stem 4 cups fully ripened berries, discarding dried fruit. Place in saucepan, add 1/3 cup water, vinegar, ground cinnamon, ground allspice, cloves, and sugar. Mix thoroughly, place over a low heat, and simmer for 30 minutes. Stir occasionally to prevent bottom burn.

Remove from the heat, drip through a jelly bag. Recover the juice. Place the mixture into a saucepan, bring to a boil. Add 3 ounces of liquid pectin, hold at a boil for 1 full minute. Skim the foam, pour into hot, sterile jelly jars, seal, and label.

CANADA MAYFLOWER–CRAB APPLE JELLY

1 qt. ripe berries
6 to 8 medium crab apples
1 cup sugar per cup juice

Select fully ripened fruit, discarding dehydrated berries. Wash and stem 1 full quart of berries, add them to a saucepan and cook in a small amount of water until berries pop and the juice runs free.

Wash and stem 6 to 8 medium-size crab apples. Remove the flower sections and core. Cut the fruit into eighths. Cook in a saucepan with 2 tablespoons of water for 20 to 30 minutes. Crush with a food masher. Combine both fruits in a food mill, extract the watery pulp, and run through a jelly bag. Do not squeeze!

Measure the juice and add 1 cup of granulated sugar to each cup of juice. Mix thoroughly, and bring the mix to a boil for 2 full minutes. Skim the colorful foam, pour into hot, sterile jelly jars, seal, and label.

The color of the jelly may blanch somewhat; this can be corrected by adding a few peels of bright colored red crab apples. This will add extra pigment to the sauce when cooking.

CANADA MAYFLOWER CONSERVE

4 cups berries	¼ cup chopped nut meats
1½ cups water	1 orange
¼ lb. seedless raisins	6 cups sugar or corn syrup

Wash and stem 4 cups of ripe berries. Add the fruit to a saucepan with 1½ cups water. Cook until the berries have softened and burst. Stir to keep the bottom from burning.

Add seedless raisins, chopped nut meats, chopped orange, and sugar. Mix thoroughly. Cook the mixture for 25 minutes, skim the colorful foam, pour the hot sauce into hot, sterile jelly jars, seal, and label.

CANADA MAYFLOWER–GINGER SAUCE

4 cups ripe berries	¼ tsp. ground ginger
¼ cup sugar	⅛ tsp. salt
1 cup boiling water	¼ cup honey

In a saucepan, blend the sugar, honey, ginger, and salt. Slowly add the boiling water and bring the mixture to a boil.

Cook at a full boil for 5 minutes. Remove from the heat and pour into hot, sterile jelly jars, label, seal, and label. Store in a dark, cool place.

DRIED CANADA MAYFLOWER

Collect as much of the delightful fruit as wanted. Wash and stem. Discard any imperfect fruit. Place on a cookie sheet and dry in a warm place. Direct sunlight is not desirable. A 140-degree oven is better and will dry the fruit in a matter of a few hours. Store in a locking plastic bag, then in a dark, cool place. Use to make sauces when the snow is on the ground.

The dried berries can be rehydrated with warm water when ready to use. The more you harvest and dry, the more you will have for winter use.

CARRION FLOWER
Smilax herbacea

THIS UNUSUAL MEMBER OF THE lily family produces a bluish-black berry that has a very pleasant flavor. Greenish-white flower clusters appear in June and have a rather noxious scent, similar to that of decaying flesh; hence its name. The unpleasant odor causes many folks to shy away from this unusual food source.

A climbing vine, it will attain heights of 10 to 15 feet. It can usually be found growing in meadows, in thickets, or over any type of shrub that thrives in open areas. It has a growth range from New Brunswick south to Georgia and west to the Rocky Mountains.

The fruit clusters appear in mid-July and ripen during late August. These berry clusters are many and several pounds of fruit may be taken from a 20-foot vine. The fruit can be eaten raw.

The dark blue-black color makes a very impressive colored jelly or sauce. The amount of pectin in the fruit is sufficient to create gelling without additional pectin. The fruit sauce adds zest and flavor to wild meats.

CARRION FLOWER JELLY

2 qts. ripe berries
½ cup of sugar per cup juice

Select, collect, wash, and stem 2 quarts of fully ripened berries. They will be a little pulpy, but quite usable. Place into a saucepan with a little water and cook over a moderate heat until fruit softens. Crush the fruit with a food masher and let cook for 5 minutes. Stir occasionally.

Remove from the heat and drip through a jelly bag. Recover the juice and measure. Add ½ cup of sugar to each cup of juice. Place the mix over a high heat and hold at a boil until sugar dissolves. Cook the mix until a "positive jelly sheet test" results. Skim the blue foam, pour into hot, sterile jelly jars, seal, and label.

SPICY CARRION FLOWER JELLY

4 cups berries	1 tsp. ground allspice
½ cup water	6 whole cloves
¾ cup cider vinegar	4 cups sugar or honey
1 tbsp. ground cinnamon	3 oz. liquid pectin

Wash and stem 4 cups of ripe berries. Place them in a saucepan with water, cider vinegar, ground cinnamon, ground allspice, cloves, and sugar. Mix the ingredients.

Place the mix over a low heat and cook for 30 minutes, stirring occasionally. Pour the sauce through a fine sieve. Place in a saucepan, add in the liquid pectin and cook for at a boil for 1 full minute. Skim the foam, pour into hot, sterile jelly jars, seal, and label.

CARRION FLOWER–BRANDY SAUCE

4 cups ripe fruit	1 cup of sugar
2 tbsp. brandy	pinch ground cinnamon
½ cup water	

Wash and stem the berries and place in a saucepan. Add in the water and cook over a moderate heat for 30 minutes. Add in the ground cinnamon and cook for 1 full minute. Run the mix through a sieve and place in a saucepan, add in your favorite brandy and mix well.

Skim the foam and pour into hot, sterile jelly jars, seal, and label. Use to flavor game meats as well as beef.

CARRION FLOWER LEATHER

2 cups berries
2 tsp. lemon juice
½ cup sugar, honey, or corn syrup

Wash and stem 2 full cups of carrion flower berries. Toss into a blender and produce a fine-looking puree. Add in 2 teaspoons of lemon juice and ½ cup of sugar, honey, or corn syrup. Mix thoroughly.

Using plastic wrap, cover a cookie sheet, spread the puree across the sheet. Place in a warm place, out of the sunlight, and allow to dry. May take 2 to 3 days. Use an oven at 140 degrees for only 5 to 6 hours of drying time. Once dried, roll and store in a locking plastic bag. Garnish with marshmallow, nuts, or whatever catches your fancy. (Some young folks use peanut butter as a garnish.)

CARRION FLOWER COOKING SAUCE

1 cup ripe berries	pinch salt
¼ cup finely chopped onions	pinch sage
3 tbsp. white wine vinegar	1 tbsp. brown sugar

Place fruit into saucepan and cook over moderate heat until fruit pops and juice runs. Run the pulpy sauce through a food mill, removing the skins and seeds.

Combine all ingredients in a saucepan and boil for 1 to 2 minutes. Skim off the foam, pour the hot sauce into hot, sterile jelly jars, seal, and label.

When ready to use, blend in ¼ cup of heavy cream, bring to a boil for 1 full minute. Cover skillet-fried chicken or cooked beef.

DRIED CARRION BERRIES

Harvest as many berries as needed. Wash and stem. Place in a shallow pan and allow to dry until stiff. Do not place in direct sunlight.

When dry, place in locking plastic bag and store in a dark, dry place.

BLACK AND RED CHERRIES
Prunus spp.

THERE ARE SEVERAL SPECIES OF WILD cherry located throughout most of the United States and southern Canada. The more common ones include: chokecherry (*Prunus virginiana*), pin cherry (*P. pennsylvanica*), sand cherry (*P. pumita*), sweet cherry (*P. avium*), chicasaw plum cherry (*P. angustifolia*), and black cherry (*P. serotina*). All have considerable merit as wild fruits. They vary in abundance, size, color, and, of course, taste. Many wild species are commonly used as ornamentals and so they are often very easy to locate.

Wild cherries are usually available from August through September. They can be eaten raw from the trees or used in making jellies and jams. These particular wild fruits do not contain high concentrations of pectin, so additional pectin will be required for gelling.

When used as a food source the cherry has 65 calories per 4 ounces of fruit and 650 IU of vitamin A. It makes either a sweet or tart jelly, depending on the particular type of wild cherry.

PIN CHERRY JELLY

12 cups pin cherries	7 cups sugar or honey
2 cups water	6 oz. liquid pectin

You may use any cherry for this recipe. Clean and stem the cherries, place in a saucepan with the water, and cook over a low heat for 20 to 30 minutes or until the fruit pops and the juice runs. Strain the juice through a jelly bag. Collect 3½ cups juice, place into a saucepan, add the sugar, mix well, and bring to a boil. Stir constantly. Add the pectin and hold at a boil for 1 full minute. Remove the foam, pour into hot, sterile jelly jars, seal, and label. Store in a cool, dark place.

CHOKECHERRY JELLY

12 cups ripe fruit	3 cups water
6 cups sugar or honey	6 oz. pectin

Clean and stem 12 cups of fully ripened cherries, place into a saucepan, add 3 cups water, and bring to a boil. Lower the heat and simmer for about 15 minutes, or until the cherries pop their skins.

Strain the juicy mix through a jelly bag. Measure 3 full cups of the juice. Place in saucepan, add 6½ cups sugar, and mix. The sauce will be a little tart. Add more sugar if you like your jellies sweet.

Bring to a boil, add 6 ounces liquid pectin and boil for 1 full minute. Remove from the heat, skim the foam, pour into hot, sterile jelly jars, seal, and label. Goes well on toast or muffins.

CHERRY-CURRANT JELLY

12 cups ripe cherries	¾ cup of water
12 cups ripe currants	7 cups sugar or honey
3 oz. liquid pectin	

Wash, stem, and crush the ripened cherries. Separately crush 12 cups red currants. Red currants are preferred as they will enhance the color of the jelly.

Combine the fruit mixes in a saucepan, add in the water, and bring to a boil, then simmer over a low heat for 10 minutes or until the juice flows from the fruit. Strain through a jelly bag.

Recover 4½ cups of juice. Add the sugar, bring to a boil, and add in the liquid pectin. Stir constantly and boil for 1 full minute. Skim off the colorful foam, pour the hot mix into hot, sterile jars, seal, and label.

BLACK CHERRY CONSERVE

1 qt. black cherries	¾ tsp. ground cinnamon
2 juice oranges	6 tbsp. lemon juice
3½ cups sugar	¾ tsp. ground allspice
2 tbsp. brandy	

Cut 2 juice oranges into very thin slices, remove the seeds, place in a saucepan, and cover with a little water. Cook until skins are tender.

Stem and clean 1 quart of wild black cherries. Run the fruit through a food mill to remove the seeds. Add the juicy pulp to the cooked orange slices and mix well. Next add the spices, lemon juice, and sugar. Mix thoroughly and simmer over a low heat until thick. Add in your choice of brandy and mix. The mixture will appear somewhat clear when ready. Remove from the heat, spoon into hot, sterile jelly jars, seal, and label.

WILD CHERRY JAM

3 lbs. wild cherries
7 cups sugar or honey
3 oz. pectin

Any of the wild cherries can be used to make this fine-tasting jam, but the amount of sugar required will vary according to the sweetness of the jam you desire.

Stem and clean 3 pounds of wild cherries. Pit and chop or mash. You may also strain the fruit through a food mill, which will remove the pits. Collect 4 cups of the juicy pulp. Add 6 or 7 cups of sugar or honey and mix well. Bring to a boil, add in 3 ounces of liquid pectin and boil for 1 full minute. Stir constantly. Remove from the heat, skim the foam, and pour into hot, sterile jars, seal, and label.

WILD CHERRY SAUCE

4 cups wild cherries
¼ cup sugar
1 tbsp. orange juice

Stew 4 cups of wild cherries for 20 minutes. Remove from heat and strain through a food mill, removing the seeds and skins. Mix 1 cup of strained cherry pulp, and sugar. Simmer over low heat for 10 minutes. Stir to prevent burning.

Remove from the heat, add in orange juice, mix, and pour into hot, sterile jar(s) and seal and label. This type of sauce can be used to baste wild meats or lamb to enhance the flavor. Can also be used as a topping for ice cream.

SWEET AND SOUR CHERRY SAUCE

1 cup juicy pulp	1½ tsp. lemon juice
½ cup boiling water	1 tbsp. butter
2 tbsp. sugar	½ cup water
¾ tsp. cornstarch	¼ tsp. salt

Place the cup of juicy cherry pulp in a saucepan, bring to a boil, add in the cornstarch, sugar, and salt, then pour boiling water over the mixture, stirring constantly. Cook the mix until it thickens. Add in the lemon juice and butter. Cook one full minute, stirring constantly.

Skim the foam, pour into hot, sterile jars, seal, and label. Makes 1 pint of sauce.

CHERRY LEATHER

2 cups cherry puree
2 tsp. lemon juice
½ cup of sugar, honey, or corn syrup

Wash and stem 2 full cups of wild cherries. Cook until the fruit pops and the juice runs freely. Run the hot mix through a food mill, collecting the juicy pulp. Add in the sugar and lemon juice. Mix thoroughly.

Using a plastic wrap, cover a cookie sheet and spread the fruit mix across the sheet. Place in bright sunlight and dry. Will take 2 to 3 days. Dries in 140-degree oven faster. When dry, roll and store in a locking plastic bag.

When ready to eat, unroll and garnish the top with nuts or jams, etc.

CHERRY COOKING SAUCE

1 cup ripe cherries	pinch salt
¼ cup finely chopped onions	pinch sage
3 tbsp. white wine vinegar	1 tbsp. brown sugar

Place the fruit in a saucepan and cook until fruit pops. Then run the mess through a food mill, removing the seeds and skins.

Combine the ingredients and boil for 1 to 2 minutes, stirring constantly to prevent burning. Pour into hot, sterile jelly jars, seal, and label.

When ready to use, blend in ¼ cup heavy cream, bring to a boil. Cover skillet-cooked chicken or other game fowl and serve hot.

CHERRY FRUIT SALSA

2 cups wild cherries	1 tbsp. honey or corn syrup
1 small apple, diced	1 tbsp. lemon juice

Run the 2 cups of wild cherries through a food mill, removing the skins and seeds. Core, stem, and peel 1 small apple, then dice.

Combine the fruit sauce with the apples, and other ingredients and mix well. Refrigerate or bring to a boil, then pour into hot, sterile jars, seal, and label. When ready to use, refrigerate and serve. Good for parties.

DRIED CHERRIES

Collect as many wild cherries as possible, then wash and stem. Discard any soft or imperfect fruit. Spread on a cookie sheet(s) and place in a warm area, but not in direct sunlight!

A 140-degree oven is best to dry this fruit, but even better is a commercial dehydrator. Store in locking plastic bags and place in a cool dry place.

When ready to use, rehydrate and run through a food mill, removing the seeds and skins.

CHICORY
Chicorium intybus

THIS NATIVE OF EUROPE LONG AGO escaped from the gardens to the wilds, where it is considered a weed species.

It thrives in marginal areas alongside the road, in pastures, drainage ditches, and in unused lands. Ranges in growth from Nova Scotia, south to Florida, and west to California and the Pacific Coast.

Height ranges from 1 to 4 feet. Branches are rigid and angular with most of the leaves located at the base of the plant. Leaves are lobed, 6 inches in length, and often curled. Flowers are often found in small, blue clusters—they are often called ragged blue sailors.

The tender young spring roots are often served like carrots and are very tasty. The roasted ground roots have been used to flavor roasted coffee; during the American Civil War, the Southerners even used chicory as a substitute for coffee.

DRIED CHICORY

Locate, then carefully dig to remove the roots, which will look like carrots. They are white in color and somewhat narrow. Wash carefully, removing all dirt. If you choose, serve for dinner. The roots can be roasted in an oven at a temperature of 200 degrees. You can tell when they are finished, as they will be crunchy.

Crush the roots and store the roasted fragments in locking plastic bags. Use as a flavoring or substitute for coffee. The roots will keep for a year or so.

When flavoring coffee it is wise to start out small. Add a small amount to your favorite coffee as a blend. If you find it needs more, you can add a larger amount the next time. By trial and error you will find that blend of chicory and coffee that appeals to your taste buds.

COCOPLUM
Chrysobalanus icaco

THIS SEMITROPICAL PLANT CAN be found in the wild from central Florida to South America. Generally planted as an ornamental shrub, it has escaped to the wild and survives very well. It can be found growing in the wild near canals, wet areas, beaches and, in Florida, dry hammock areas.

The leathery, nearly round leaves alternate on the stem, ranging in length from 2 to 3 inches. The small clusters of white flowers yield a fleshy, dry, berrylike drupe, dark purple in color. The flesh clings to a large stone and does not taste especially good when eaten raw. Cooking greatly improves the flavor and makes excellent jellies and cooking sauces.

COCOPLUM JELLY

ripe fruit	4 tbsp. lemon or lime juice
3 cups sugar or honey	3 oz. liquid pectin

Gather enough ripe cocoplums and cook down to make 3 cups of juice. Add a little water and place cocoplums in a saucepan, cook until the juice runs freely. Measure and run through a jelly bag to clarify.

Add the juice to a saucepan, bring to a boil, and add in the lemon or lime juice and the sugar. Bring to a boil, then add in the pectin and bring to boil. Remove the colorful foam, pour into hot, sterile jelly jars, seal, and label. Goes well with chicken dishes.

COCOPLUM JAM

ripe fruit	3 tbsp. lemon juice
¾ cup sugar per cup sauce	3 oz. liquid pectin

Collect about 1½ quarts of ripe cocoplums. They vary in size, which means the amount will also vary. Place in a saucepan and cook until the fruit softens and the juices run. Run through a food mill and remove the seeds and skins. Measure. Place the juicy pulp in a saucepan and bring to a boil. Add in the lemon juice and add ¾ cup sugar to each cup of juicy pulp. Bring to a boil, add in the liquid pectin, and bring to a boil for 1 full minute.

Skim the colorful foam, pour into hot, sterile jelly jars, seal, and label. Goes well on hot French toast.

COCOPLUM SAUCE

1 qt. ripe fruit	pinch ground cinnamon
½ cup sugar or honey	1 tbsp. orange juice

Stew 1 quart of ripe cocoplums for about 20 minutes. Remove from the heat and strain through a food mill. Remove the seeds and skins.

Mix 1 full cup of juicy pulp with ½ cup sugar or honey and simmer over a low heat for 10 minutes. Stir constantly to prevent burning.

Remove from the heat, add in the orange juice, and mix well. Used directly at the table to enhance wild meats or lamb dishes, or topping to ice creams. If desired, pour into hot, sterile jelly jar, seal, and label.

COCOPLUM-AMARETTO SAUCE

2 cups ripe cocoplums
½ cup sugar or honey
pinch allspice

1 tbsp. lemon juice
¼ cup Amaretto

Cook cocoplums until soft and the juice runs. Run through a food mill to remove the skins and seeds. Combine the sugar and juicy pulp in a saucepan. Cook over a low heat for 10 minutes. Cool slightly and place in a blender with the lemon juice and the Amaretto. Puree.

Add to hot, sterile jars, seal, and label. Excellent when used as a sauce on cakes and other bakery products, as well as ice cream.

COCOPLUM CONSERVE

1 qt. ripe fruit
¾ tsp. ground cinnamon
3½ cups sugar or honey

2 juice oranges
6 tbsp. lemon juice

Cut 2 juice oranges into very thin slices, remove the seeds, place in a deep saucepan, cover with water, and cook until skins are tender.

Wash and stem 1 quart of ripe cocoplums. Strain the fruit through a food mill, removing the skins and seeds. Add the juicy pulp to the cooked orange slices and mix well. Next add the spices, lemon juice, and sugar. Mix and simmer over a low heat until thick. Remove from the heat, spoon the mix into hot, sterile jelly jars, seal, and label. Goes well on English muffins.

COCOPLUM LEATHER

2 cups cocoplums
½ cup sugar or corn syrup

2 tsp. lemon juice
pinch ground cinnamon

Wash and stem 2 full cups cocoplum fruit. Toss into a blender to produce a colorful puree. Add in 2 teaspoons of lemon juice and ½ cup of sugar or corn syrup. Mix thoroughly.

Cover the cookie sheet with plastic wrap and then spread the mix evenly across the sheet. Place in a warm shaded area but cover to keep off visiting insects. Place in a 140-degree oven to dry faster. When dry, roll then store in a locking plastic bag.

Garnish when ready to eat with crushed nuts, etc.

DRIED COCOPLUMS

Despite the large seeds, cocoplum yields an excellent dried fruit. Collect as many as you need, wash thoroughly, and remove stems and debris. Place in a sunlit area and allow to dry for three to four days. You may also dry in a oven at 145-degree heat for 3 to 4 hours. Once dry, place in a locking plastic bag and store in a dark, dry area.

When ready to use, rehydrate with warm water. If you prefer, they can also be served dry.

CRAB APPLE
Malus spp.

CRAB APPLE TREES ARE FOUND primarily in the northern states. They range from Ontario and New England south to Florida. There are several species of crab apple, and often all can be found in the same area. Narrow-leaved crab apples *(Malus angustifolia)* can be found growing from southern New England south to Florida and west to Kansas. The western crab apple (M. *ioensis)* has a range throughout the midwestern U.S. The American crab apple (M. *coronaria)* ranges from Ontario south to the Carolinas and west to Iowa. The California crab apple (M. *fusca)* ranges from California north to Alaska, along the coastal areas. The Siberian crab apple (M. *baccata)* is a small, cultivated tree used primarily as an ornamental. In recent years it has escaped to nearby wilds and other areas where crab apples might be found. The fruit is abundant and quite edible, although somewhat smaller.

Crab apple leaves are narrow or ovate, dark green, and up to 3 inches in length with toothed edges. The blossoms are white-pink and yield a small 1½-inch fruit that resembles an apple and is red when fully ripe. The fruit is somewhat sour but is excellent when cooked or pickled.

Most wild crab apple trees bear an abundance of fruit and are ready for harvest just after the first frost, which helps to color the fruit. The crab apple has a high concentration of natural pectin just below the outer skin layer. When selecting fruit it is wise to select partially ripened crab apples, as they yield a much better flavor than fully ripened fruit, and contain more pectin.

CRAB APPLE JELLY

5 lbs. partially ripe fruit
5 cups water
8 cups sugar

Select 5 pounds of partially ripened crab apples, discarding any soft or rotten fruit. Remove the stem and flowers ends. Cut the fruit into thin slices, leaving the peels and cores intact. Place the fruit into a saucepan, add 5 cups of water, cover and simmer over a low heat for 10 minutes. Use a hand masher and crush the fruit completely, producing a juicy sauce. Allow the mix to simmer for 5 to 10 minutes longer.

Remove from the heat, strain through a jelly bag. Save the pulp and make a delicious apple butter.

Recover the juice, place in a saucepan, add 8 cups of sugar, and stir constantly over a medium heat until sugar is dissolved. Bring to a boil for 1 full minute, pour into hot, sterile jelly jars, seal, and label.

CRAB APPLE–MINT JELLY

5 lbs. partially ripe fruit   5 cups water
8 cups sugar   1 bunch fresh mint leaves

Use the preceding recipe for crab apple jelly. After you have completely dissolved the sugar, add in the mint leaves, but first bruise the leaves and stems. Tie them in a bundle, pass the bundle through the hot crab apple sauce until you obtain the desired mint flavor. The longer the mint remains in the sauce the better the flavor.

When the desired mint flavor is obtained, remove the mint leaves and bring the mixture to a boil for 1 full minute. Then pour the hot sauce into hot, sterile jars, seal, and label.

CRAB APPLE–QUINCE JELLY

3 qts. crab apples
3 pints ripe quince
1 cup sugar per cup juice

Select, wash, and stem the partially ripened apples. Remove the blossom ends and cut the fruit into pieces. Wash the ripe quince, peel, and cut into slices. Cook the fruit in separate saucepans until soft and the juice flows. Separately pass the juicy sauce through a jelly bag. Combine the two juices in a saucepan. For each cup of juice add 1 cup of granulated sugar.

Cook the combined sauce until the sugar dissolves. Bring to a full boil for 1 minute. Pour the hot sauce into hot, sterile jelly jars, seal, and label.

CRAB APPLE PRESERVES

2 qts. ripe fruit	1 sliced lemon
1 sliced juice orange	1 cup sugar per cup of juice
pinch ground cinnamon	pinch ground allspice

Wash and stem and remove flower ends from partially ripened fruit. Slice the fruit into quarters, core and peel. Place the peelings in a saucepan and just cover with water. Add 1 thinly sliced juice orange and lemon. Mix well and simmer until the peelings are soft. Save the citrus peels!

Strain the mixture, saving the juice. Place the juice in a saucepan, add cooked citrus peels, apple slices, and sugar and mix thoroughly.

Bring to a boil, then reduce heat and simmer until apple slices soften. Then, pour the mixture into hot, sterile jars, covering the fruit with the hot sauce. Seal and label.

CRAB APPLE PICKLES

6 lbs. crab apples	2 sticks cinnamon
2 cups sugar	1 qt. cider vinegar
1 tbsp. whole cloves	pinch allspice

Select 6 pounds uniformly colored fruit. Wash, but do not remove the stems or flower remnants. Use the apple intact. Puncture the skin a few times using a toothpick.

Make a spice bag. Place the apples in a saucepan, add 1 quart of cider vinegar and 2 cups of sugar, and suspend the spice bag in the mixture. Place over moderate heat, bringing the mix to a slow boil. Cook at a soft boil for 20 minutes, stirring occasionally. Remove the fruit, pack into hot, sterile jars, cover with the hot syrup, seal, and label. Allow the pickled fruit to age for 1 month before serving.

CRAB APPLE SALSA

2 cups cleaned, diced apples	1 tbsp. honey
2 tbsp. cider vinegar	1 tbsp. corn syrup
1 tbsp. lemon juice	1 cup seedless raisins

The crab apples should be stemmed, flowers removed as well as seeds. Cut into small pieces. Cook the raisins until soft. Combine all ingredients and refrigerate. Can be placed in a plastic freezer container and frozen for future use.

CRAB APPLE–GINGER SAUCE

4 cups ripe fruit	¼ tsp. ground ginger
¼ cup sugar	⅛ tsp. salt
1 cup boiling water	¼ cup honey

Stem, wash, and core apples. Dice and place in a saucepan; cook until fruit softens and the juice runs free. Remove and run through a food mill, removing the skins and seeds.

Separately blend sugar, honey, salt, and ginger in a saucepan, slowly adding the water. Stir constantly and bring to a boil. Add in the cooked sauce and mix thoroughly. Cook over a moderate heat for 5 minutes.

Remove from the heat, pour the mix into hot, sterile jars, seal, and label. Sauce goes well with meats, cake toppings and is delicious with ice cream.

DRIED CRAB APPLES

Wash stem and core the fruit, place on cookie sheets, and dry in the sun. May take 3 to 4 days to dry. Dry faster in a 140-degree oven in 5 to 7 hours. Store in plastic locking bags and store in a dark place.

Can be eaten dry or rehydrated with warm water.

BOG CRANBERRY

Vaccinium spp.

THIS SMALL BOG PLANT IS A RELATIVE OF the blueberry. We are all familiar with the commercial varieties that decorate the table at Thanksgiving and Christmas. Few folks realize that this wonderful fruit grows wild in boggy areas throughout the northeastern and north-central United States and southern Canada, as well as some areas of Alaska.

The bog cranberry (*Vaccinium macrocarpus*) is a creeping, somewhat brittle vine, from 3 to 4 inches to sometimes 12 inches in length. The short, stubby branches have oval, evergreen leaves. The fruit is bright red when ripe, firm, and about ½ to 1 inch in size.

Mountain cranberry (*V. vitis-idaea*) can also be used much in the same manner. As the name indicates, this small but abundant scraggly plant is usually found at higher elevations. The leaves are similar to those of the bog cranberry and it bears bright red fruit. The fruit is much smaller and less tart than the bog cranberry's and tends to become quite dry and pulpy when it remains on the vine too long.

CRANBERRY JELLY

4 cups ripe berries
2 cups sugar or honey
2 cups water

Wash and stem the berries and drain. Place in a saucepan, add 2 cups water and bring to a boil. Cook at a soft boil until berries soften and juice runs freely. Remove from the heat and strain through a jelly bag.

Bring the juice to a boil, add 2 cups sugar or honey and boil until the sugar is completely dissolved. Skim the foam, pour into hot, sterile jelly jars, seal, and label. Store in dark place.

CRANBERRY-GRAPE JELLY

1 cup ripe berries
2 cups ripe grapes

1 tbsp. lemon juice
3 oz. liquid pectin

You will need the juices of wild cranberries and grapes. Boil 1 cup ripe cranberries in $\frac{1}{2}$ cup water for 20 minutes. Squeeze the juicy sauce through a food mill, then pass the juice through a jelly bag,

At the same time, boil the grapes in 1 cup of water until all the grapes pop and juice runs freely. Pass the mess through a jelly bag and save the juice.

Mix the two juices, adding the pectin and lemon juice. Bring to a boil and cook for 5 minutes. Pour into hot, sterile jelly jars, seal, and label. Store in a dark place.

SPICED CRANBERRY CONSERVE

4 cups cranberries	¼ lb. seedless raisins
1½ cups water	½ cup chopped nut meats
1 orange	pinch of mace and allspice
6 cups sugar	1 tsp. cider vinegar

Wash and stem 4 cups ripe cranberries. Add the berries to a saucepan with 1½ cups water. Cook until the berries pop. Stir to keep from burning.

Add chopped raisins, nut meats, finely chopped orange, and sugar. Mix thoroughly. Cook the concoction for 25 minutes. Skim the foam, pour the sauce into hot, sterile jars, seal, and label.

CRANBERRY SAUCE

4 cups ripe berries	1 grated orange rind
2 cups water	2 cups sugar

Place 2 cups of water in a saucepan, the grated rind of 1 orange, and 2 cups of sugar. Mix thoroughly and cook over moderate eat for 5 minutes.

Add the cleaned cranberries and cook until berries burst, When cooking is complete, place the hot sauce in hot, sterile jelly jars, seal, and label.

DRIED CRANBERRIES

Collect as many berries as needed, wash, and stem. Place on cookie sheet(s) in warm sunlight to dry. May take up to 3 to 4 days. Drying in an oven at 140 degrees will take 6 to 8 hours. Diced cranberries will dry faster than whole berries. Place in locking plastic bags and store in dark, dry place. May be eaten as is, used to make gorp, or put on hot cereals in the winter months.

CRANBERRY PRESERVES

2 qts. ripe berries
6 cups sugar or corn syrup
½ cup water

Place all ingredients in a saucepan, heat until all the sugar dissolves. Cook at a boil for 5 minutes. Reduce the heat and cook at a simmer until the mix passes the jelly test. Pour the mixture, whole berries and all, into hot, sterile jars, seal, and label. Makes a great addition to the holiday table.

CRANBERRY LEATHER

2 cups cranberry puree   2 tsp. lemon juice
½ cup sugar or corn syrup   pinch ground cinnamon

Place enough ripe berries in a blender to obtain 2 full cups of puree. Place in a saucepan, add in lemon juice and sugar, and mix well.

Using plastic wrap, cover a cookie sheet and spread puree across sheet. Place in 140-degree oven and dry. When dry, roll the leather and place in a locking plastic bag and store in a dark place. When ready to use, garnish with a spread, finely chopped nuts, or whatever catches the eye.

HIGHBUSH CRANBERRY
Viburnum trilobum

A TALL SHRUB, RANGING IN height from 3 to 15 feet. The leaves are similar to the three-lobed maple leaves. White flower clusters yield a bright, red, waxy fruit during late September and early October. The fruit is firm but softens soon after the first frost. It is juicy and tart, with large seeds. Can be used as a wonderful substitute for the bog cranberry.

This ornamental shrub has taken to the wild and thrives in wetland areas, from Newfoundland south to the Middle Atlantic states and west to Oregon. It has become a familiar roadside ornamental shrub.

HIGHBUSH CRANBERRY JELLY

4 cups ripe fruit
2 cups sugar
2 cups water

Wash and stem 4 cups ripe highbush cranberries. Place in a saucepan, add in water, and cook until fruit softens and juice runs freely. Remove from heat and run through a jelly bag.

Place the juice in a saucepan, add sugar, and boil until sugar completely dissolves. Skim the foam, pour into hot, sterile jars, seal, and label. Goes well on toast.

CRANBERRY–CRAB APPLE JELLY

> 1 qt. ripe berries
> 5 to 6 ripe crab apples
> 1 cup sugar per cup juice

Cook the berries with a little water until the fruit pops. Wash, stem, deflower, and core the crab apples. Cut the fruit into eighths, cook until fruit softens, then crush with a masher. Strain both fruits through jelly bags. Do not squeeze the pulp!

Measure the juices and combine in a saucepan. Add 1 cup sugar to each cup of juice. Bring the mixture to a boil and cook until sugar completely dissolves. Cook until mixture begins to thicken. Pour into hot, sterile jars, seal, and label.

SPICY HIGHBUSH CRANBERRY SAUCE

> 4 cups cranberries   1 grated orange rind
> 2 cups water $\frac{1}{2}$ tsp. ground cinnamon
> 2 cups sugar $\frac{1}{2}$ tsp. allspice

Place 2 cups water, the grated rind of 1 orange and 2 cups sugar and spices in a saucepan, mix thoroughly and cook over moderate heat for 5 minutes.

Cook the highbush cranberries in a separate saucepan until fruit pops and juice runs freely. Run through a food mill to remove the many seeds. Combine with the spicy mixture and mix thoroughly. Pour into hot, sterile jars, seal, and label. Goes well with meats and bakery topping.

SPICED HIGHBUSH CRANBERRY CONSERVE

4 cups ripe berries	¼ lb. chopped seedless raisins
1 orange, finely chopped	½ cup finely chopped nuts
6 cups sugar	pinch mace and allspice
1½ cups water	1 tsp. cider vinegar

Wash and stem 4 cups of ripe highbush cranberries; place the berries and the water in a saucepan. Cook until berries soften and juice flows. Run through a food mill to remove seeds.

Place the juicy pulp in a saucepan, add in the remaining ingredients, mix thoroughly. Cook for 25 minutes over moderate heat. Skim off the foam, pour into hot, sterile jars, seal, and label.

SWEET AND SOUR HIGHBUSH CRANBERRY SAUCE

1 cup berries	1½ tsp. lemon juice
½ cup water	1 tbsp. butter
2 tbsp. sugar	½ cup water
¾ tsp. corn starch	¼ tsp. salt

Bring the berries, in a little water, to a boil. Run through a food mill removing the seeds. Combine with the cornstarch, sugar, and salt, then pour the boiling water over the mix, stirring constantly.

Cook until the mix thickens. Add in the lemon juice and butter. Stir well. Cook 1 minute longer, stirring. Pour the hot mixture into hot, sterile jars, seal, and label. Excellent cooking sauce for stir-fry veggies.

HIGHBUSH CRANBERRY LEATHER

Collect as many berries as you need, wash, and stem. Remove any damaged fruit! Prepare 2 cups puree. Do not use a blender as the seeds are too many and too large. Use a hand masher. Crush the fruit and run through a food mill. Save the juicy pulp!

Place in a saucepan, add in the sugar, honey, or corn syrup. Mix.

Using a plastic wrap, cover a cookie sheet and spread the mix across the surface. Best dried in an oven, although sunlight will work. Use a 140-degree oven. Will take 5 to 6 hours.

When dry, roll and place in a locking plastic bag and store in dark place. Use desired garnish when served.

DRIED HIGHBUSH CRANBERRIES

Collect as many ripe berries as needed, wash and sort out the bad fruit. Place on cookie sheets and place in bright sunlight. Oven is best at 140 degrees. Remember there are large seeds still inside the fruit. Place the dried fruit in locking plastic bags and store in dark place.

FROZEN HIGHBUSH CRANBERRIES

Collect as much of the ripened fruit as needed. Wash and stem. Allow to air dry for several minutes. When dry, place the fruit in a locking plastic bag, label, and place in the freezer. Will keep for several months. Can be thawed, then used for sauces, etc.

CROWBERRY
Empetrum nigrum

THE CROWBERRY IS A LOW, SPREADING bush. Highly branched, it has leaves that are small, slender, and needlelike.

The plant bears small, almost inconspicuous purple flowers, usually in the axils of the leaves. The small, delicate flowers yield a drupe, a juicy berrylike fruit with a purple-black color. The fruit matures in the early fall and may remain on the bush throughout the early winter months. It is somewhat tasteless and mealy when eaten raw. Cooking enhances the flavor greatly.

The crowberry can be found throughout the Arctic region, Newfoundland, and south along the mountains of New York, New England, and California. It thrives in small patches of soil in rocky outcrops.

CROWBERRY JELLY

1 qt. ripe fruit	1½ cups sugar per cup juice
1 tbsp. lemon juice	3 oz. liquid pectin

Wash the ripe fruit, even the dehydrated ones. Place in a saucepan with a little water, and cook until fruit pops. Allow to simmer for 15 minutes. Run through a jelly bag and save the fine colored juice.

Measure the juice, add to saucepan, stir in the lemon juice and 1 cup sugar to each cup of juice, and bring to a boil. Add 3 oz. of liquid pectin and boil for 3 minutes.

Remove the foam, pour into hot, sterile jars, seal, and label. The final product will have an umber or bright brown color. Goes well as fruit topping on cakes and other pastries.

CROWBERRY SAUCE

4 cups ripe berries	2 cups water
1 grated orange rind	2 cups sugar

Place 2 cups of water, the grated rind of 1 orange, and 2 cups of granulated sugar into a saucepan, mix thoroughly, and cook over a moderate heat for 5 minutes.

Next add 4 cups of fully ripened berries, washed and stemmed. Cook until the berries begin to pop. When cooking is complete, serve chilled.

CURRANT
Ribes spp.

A SHRUB; WILD CURRANTS ARE almost vinelike, with low, hanging branches that will root freely where they touch the ground. The fruit of the red currant (*Ribes satinum*) is juicy, red, smooth, translucent, and tart. It is an upright shrub, with heart-shaped leaves that have fine lobes and are often hairy on the undersides. The shrub may attain heights of 5 feet and bears fruit in late June or early July.

The swamp red currant (*R. triste*) is similar, but it may have leaves of 3 to 5 lobes. This species has a foul smell but the fruit is edible.

The black currant (*R. nigrum*) has escaped cultivation and bears fruit similar to the American black currant (*R. americanum*): black, smooth, and translucent. These currants grow in damp, moist places and range across much of the mountainous land of North America.

Canadian black currants (*R. hudsonianum*) grow from Alaska south to Iowa, Oregon, and Michigan. The golden currant (*R. aureum*) is a rather tall western currant with a range from California north to southern Alaska.

There are many more wild currants and gooseberries, but the above are most commonly found in the greatest abundance. The fruit of all these species is deliciously tart and edible but lacks pectin.

CURRANT JELLY

2 qts. ripe fruit	1 cup water
2 cups water	3 oz. liquid pectin

Select 2 quarts ripe currants (red, black, or white), wash, and stem. Place in a saucepan and add 1 cup of water. Bring to a boil and cook at a soft boil for 15 minutes. The fruit will develop a whitish color when ready.

Strain the mixture through a jelly bag. Do not squeeze the pulp through the bag. Collect the juice and place in a saucepan and heat to boiling. Add 2 cups granulated sugar and the pectin. Bring to a boil for 5 minutes, stirring constantly. Skim the foam, pour into hot, sterile jars, seal, and label.

SPICED CURRANT JELLY

4 cups ripe currants	1 tsp. cinnamon
¼ cup cider vinegar	1 tsp. ground cloves
6 cups sugar or honey	3 oz. liquid pectin

Wash and clean 4 cups of ripe berries. Crush in a saucepan or blender. Add ¼ cup cold water and ¼ cup cider vinegar. Add the spices and mix the contents thoroughly. Place over a high heat, bring to a boil, stirring constantly. Then simmer over a low heat for 10 minutes.

Add 6 cups of sugar or honey and stir well. Bring to a boil until sugar dissolves. Add the pectin; bring to a boil for 1 full minute. Remove from the heat, skim the foam, and pour into hot, sterile jars, seal, and label.

CURRANT-MINT JELLY

2 qts. ripe berries	¼ cup cider vinegar
1 cup water	3 ½ cups sugar
3 oz. liquid pectin	3 cups fresh mint leaves

Select 2 quarts of ripe fruit and wash. Place in a saucepan, bring to a boil and simmer until juices run freely. Strain through a jelly bag. Place the juice in a saucepan.

Add 1 cup of water, fresh mint leaves, vinegar, sugar and mix thoroughly. Bring to a hard boil for 3 minutes, stir constantly. Add 3 oz. of liquid pectin and boil for 5 minutes. Skim colorful foam, strain out the leaves and debris, pour into hot, sterile jars, seal, and label.

CURRANT MARMALADE

4 cups ripe fruit	2 oranges
2 ½ cups sugar	1 lemon
1 ¾ cups water	⅛ tsp. baking soda
3 oz. liquid pectin	pinch ground cloves

Remove the seeds from the citrus fruit and cut into thin slices. Grind the fruit in a blender. Add the baking soda and water, cover, and cook at a simmer for 20 minutes. Add in the fruit and cook at a simmer for 10 minutes.

Measure 5 cups, place in a saucepan, and add in sugar or honey. Bring to a boil for 1 minute. Remove from the heat and add in the pectin, stir, and cook at a boil for 1 full minute. Skim the foam, pour into hot, sterile jars, seal, and label. Great garnish for hot toast or muffins.

CURRANT LEATHER

> 2 cups ripe fruit
> 2 tsp. lemon juice
> $\frac{1}{2}$ cup sugar, honey, or corn syrup

Wash and clean, removing any stems. Toss into a blender and puree. Add in 2 teaspoons of lemon juice and the sugar and mix thoroughly.

Using a plastic wrap, cover a cookie sheet and spread the mix across the sheet. Place in direct sunlight to dry. May take a few days, or you can dry in a 140-degree oven in a few hours. When dry, roll and store in a locking plastic bag. Garnish with nuts, etc., when ready to eat.

DRIED CURRANTS

Collect as much of the fruit as you want, wash, and stem. Place on a cookie sheet and dry in bright sunlight. May take a few days, or dry in an oven at 140 degrees in a day. Store in locking plastic bags, in a cool dark place.

Serve dry or rehydrate in warm water. Can be utilized as stock material for more jam or jelly.

ELDERBERRY
Sambucus spp.

THE COMMON ELDERBERRY OR black-berried elder (*Sambucus canadensis*) is one of the most abundant wild fruits of the northern United States. Considered a shrub, this plant may attain heights of 10 feet or more. It can be found growing along the roadways, railroads, hedgerows, woodlands, drainage ditches, and thickets. There are usually several bushes in a single area.

The twigs are somewhat brittle with a white, pithy center. The leaves are compound, with 5 to 11 leaflets, coarse-toothed edges, and an elliptical shape.

The flowers appear in large white clusters or umbels, about 4 to 6 inches in diameter. It is best to locate elderberry when the flowers are in bloom; note the location and return in the fall to harvest the large clusters of black-colored berries. The clusters are so heavy with ripe fruit that their weight pulls the branches downward.

The fruit is sweet with a deep purple or black color. It is about ¼ inch in diameter and contains 3 to 4 nutlets as seeds. The flowers open in June and the fruit ripens in late summer or early autumn. The fruit has a high concentration of vitamin C: 100 mg of ascorbic acid for each ounce of fruit.

All parts of the plant contain the poison hydrocyanic acid, which is destroyed by cooking. Red elderberry (*S. pubens*) is considered poisonous and should not be used, as cooking does not destroy enough of the toxin.

ELDERBERRY JELLY

3 lbs. ripe berries	½ cup lemon juice
6 cups sugar	6 oz. liquid pectin

Wash and stem 3 pounds freshly picked ripe berries. Place in a saucepan and cook over a moderate heat for 15 minutes. Crush with a masher. Then run the mess through a jelly bag and recover 3 cups of juice. Place into a saucepan. Add in the lemon and mix thoroughly. Add in the sugar and boil until dissolved.

Add 6 oz. liquid pectin, bring to a boil for 1 full minute, and stir constantly. Skim the foam, pour into hot, sterile jars, seal and label. Goes well with hot biscuits or toast.

ELDERBERRY-APPLE JELLY

2 qts. ripe fruit	2 qts. water
4 medium apples	1 cup sugar per cup juice
1 tbsp. lemon juice	

Cook 2 quarts ripe berries until the juice rolls. Crush the mess with a hand crusher.

Wash, stem, and remove blossom remnants of 4 medium cooking apples. Cut the apples into quarters, add to the berries, and mash with a potato masher. Add 2 quarts of water and simmer for 20 minutes. Stir occasionally to prevent bottom burn.

Strain the mixture through a jelly bag. Measure the juice, place in a saucepan, add 1 cup of sugar per cup of juice, stir in the lemon juice, and bring to a boil for 1 full minute. Lower the heat and cook until the sauce "sheets." Pour into hot, sterile jars, seal, and label.

ELDERBERRY JAM

4 cups cooked crushed fruit
3 cups sugar
3 oz. liquid pectin

Cook and crush enough fruit to obtain 4 cups of cooked sauce. Cook at a moderate heat for 15 minutes, then strain through a food mill to remove the skins and seeds. Combine the juicy pulp and sugar in a saucepan and cook until sugar dissolves. Add the pectin, bring to a boil for 1 full minute. Skim the foam, pour into hot, sterile jars, seal, and label.

SWEET AND SOUR ELDERBERRY COOKING SAUCE

1 cup juicy pulp	1½ tsp. lemon juice
½ cup water	1 tbsp. butter
2 tbsp. sugar	¼ tsp. salt
¾ tsp. corn starch	1 tsp. soy sauce

Bring the juicy fruit pulp to a boil. Add in the corn starch, sugar, and salt, pouring boiling water over and stirring constantly. Cook until thickens, then add in lemon juice, soy sauce, and butter. Cook and stir constantly. Cook for one full minute. Pour into hot, sterile jars, seal, and label. Goes well with stir-fry veggies.

DRIED ELDERBERRIES

Wash and stem as many berries as you wish. Spread on a cookie sheet and dry in the sun. This usually takes 2 days. Store in locking plastic bags, in a dry, cool, dark area. Remember the seeds are still intact when ready to use. Reconstitute with water, run through a food mill, and remove the seeds.

RY-GINGER SAUCE

fruit	¼ tsp. ground ginger
¼ cup sugar	⅛ tsp. salt
1 cup boiling water	¼ cup honey or corn syrup

Cook the fruit until berries pop and then run through a food mill to remove the seeds and skins. Blend the colorful sauce, sugar or corn syrup, ginger, and salt in a saucepan. Slowly add the water, stirring constantly. Bring to a boil and cook for 5 minutes, stirring to prevent bottom burn. Pour into hot, sterile jars, seal, and label.

Makes an excellent topping for pastries, waffles, and pancakes.

FALSE SOLOMON'S SEAL

Smilacina racemosa

FALSE SPIKENARD OR FALSE SOLOMON'S seal grows from a fleshy underground rhizome. It can be found growing in shaded, wooded areas with moist soils from Nova Scotia south along the mountains to Georgia. The so-called stem may attain heights of 2 feet. The stem may bear 5 to 10 leaves, which are oval and pointed at the ends.

The flowers appear in a cluster at the end of the stem. They yield a cluster of freckled pink berries that turn bright red when ripe. They are quite aromatic and tart. The berries can be eaten raw, as you find them, or used for jellies and sauces.

FALSE SOLOMON'S SEAL JELLY

    1 quart ripe berries
    1 cup of sugar per cup juice
    3 oz. liquid pectin

Gather 1 full quart of ripe berries. Do not use berries that are speckled and pink. Wash, stem, place in a saucepan, add in a little water, cover, and cook over moderate heat until fruit pops and juice runs freely.

Strain through a jelly bag. Measure the juice and to each cup of add 1 cup of sugar and mix well. Bring to a boil and cook until all sugar dissolves. Stir constantly.

Add in 3 ounces of pectin and hold at a boil for 1 full minute. Skim the foam, pour into hot, sterile jars, seal, and label.

FALSE SOLOMON'S SEAL JAM

    1 qt. ripe berries
    1 cup sugar per cup sauce
    3 oz. liquid pectin

Wash and stem the berries, place in a saucepan, add in a little water, cover, and cook over moderate heat until juices run free.

Strain the juicy pulp through a food mill, removing the seeds and skins. Measure the juicy pulp, add 1 cup of sugar to each cup of juicy pulp. Bring to a boil, stirring constantly until all sugar dissolves.

Add the pectin, hold at a boil for 1 full minute. Stir. Skim the colorful foam, pour into hot, sterile jars, seal, and label.

FALSE SOLOMON'S SEAL LEATHER

    2 cups puree
    2 tsp. lemon juice
    ½ cup sugar or corn syrup

Wash the berries and toss in a blender. Place the puree in a saucepan, add in the lemon juice and sugar or corn syrup. Mix thoroughly.

Using a plastic wrap, cover a cookie sheet and spread the mixture across the surface evenly. Place in the sunshine to dry or in a 140-degree oven. When dry, roll and store in a locking plastic bag. Add garnish when ready to use.

SPICY FALSE SOLOMON'S SEAL SAUCE

4 cups ripe berries	2 cups sugar
1 grated orange rind	¼ tsp. ground cinnamon
2 cups water	pinch ground cloves

Combine the grated rind of 1 orange, 2 cups water, and 2 cups sugar in a saucepan. Mix and cook over moderate heat for 10 minutes. Add the berries and cook until the juice runs freely. Add ground cinnamon and ground cloves. Cook for 5 minutes, stirring frequently. Spoon into hot, sterile jars.

FALSE SOLOMON'S SEAL DRESSING

2 cups fruit	2 tbsp. soybean oil
1 cup red wine	½ cup corn syrup
1 tbsp. lemon juice	

Cook the berries in a little water over a moderate heat until the juice runs freely. Run the juice through a jelly bag and place in a saucepan. Add in the soybean oil, red wine, lemon juice, and corn syrup, mix thoroughly, and bring to a boil for 1 full minute. Can be used as an excellent salad dressing.

FALSE SOLOMON'S SEAL CONSERVE

4 cups berries	1½ cups water
¼ lb. seedless raisins	½ cup chopped nut meats
1 chopped orange	6 cups sugar
1 tsp. allspice	

Wash and stem 4 cups berries. Add the berries to a saucepan with the water and cook until the berries have softened and burst. Stir to prevent bottom burning.

Add chopped raisins, nut meats, thinly sliced oranges, allspice, and sugar. Mix thoroughly. Cook for 25 minutes, then skim the foam, and pour the mix into hot, sterile jars, seal, and label.

DRIED FALSE SOLOMON'S SEAL

Collect as many berries as needed. Wash and stem, then place on a cookie sheet and dry in full sunshine. May take 2 to 3 days to completely dry. A 140-degree oven will accomplish this in one day. When dry, place the fruit in locking plastic bags and store in a dry, dark place.

Can be served dried as an ingredient for trail mixes or rehydrated with warm water and served as a sauce or to make more jam or jelly.

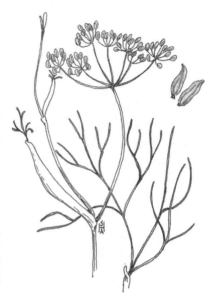

FENNEL
Foeniculum vulgare

THIS HIGHLY AROMATIC PERENnial reaches heights to 4 to 5 feet. A native of Europe, it has escaped from gardens to the wild, especially in California, where it is highly cultivated. Common from New England south to the Carolinas, and west to California and the Pacific Coast. It can be found growing near open fields, roadsides, field edges, open slopes, and generally anywhere with good, open soils.

The leaves are compound, featherlike, and narrow, with long, sheathed petioles. Flowers are yellow and appear in large, loose clusters. Ripe fruits are ¼ inch long, narrow, oblong, and somewhat round. All parts of the plant contain the oils of anethole and fenchone and therefore can be used fresh or dried. Fennel seed has long been used as a seasoning to flavor soups, rolls, and breads.

DRIED FENNEL

Harvest only healthy-looking stems, leaves, or seed pods. The seed pods should be removed, cleaned, and then spread on a cookie sheet then dried in a warm shady area. Should take two days to dry completely. Open the seed pods, then be certain the seeds are crunchy and dry. When dry, place in a locking plastic bag and store in a dark, dry area.

Harvesting the stem requires identifying the day before harvest. The following morning, after the dew has dried from the plants, cut the stems low to the ground. Tie in bundles of three or four stems. Hang upside down in a warm dark place. A garage will do nicely.

The stem and leaves can be utilized as seasoning, but should be finely chopped before drying. The chopped greens can then be spread on a shallow pan and dried in the warm shade. Should take about a single day, perhaps two, depending on the moisture in the air. When dry, place in airtight containers and store in a dark, dry place.

Fennel seed can be used as a garnish on rolls, rye bread, and other baked goods. Adds zest to bean or lentil soups.

STRANGLER FIG

Ficus aurea

THIS MEMBER OF THE MULBERRY family is a vinelike shrub that matures into a thick vine that strangles the host tree it grows on. In Florida, the strangler fig can be found growing on cabbage palmetto palms.

Plant has multiple stems, rounded, with hanging roots and attaining heights to 100 feet. The leaves are 5 to 6 inches long, elliptical or ovate, evergreen, and thick.

The fruit is rounded and hard, with colors ranging from yellow to red. Can be found growing throughout central and southern Florida, in hammocks and especially on the coastal islands. The fruit is ripe when soft. Harvesting can be done by simply picking the fruit from the ground, if the small creatures don't beat you to it.

FIG JAM (WITHOUT PECTIN)

4 cups ripe figs	juice 1 lime or lemon
1 cup water	2½ cups sugar

Collect and wash the figs thoroughly, discarding imperfect fruit. Use a food masher, processor, or blender and chop the fruit into small pieces.

Place the mashed fruit in a saucepan, add in the water and lime or lemon juice. Mix thoroughly. Cook over a medium to low heat until the mess thickens. Spoon the mix into hot, sterile jars, seal, and label.

FIG JAM (WITH PECTIN)

4 cups ripe figs	juice of 1 lime or lemon
1 cup water	2 ½ cups sugar
3 oz. liquid pectin	

Wash and stem the ripe figs. Using a blender, food processor, or hand masher, chop the fruit into small pieces. Place the mashed fruit into a saucepan, add the water and lime or orange juice, mixing thoroughly. Cook over a medium heat until mix thickens.

When the mixture has properly thickened, add in the liquid pectin and bring to a boil for 1 full minute. Skim and spoon the mixture into hot, sterile jars, seal, and label.

FIG MARMALADE

3 lbs. ripe figs	1 cup chopped orange peel
2 tbsp. lemon juice	6 cups sugar
6 oz. liquid pectin	pinch allspice

Wash and clean, using hot water, 3 pounds of ripe figs. Chop the fruit into small pieces. Place in a saucepan, add in the lemon juice, diced orange peel. Mix thoroughly. Bring to a boil and cook over a moderate heat for 30 minutes. Remove and add 6 cups sugar. Mix thoroughly.

Add in the liquid pectin and mix thoroughly, then bring to a boil for 2 full minutes. When ready, spoon the mixture into hot, sterile jars, seal, and label.

FIG SAUCE

4 cups diced ripe figs	1 grated orange rind
2 cups water	2 cups sugar
pinch allspice	pinch ground cinnamon

Wash enough ripe figs to obtain 4 cups of diced fruit. Place in a saucepan, add in water, grated rind of orange, spices, and sugar. Mix thoroughly and cook over a moderate heat for 5 minutes.

Add in the diced figs and mix. Cook for 30 minutes, then strain the mix, removing the many seeds and pulp. Place the juice in a bowl, chill, and serve. To preserve, while still hot, spoon the mix into hot, sterile jars, seal, and label. Serve chilled on ice cream or other desserts.

FIG SYRUP

4 cups diced fruit	2 cups sugar
2 cups water	6 tbsp. grated lemon rind
4 tbsp. corn syrup	pinch ground ginger

Combine the ingredients in a saucepan and mix thoroughly. Cook over a medium heat until the sugar is dissolved. Simmer for 30 minutes.

Remove all pulp using a strainer or food mill, producing a yellow-brown liquid. Use immediately on waffles, pancakes, etc. Store in refrigerator until ready to use.

FIG CONSERVE

4 cups ripe fruit	½ cup chopped nut meats
1½ cups water	3 cups sugar
1 cup chopped seedless raisins	1 chopped orange

Remove seeds then dice the figs. Place in a saucepan, add in the water, mix, and bring to a boil. Simmer for 30 minutes. Using a potato masher, crush the fruit. Add in the raisins, chopped orange (rind included), and sugar. Mix sauce thoroughly and bring to a boil, then reduce heat to medium and cook for 20 minutes. Add finely chopped nut meats.

Simmer for an additional 10 minutes, stirring frequently. Remove from the heat, pour into hot, sterile jars, seal, and label.

PICKLED FIGS

2 lbs. fresh figs	2 cups brown sugar
¼ tsp. salt	2 sticks cinnamon
1 qt. water	2 to 3 whole cloves
1 cup cider vinegar	pinch allspice

Combine the ingredients in a saucepan, mix well, and bring to a boil. Cook over a medium heat for 5 minutes.

Remove and spoon the fruit into hot, sterile jars, cover the fruit with the liquid sauce, seal, and cover.

FIG RELISH

3 cups figs	¼ cup sugar
¼ cup raisins	1 tsp. ground cinnamon
½ cup apples, peeled and diced	pinch ground cloves
	½ cup cider vinegar

Remove the seeds from the figs and cut into small pieces and place in a saucepan. Add in remaining ingredients and mix thoroughly. Bring the mix to a boil, then simmer over moderate heat until the fruit softens and the mixture thickens. Stir frequently to prevent burning. Spoon into hot, sterile jars, seal, and label.

WILD FIG LEATHER

2 cups fig puree	2 tsp. lemon juice
½ cup sugar or corn syrup	pinch ground ginger

Wash and clean fresh figs, remove the seeds, and chop in a blender or food processor. Place the puree in a saucepan, add in the lemon juice, sugar, and ground ginger. Mix thoroughly.

Using plastic wrap, cover a cookie sheet and spread the mix evenly across the sheet. Place in bright sunlight or in a 145-degree oven until dry. Drying time may take 2 to 3 hours in the oven, 1 to 2 days in sunlight.

Once dried, roll and store in a locking plastic bag. Serve with your desired garnish.

FIG FRUIT SALSA

2 cups diced figs	1 tbsp. honey or corn syrup
1 small apple, diced	1 tbsp. lemon juice

Remove the seeds from the figs, and dice. Peel, core, and dice one small apple. Combine the ingredients in a saucepan and mix well. Allow to sit for 1 hour to flavor. Serve chilled; or, spoon into sterile freezer container(s) and refrigerate until ready to use. Good for parties.

FIG RUM SAUCE

½ cup fig juice	½ cup rum
½ cup sugar	¼ cup water
⅓ cup orange juice	

Cook 2 cups ripe figs in a saucepan with a little water. Strain the mixture through a strainer and collect ½ cup juice. Combine the juice, sugar, and water, and boil for 1 full minute. Cool the mix, then add in the orange juice and your favorite rum. Bring to a quick boil, remove, and pour into hot, sterile jar(s), seal, and label. Best used on cakes and similar desserts.

DRIED FIGS

Harvest as many figs as needed. Wash and stem. Gently press down on each fig until somewhat flat. Place the flattened figs onto a shallow pan and dry in bright sunshine.

This process may take 3 or 4 days. Drying in an oven at 140 degrees is much faster. When dry, garnish with a little sugar, place in plastic bags, and store in a dark, dry area.

DRIED FIGS (SYRUP METHOD)

3 lbs. fresh figs
1 cup sugar
3 cups water

The syrup method produces a sweeter fig. Wash and stem the ripe fruit, then cut into small pieces or use whole. Place the water and sugar in a saucepan, bring to a boil, and add in figs. Simmer for 10 minutes. Remove from the heat and allow the fruit to stand for 10 to 15 minutes

Drain thoroughly, then spread on a cookie sheet and place in oven at 110 degrees. Allow to dry until fruit is leathery and elastic, but sticky. Then, complete drying process at a temperature of 145 to 150 degrees. The drying process may take 2 to 3 hours. Can also be dried in bright sunlight, but may take 1 or 2 days.

When dried, place in locking plastic bags and store in dry, dark place. Excellent addition to dried fruit snacks, gorp, or other trail foods.

AIR-DRIED FIGS

3 lbs. fresh-picked figs

Collect only ripened fruit. Wash thoroughly and remove the stems. Cut into halves and place the cut section face up in a shallow pan. Place the sections in direct sunlight and allow to dry for as long as necessary, perhaps 2 or 3 days.

Turning the fruit over once or twice a day will help speed the drying process.

When dry, place the fruit into locking plastic bags and store in a dark, dry place until ready to use.

FIRETHORN
Pyracantha spp.

SCARLET FIRETHORN (*PYRACANTHA angustifolia*), a member of the rose family, is widely planted as a landscape shrub. Generally used as a hedge plant due to the branching trunks, which are laden with many long thorns.

Attains heights of 5 to 7 feet and will spread over an area of 6 to 10 square feet. The foliage is evergreen, with simple leaves that alternate on the stem. The foliage color is bronze-green. The white flowers, which grow in clusters, appear in early May. The berries appear later in the summer; they are ¼ inch long and red-orange and grow in clusters along the branch.

Several varieties may be found growing near open areas, the edges of fields, and hedgerows. Ranges in growth from New England south to Alabama and west through Texas and Arkansas. Can be found on the West Coast in Oregon and Washington State.

FIRETHORN JELLY

1 qt. ripe berries	1 tsp. lemon juice
4 cups sugar or honey	3 oz. liquid pectin

Wash 1 quart of ripened berries and stem. Place the fruit in a saucepan, add a little water, and cook at a boil until the berries pop and the juice flows freely.

Strain the juicy pulp through a jelly bag. To the juice add the lemon juice and sugar. Bring to a boil and cook for 5 minutes. Remove from the heat, mix in the liquid pectin, and bring to a boil. Pour the mix into hot, sterile jars, seal, and label.

FIRETHORN JAM

1 qt. ripe berries	1 tsp. lemon juice
4 cups sugar or honey	3 oz. liquid pectin

Wash and stem 1 quart fully ripened berries. Place in a saucepan and crush the berries with a potato masher. Cover the berries with a little water and cook over a low heat for 20 minutes. Remove from the heat and strain through a food mill to remove the seeds and skins.

Place the juicy pulp in a saucepan, add in the lemon juice and sugar, and mix thoroughly. Bring to a slow boil and cook for 2 minutes. Add in the liquid pectin and bring to a fast boil for 3 full minutes.

Skim off the orange-colored foam, pour the juice into hot, sterile jars, seal, and label.

FIRETHORN RELISH DRESSING

½ cup diced fruit	1 tsp. chopped green pepper
1 cup French dressing	1 tsp. catsup
pinch ground horseradish	

Dice enough ripe fruit to obtain ½ cup. Combine the remaining ingredients in a bowl and mix thoroughly. Place the mixture in a blender to make a delightful-looking dressing.

Makes an excellent salad dressing and can be used to add zest to cold meats.

FIRETHORN RUM SAUCE

½ cup fruit juice	½ cup favorite rum
½ cup sugar	¼ cup water
⅓ cup orange juice	pinch ground cinnamon

Combine the washed and stemmed berries and sugar in a saucepan and bring to a boil for 1 full minute. Cool and add in the orange juice and rum. Bring to a fast boil. Place in a container and refrigerate. You may, after bringing the mix to a boil, pour into a hot, sterile jar, seal, and label. Will keep for about a month. Use warmed sauce on pastries and meats. Will have a delightful orange color.

FIRETHORN SAUCE

4 cups ripe berries	2 cups water
1 grated orange rind	2 cups sugar

Place 2 cups of water, the grated orange rind, and 2 cups of sugar in a saucepan, mix thoroughly, and cook over moderate heat for 5 minutes.

Add the cleaned berries and cook until the fruit pops its skin. When cooking is complete, place the sauce in a bowl and serve chilled. It will be slightly runny and not gelled. You may also, after cooking, store in hot, sterile jars, sealed and labeled.

FIRETHORN CONSERVE

4 cups ripe berries	1½ cups water
¼ lb. seedless raisins	½ cup chopped nut meats
1 grated orange rind	pinch allspice

Wash and stem 4 cups of ripe berries. Add to a saucepan with the water. Cook until the berries soften and juice runs. Stir to prevent burning.

Add the chopped seedless raisins, orange rind, chopped nut meats, diced orange rind, and the sugar. Mix thoroughly. Cook over moderate heat for 25 minutes. Skim the foam, pour into hot, sterile jars, seal, and label.

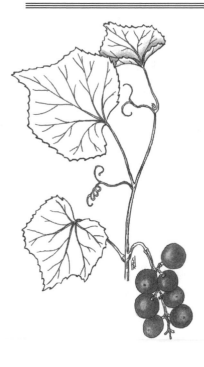

GRAPE
Vitis spp.

THERE ARE MANY DIFFERENT SPECIES of wild grapes that are found throughout Canada and the United States. In the northeastern United States and Canada, the fox grape (*V. labrusca*), the summer grape (*V. aestivalis*), the river grape (*V. vulpina*), and the winter grape (*V. bicolor*) are the most common. They range from New Brunswick south to Maryland.

Sweet winter grape (*V. cinerea*), red grape (*V. palmata*), muscadine (*V. rotundifolia*), and the sand grape (*V. rupestris*) are common in the southern portions of the United States, from Texas east to Florida and the Carolinas.

The fox grape (*V. labrusca*) is perhaps the most common and is usually found growing in large thickets, climbing over small trees and shrubs. The fruit is a sparse cluster, ¾ inch in size, and dark purple in color.

The fruit ripens in September or early October and is covered with a fine coating of wild yeast; thus giving it a musky odor. When using wild grapes for jellies or jams, it is best to select them partially ripened as they have a higher concentration of natural pectin and a much better flavor.

WILD GRAPE JELLY

5 lbs. wild grapes	½ cup water
8 cups sugar	2 oz. liquid pectin

Stem and wash 5 pounds of wild grapes. Use a ratio of 3 pounds partially ripe grapes to 2 pounds ripe grapes. Discard any imperfect fruit. Place into a saucepan, crush with a masher, add water, and bring to a boil. Cover and simmer for 15 minutes.

Strain the cooked fruit through a food mill then through a jelly bag. Save the pulp for grape butter. Place the juice in a saucepan, add the sugar, and bring to a boil. Add the liquid pectin and boil for 1 full minute. Skim the colorful foam, pour into hot, sterile jars, seal, and label.

SPICED GRAPE JELLY

5 lbs. grapes	1 tsp. ground allspice
8 cups sugar	1 tsp. whole cloves
½ cup water	1 tsp. ground cinnamon
2 oz. liquid pectin	

Use any of the wild grapes. Stem and wash. Use 3 pounds of partially ripened grapes to 2 pounds of ripe grapes. Place in a saucepan and crush. Add in the spices, water and mix thoroughly. Cover, bring to a boil, and then simmer for 15 minutes.

Strain the mixture through a food mill, then a jelly bag. Save the spicy pulp to make grape butter. Place the juice in a saucepan, add the sugar, and boil until the sugar dissolves. Then add the liquid pectin, hold at a boil for 2 full minutes. Skim the foam, pour into hot, sterile jars, seal, and label.

GRAPE JAM

3 lbs. ripe grapes	1 cup sugar per sauce
½ cup water	3 oz. liquid pectin

Stem and wash the grapes. Use partially ripe and ripe fruit. Crush in a saucepan, add in the water, and bring to a boil. Simmer for 10 minutes.

Strain the mixture through a food mill. Measure the juicy pulp into a saucepan and add 1 cup sugar to each cup of juicy pulp. Boil for 1 minute, then add 3 ounces of liquid pectin and boil again for 1 full minute. Skim the foam, pour into hot, sterile jars, seal, and label. Goes well on hot toast, bagels, and muffins.

GRAPE CONSERVE

3 qts. wild grapes	1 cup water
4 cups sugar	1 cup orange pulp
2 cups seedless raisins	pinch cinnamon

Stem and wash 3 quarts of fully ripened grapes. Peel the skins and place the skins in a saucepan with 1 cup water. Cook for 15 minutes. Cook the peeled grapes without water for 10 minutes. Remove the mixture and press through a food mill.

Combine the two juices, add 4 cups sugar, diced orange pulp, and chopped seedless raisins; cook over a medium heat for 40 minutes. Stir frequently.

Skim the foam, pour into hot, sterile jars, seal, and label. Allow 1 month before serving.

WILD GRAPE BUTTER

5 lbs. ripe fruit	6 cups sugar
6 cups cider vinegar	½ tsp. ground cinnamon
½ tsp. ground allspice	

Wash, stem, and place the fruit in a saucepan, add the water, and bring to a boil. Allow to simmer, until the juices flows. Remove and run the cooked fruit through a food mill. This will remove the skins and seeds. If you have leftover pulp from making jelly, you may use that.

Place the juicy pulp into a saucepan, add the sugar and cider vinegar, and mix thoroughly. Add the spices. Mix thoroughly again and spoon the mixture into a baking pan. Place in the oven and bake for 4 hour at 250 degrees. Occasionally stir the mix. When the juice can no longer be separated from the pulp, the butter is finished.

Remove from the oven and spoon into hot, sterile jars, seal, and label. The amount of sugar to sweeten depends on your taste.

WILD GRAPE LEATHER

2 cups grape puree	2 tsp. lemon juice
½ cup corn syrup	pinch allspice

Wash enough grapes to obtain 2 cups puree. Run the grapes through a food mill to remove the seeds and skin. Place the mess into a blender, then puree.

Place in a saucepan, add in the lemon juice and corn syrup. Mix thoroughly.

Using a plastic wrap, cover a cookie sheet, spread the puree across the sheet. Place in a 145-degree oven and dry. Should take 5 to 6 hours. When dry, roll and place in locking plastic bags and store in a dark, dry place.

SPICY WILD GRAPE SAUCE

6 cups wild grapes	2 cups sugar
1 grated orange rind	½ tsp. ground cinnamon
2 cups water	pinch ground cloves

Combine the grated rind of 1 orange, water, and sugar. Mix and cook over a moderate heat for 10 minutes. Add 4 cups of cleaned berries. Cook until the berries pop and the juice runs. Run through a food mill and place in a saucepan. Now add ¼ teaspoon of ground cinnamon and a pinch of ground cloves. Cook for 5 minutes, stirring frequently. Spoon the mixture into hot, sterile jars, seal, and label. Great sauce for pork or lamb.

WILD GRAPE RUM SAUCE

½ cup grape juice	½ cup rum
½ cup sugar	¼ cup water
⅓ cup orange juice	

Combine the grape fruit juice, water. Bring to a full boil for 1 full minute. Cool, then add in orange juice and favorite rum and bring to a boil. Pour into hot, sterile jars, seal, and label. Store cool in the refrigerator and use at a meal.

DRIED WILD GRAPES

Everyone is familiar with raisins, but there are many folks who do not know that dried grapes are really raisins. Gather as many fully ripened grapes as needed. Wash them carefully, discarding the poor-quality fruit.

Place the fruit on a cookie sheet in direct sunlight. This will take 6 or more days to dry and produce the familiar raisin. When dry, place the fruit in locking plastic bags and seal. Store in a cool dry place. Goes well with homemade gorp or snacks.

WILD GRAPE AMARETTO SAUCE

2 cups grapes	1 tsp. lemon juice
½ cup sugar or honey	¼ cup Amaretto

Combine the grapes and sugar in a saucepan and cook on a low heat for 10 minutes.

Cool the mixture slightly and run through a food mill, removing the skins and seeds. Place the juicy pulp in a blender, add in the lemon juice and Amaretto. Puree.

Bring to a quick boil, spoon into hot, sterile jars, seal, and label. Goes well as a sauce for cakes and other pastries.

WILD GRAPE DRESSING

½ cup diced grapes	1 chopped green pepper
1 cup French dressing	pinch ground horseradish
1 tsp. catsup	

Remove the seeds, place in a blender with the French dressing, finely chopped green pepper, catsup, and horseradish. Serve the dressing or refrigerate and use at another time. Goes well with salads.

GREENBRIER
Smilax spp.

GREENBRIERS HAVE A BRIGHT GREEN, woody vine, often with scattered prickles. It uses paired tendrils as a means of climbing. Leaves are ovate or egg-shaped and glassy on both sides.

Two common plants are greenbrier (*S. rotundifolia*) and bristly greenbrier (*S. tamnoides*). Small, yellowish-white flowers are located in the axils of the leaves; they yield a small cluster of blue-black berries, which are edible but best when cooked.

Greenbriers are common from Nova Scotia south to Florida and west to Texas and Minnesota. They thrive in open fields and especially at forest edges.

GREENBRIER JELLY

2 qts. ripe berries	1 cup water
2 cups sugar or honey	3 oz. liquid pectin

Select 2 quarts of ripe berries, wash, and stem. Place the fruit in a saucepan, add 1 cup water, and bring to a boil. Then, cook at a soft boil for 15 minutes. The fruit will pop and the juices will run free.

Strain the mixture through a jelly bag. Do not squeeze! Collect the juice, place in a saucepan, and bring to a boil. Add in the pectin and hold at a boil for 1 full minute. Skim the foam, pour into hot, sterile jars, seal, and label. Goes well on toast and biscuits.

SPICED GREENBRIER JELLY

2 qts. ripe fruit	3 oz. liquid pectin
6 cups sugar	1 tsp. cinnamon
¼ cup cider vinegar	1 tsp. cloves
1 cup water	

Wash and stem the fruit, crush with a potato masher or blender, and place in a saucepan. Add in the water, vinegar, and spices and mix thoroughly. Place over a high heat, bring to a boil, stirring constantly. Then simmer over a low heat for 10 minutes.

Add in the sugar and stir well. Bring to a boil until sugar dissolves. Add in the liquid pectin and hold at a boil for 1 full minute. Skim the foam, pour into hot, sterile jars, seal, and label.

GREENBRIER RUM SAUCE

4 cups berries	1 grated orange rind
2 cups water	2 cups sugar
¼ cup rum	

Place 2 cups of water, the grated orange rind, and the sugar into a saucepan and cook over a moderate heat for 5 minutes.

Next add the washed and stemmed berries. Cook until the berries begin to pop and the juice runs freely. Place the sauce in a food mill and strain out the seeds. Place in a saucepan and add in the rum. Bring to a quick boil and pour into hot, sterile jars, seal, and label. Goes great with meats of any type.

GREENBRIER RELISH DRESSING

½ cup diced berries
1 cup French dressing
pinch ground horseradish

1 tsp. finely chopped nuts
1 tsp. catsup

Place all ingredients in a blender. Produce a very thin puree. You may serve or store in a refrigerator as you would any dressing.

DRIED GREENBRIER BERRIES

Collect amount desired and wash and stem thoroughly. Discard any soft or imperfect berries. Spread on a cookie sheet and dry in bright sunlight. May take 2 to 3 days. When using dried berries cook before eating: the dried taste is not very impressive.

GREENBRIER LEATHER

2 cups ripe fruit
2 tsp. lemon juice
½ cup sugar or corn syrup

Wash and stem 2 full cups of ripe berries. Toss into a blender and puree. Add in the lemon juice and sugar or corn syrup. With greenbrier berries corn syrup is tastier.

Using plastic wrap, cover a cookie sheet and spread the puree evenly. Place in bright sunlight and allow to dry all day. When dry, roll and store in a locking plastic bag and keep in dry, dark place. When ready to use, cover with a special garnish.

GREENBRIER CURRY SAUCE

½ cup chopped berries	1 tbsp. butter
1 cup beef stock	3 tbsp. flour
½ tsp. salt	pinch pepper
1 tbsp. minced onion	1 tsp. curry powder

Make up a brown sauce by melting the butter in a saucepan, over a low heat, add in the flour, stir until brown. Add in the beef stock, salt, pepper, and berries. Bring to a boil and simmer for 5 minutes. Blend in the minced onion, curry powder and mix thoroughly. Boil for 1 full minute. Pour into hot, sterile jars, seal, and label. Can be used for flavoring fowl, meats, or veggie dishes.

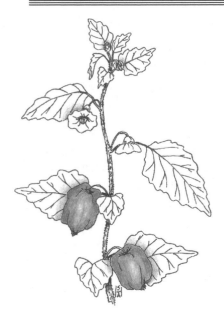

GROUND-CHERRY

Physalis spp.

THE GROUND-CHERRY HAS BEEN cultivated for over 100 years in North America as a garden vegetable and as a floral arrangement. It has, as have many plants, escaped to the wild.

It thrives along fence rows, waste areas, and abandoned farmlands. There are two widely used species, the Mexican ground tomato (*Physalis ixocarpa*) and the ground-cherry (*P. heterophylla*).

The plant attains a height of 2 feet, usually sprawling over the ground. The greenish-yellow flowers are borne in the leaf axils, yielding a fruit that is enclosed in a calyx or husk similar to a the Japanese lantern. The berry, when ripe, is either yellow or red and about ½ inch in diameter.

Ground-cherries can be eaten raw when ripe or used in jams, sauces, or pies. The unripe fruit, undesirable because of the repugnant taste, can also cause intestinal problems.

The stem is either erect or sprawling and is sometimes hairy and sticky. The leaves alternate on the stem, are bluntly toothed, and range from 3 to 4 inches in length.

The ground-cherry has a growth range extending from New Brunswick south to Florida and west to Colorado.

GROUND-CHERRY SAUCE

2 cups ripe fruit	2 cups sugar
1 grated orange rind	2 cups water
pinch cloves and cinnamon	

Combine the grated rind of 1 orange, 2 cups water, sugar and cook over a moderate heat for 10 minutes. Add the fruit and cook until berries pop. Add in the seasonings, stir well, and cook 5 minutes, stirring frequently. Pour into hot, sterile jars, seal, and label.

DRIED GROUND-CHERRIES

Collect as much ripe fruit as you can locate. Wash and remove the stems. Place the fruit on a shallow pan and dry in the warm shade. You may speed the drying process using a commercial dryer or place the fruit in the oven at 140 degrees for 2 to 3 hours.

When completely dry, place in locking plastic bags and store in a dry, dark area. When ready to use, rehydrate with warm water and use as you would fresh-picked fruit.

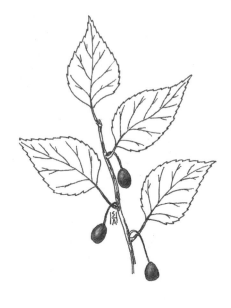

HACKBERRY
Celtis occidentalis

HACKBERRY TREES WILL ATTAIN heights of 100 feet or more. There are several species found throughout the United States. The southern hackberry, or sugarberry, ranges from New England south to the Carolinas and west to Oklahoma. Western hackberry (*C. mississippiensis*) is found throughout the southern United States.

The leaves resemble those of the American elm, with unequal sides, saw-toothed edges, a light olive-green upper surface, and a much lighter underside. They range in length from 2 to 4 inches.

The fruit is a cherrylike drupe, about ⅓ inch in diameter with an orange to blue-black color. The pulp is quite sweet and leaves a very pleasant aftertaste. The large seed takes up most of the volume, making it necessary to collect large amounts of the fruit if you wish to make jellies or jams.

HACKBERRY JELLY

1 qt. ripe fruit
½ cup sugar per cup juice
3 oz. liquid pectin

Select 1 quart of fully ripened berries, wash, and stem. Place into a saucepan, add a little water, and cook over a moderate heat until fruit pops. Crush with a food masher and cook for another 5 minutes. Remove from heat and strain through a jelly bag.

Measure the juice and add ½ cup of sugar to each cup of juice. Bring to a boil until sugar dissolves, constantly stirring. Add in the pectin and boil for 2 minutes. Skim off the foam, pour into hot, sterile jars, seal, and label.

HACKBERRY-CLOVE JELLY

4 cups ripe fruit	½ cup water
5 cups sugar	12 whole cloves
3 oz. liquid pectin	

Wash and stem the fruit. Place in a saucepan, add in the water, and cook until fruit pops and the juice runs freely. Run the mess through a food mill and collect the juice through a jelly bag.

Pour the juice into a saucepan, add in the sugar and cloves. Mix thoroughly. Place the mix over a low heat and cook for 30 minutes. Add in the liquid pectin and boil for 1 full minute. Skim the foam and pour into hot, sterile jars, seal, and label.

HACKBERRY LEATHER

2 cups puree
2 tsp. lemon juice
½ cup sugar or corn syrup

Wash and stem enough fruit to produce 2 cups of puree. Cook the berries until the juice runs, Strain the mess through a food mill and place in a blender until mixed. Add in the lemon juice and sugar. Mix thoroughly.

Using a plastic wrap, cover a cookie sheet, spread the puree evenly across the sheet. Place in bright sunshine and allow to dry. Cover with cheesecloth to keep away the hungry insects.

May take 1 to 2 days. Dry in the oven at 145 degrees for 6 to 8 hours. When dry, roll and place in a locking plastic bag and store in a dark, dry place. Garnish when ready to use.

HACKBERRY SAUCE

4 cups ripe fruit	2 cups sugar
1 grated orange rind	2 cups water
1/4 tsp. ground cinnamon	pinch ground cloves

Combine the grated rind of 1 orange, water, and sugar in a saucepan. Mix and cook over a moderate heat for 10 minutes. Add 4 cups of cleaned berries. Cook until the fruit pops. Now add ground cinnamon and ground cloves, and cook for 5 minutes. Run the mixture through a food mill to remove the skins and large seeds. Bring the mix to a quick boil and then skim the foam, pour into hot, sterile jars, seal, and label.

SWEET AND SOUR HACKBERRY SAUCE

1 cup fruit	1 1/2 tsp. lemon juice
1/2 cup water	1 tbsp. butter
1 tbsp. sugar	1 tsp. soy sauce
3/4 tsp. cornstarch	1/4 tsp. salt
2 tbsp. vinegar	

Cook the washed and stemmed berries until the fruit pops. Run through a food mill to remove the skins and large seeds. Place in a saucepan, combine the cornstarch, sugar, and salt, then pour boiling water over the mess, constantly stirring. Cook the mixture until it thickens. Add in the lemon juice and butter. Cook 1 minute longer, then pour into hot, sterile jars, seal, and label. Use to stir-fry vegetables and fowl.

HACKBERRY-GINGER SAUCE

2 cups ripe berries	$\frac{1}{4}$ tsp. ground ginger
$\frac{1}{4}$ cup sugar	$\frac{1}{8}$ tsp. salt
1 cup boiling water	$\frac{1}{4}$ cup honey
pinch ground cloves	

Cook the ripe berries in a saucepan until the juice flows freely. Run the juicy mix through a food mill to remove the skins and large seeds.

To the juicy pulp blend in the sugar, ginger, ground cloves, and salt. Slowly add the water and stir constantly. Bring to a boil and cook for 5 minutes. Remove the foam and pour into a hot, sterile jar, seal, and label. Goes well on fruit dishes and cakes as a topping.

DRIED HACKBERRIES

Collect as much fruit as needed. Wash thoroughly, remove stems, and place in a shallow, wide pan and dry in a warm, shaded area. If desired, place the fruit in a 140-degree oven and dry for 2 to 3 hours.

When dry, place the fruit in locking plastic bags and store in a dry, dark area. When ready to use, rehydrate with warm water or eat as is.

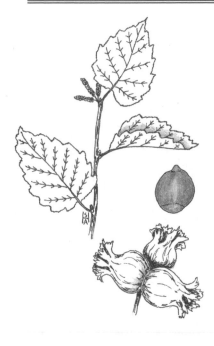

HAZELNUT
Corylus spp.

SEVERAL SPECIES OF HAZELNUTS grow throughout North America. American hazelnut *(Corylus americana)* can be found growing alongside beaked hazelnut (*C. cornuta*). Grows as a large shrub or small tree, with heights up to 15 feet.

Ranges from Nova Scotia across the United States and southern Canada, west to British Columbia and south to Kansas, northern Texas, and Florida. Prefers good soils, such as bottomlands, old farm fields, and hedgerows.

Nuts have a bristly, thin covering that peels back as the fruit matures. Fruits usually ripen in late summer and early fall. They are usually ½ to ¾ inch in diameter and have a rich brown color. Can be harvested by the bushel, if squirrels and other wild foragers do not get there before you.

Hazelnuts are high in fat. In fact, 63 percent of the kernel is concentrated oil and fat.

DRYING HAZELNUTS

Collect as many hazelnuts as you need. Remove the outer covering, Place the nuts on a flat cookie sheet and allow to dry in a warm shade. *Do not attempt to dry in the sun*: the oils will vaporize and you will lose much of the flavor and content. Once dried, run the nuts between your hands to remove the husks. Gloves are a good idea.

Do not crack the shell but store as is in a dry place, preferably in a net bag to allow the air to circulate.

If the small nutlets are chopped in half and dried, they can be used to flavor trail mixes. When finely chopped the nut may be utilized as a garnish for ice cream and other desserts.

If you wish, the finely ground nut meats, when properly dried, can be added, in small amount, to flavor coffee. The addition of hazelnuts to coffee will require some experimentation to determine the correct amount to be used.

Using ground nut meats in coffee as a blend does not allow the blended coffee to be stored for more than a month.

HICKORY NUT
Carya spp.

HICKORY TRESS MAY REACH HEIGHTS of 100 feet or more. The leaves are large and compound, with 5 to 7 leaflets. The nuts are commonly known as pignuts (*Carya glabra*) as they have been used as fodder for pigs.

Hickory grows on dry hillsides and is usually found scattered in mixed hardwood forests. Ranges from northern Maine and Ontario south to northern Florida and west to Texas and Nebraska.

The fruit can grow up to 2 inches in diameter. It is oval-shaped and red-brown and has a thin husk as a covering. The inner nut meat has a thick, woody shell and is typically in two sections. Some find the nut meat sweet to the taste, others bitter.

Hickory wood is strong, dense, and beautifully grained. It was long used to make skis and baseball bats.

DRIED HICKORY NUTS

Gather as many nuts as you need. Place them on a dry surface and allow to dry in the shade for 2 to 3 weeks. The thick outer husk will open and almost fall off when dry. Allow the nuts to dry for another week, depending on weather conditions. Warm, dry air is best. Drying in the oven will take too much time and energy.

Once the nuts are dry, you may store shelled or as is. If storage is with the shells intact, place in a net bag and store in a dry warm place. Shelling takes time, but with just the nut meats less storage space is required. Place in a locking plastic bag and store in a dry place.

After properly grinding the nut meats and drying them, they may be used as a garnish for desserts and baked products. The finely ground nut meats can be stored in jars or plastic containers and will keep for several months.

Finely ground nut meats can also be utilized to flavor coffee. This will require some experimentation on your part to determine the right amount to blend.

SALTED HICKORY NUTS

After you have collected the wild nuts and shelled them, place them on a shallow pan and roast in a 140-degree oven for a few hours. When ready, oils will coat nut meats; remove and gently salt. Allow to cool, then place in a locking plastic bag and store in a dark, dry place.

HOARHOUND
Marrubium vulgare

ALSO KNOWN AS HOREHOUND, THIS PLANT belongs to the mint family and has escaped from the family herb garden. A perennial plant, it is hairy and aromatic, with a square stem. The leaves are oval-shaped and whitish in color; they appear in opposite pairs on the stem. Leaves may range in length from ½ inch to 2 inches. Flowers are found in tight clusters at the axils of the leaves. The fruit is very small and contains the aromatic oil.

Hoarhound can be located growing near deserted farmlands, roadsides, abandoned fields, and forest edges.

Because hoarhound has been grown as an herb in local gardens for many years and has escaped to the wild, it can be found growing throughout most of the United States and southern Canada. The entire plant can be boiled down and the juice made into a cough or cold medicine. Many folks like the strange taste and use it as a candy. In the past, it was used to make an excellent but bitter beer. It is often found being sold in historical museums.

DRIED HOARHOUND

Identify the plants you wish to use the day before picking and drying. Pick them the following day just after the dew has dried. Discard any imperfect stems. Wash the stems and leaves carefully, then hang small bundles of the plant in a warm but dark garage. Allow to dry for 3 or 4 days. When dry, cut to desired lengths, place in a locking plastic bag, and store.

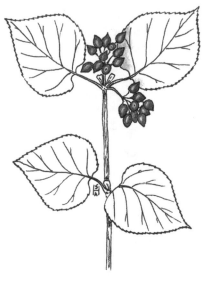

HOBBLEBUSH
Viburnum alnifolium

ONE OF THE MANY VIBURNUM species, hobblebush, or American wayfaring bush, can be found growing in the wild from New Brunswick, Canada, south to the Carolinas and west to Michigan. It is most common in mountainous areas, especially in open fields. It will attain heights of 10 to 15 feet, with branches that grow parallel to the ground and often take root where they touch the ground.

The leaves are large—they are 4 to 8 inches across—and somewhat heart-shaped with fine-toothed edges. The flowers are white and small, appearing in clusters 6 to 8 inches in diameter. The flowers yield berries that are at first pink, then red, and eventually blue when they are fully ripened. The fruit is quite sweet and edible when ripe, which is usually early autumn. When the berries dehydrate on the vine and shrivel up, they can still be harvested. You can rehydrate them by soaking them in warm water.

HOBBLEBUSH JELLY

3 lbs. ripe fruit	1 cup sugar per cup juice
3 oz. liquid pectin	½ tsp. lemon juice

Select and wash only ripe fruit. Place in a saucepan and crush with a potato masher. Bring the pulpy fruit to a boil, then simmer for 15 minutes. Strain the mess through a jelly bag.

Measure the fruit juice and add 1 cup of sugar per cup of juice. Mix thoroughly and add in the lemon juice. Bring the mixture to a boil and add in the pectin. Boil for 1 full minute. Skim the foam and pour into hot, sterile jars, seal, and label. Goes well on toast, bagels, and muffins.

HOBBLEBUSH-APPLE JELLY

3 cups berry juice	7 cups sugar or honey
3 cups apple juice	2 tbsp. lemon juice

Select partially ripened apples (these provide an excellent source of pectin), remove the stems, flowers remnants, and cores. Slice into sections, add a little cooking water and bring to a boil. Cover and simmer for 15 minutes. Crush the apple sections and continue to cook for another 5 minutes. Remove from the heat and strain the juice through a jelly bag.

Place enough cleaned hobblebush fruit in a saucepan to yield 3 cups of juice. Add a little cooking water and bring to a boil, then simmer for 15 minutes. Strain the juicy pulp through a jelly bag. Recover 3 cups of juice.

Blend the apple and hobblebush juices in a saucepan and cook for 5 minutes. Add 7 cups of sugar, lemon juice, mix thoroughly, then bring to a boil. Boil for 3 full minutes, stirring constantly. Skim the foam, pour into hot, sterile jars, seal, and label.

HOBBLEBUSH JAM

3 lbs. ripe fruit
1 cup sugar per cup juicy pulp
3 oz. liquid pectin

Clean and stem 3 pounds ripe berries, place in a saucepan, and simmer until the fruit pops the skins. Strain the juicy pulp through a food mill. This will remove the seeds and skins.

Measure the juicy pulp, add 1 cup of sugar per cup of sauce, and stir thoroughly. Bring to a boil, add in the pectin, and boil for 2 full minutes. Stir constantly. Skim the colorful foam, pour into hot, sterile jars, seal, and label.

Adds flavor and color to toasted pastries.

HOBBLEBUSH-BRANDY SAUCE

2 cups ripe fruit
1 cup sugar
2 tbsp. brandy

Wash and stem 2 full cups ripe fruit, place in a saucepan, and bring to a boil. Simmer for 15 minutes. Remove from the heat and run the mess through a food mill

Place in a saucepan, add in the sugar, stir the mixture, and bring to a boil. Cook until the sugar dissolves. Add in your favorite brandy, and mix thoroughly. Pour into hot, sterile jars, seal, and label. Excellent garnish for bakery products, cakes, etc.

HOBBLEBUSH LEATHER

2 cups hobblebush puree
2 tsp. lemon juice
$\frac{1}{2}$ cup sugar or corn syrup

Wash and stem 2 full cups ripe berries. Run through a food mill to remove the skins and seeds. Toss the juicy pulp into a blender and produce a puree. Add 2 teaspoons of lemon juice and $\frac{1}{2}$ cup of granulated sugar or corn syrup. Mix thoroughly.

Using a plastic wrap, cover a cookie sheet, spread the puree evenly across the sheet. Place in a warm, shaded area and allow to dry. A 140-degree oven will speed the process. When dry, roll the leather and store in a locking plastic bag. Garnish with pleasing spread.

HOBBLEBUSH BUTTER

3 lbs. ripe fruit	6 cups sugar
1 cup cider vinegar	½ tsp. ground cinnamon
½ tsp. ground allspice	pinch ground cloves

Wash, stem, and place the fruit in a saucepan. Add a little water and bring to a boil. Cook until the fruit pops and juices flow.

Run though a food mill and remove the skins and seeds. Place the pulp in a saucepan, add in the sugar, vinegar, and mix thoroughly. Blend in the spices, mix, then spoon the mix into a baking pan and bake for 4 hours at 250 degrees. Occasionally stir the mix. When the juice can no longer be separated from the pulp, the butter is finished. Remove from the oven, spoon into hot, sterile jars, seal, and label. Goes well on toast and biscuits.

HOBBLEBUSH CONSERVE

1½ qts. ripe fruit	2 juice oranges
3 tbsp. lemon juice	¾ tsp. ground cinnamon
3 cups sugar	pinch of ground cloves

Slice 2 juice oranges into very thin sections, removing the seeds. Cook the slices in a little water until tender.

Clean and stem about 1½ quarts of hobblebush berries. Crush the fruit in a saucepan with a hand masher. Do not use a blender, because it will pulverize the seeds. Strain the juicy pulp through a food mill, removing the seeds. Add the juicy pulp to the cooked oranges and mix well.

Add the lemon juice, spices, sugar, and mix thoroughly. Cook over a moderate heat until the sauce thickens. Allow to cool, then spoon the conserve into hot, sterile jars, seal, and label.

HOBBLEBUSH RELISH

2 qts. ripe fruit	3 cups vinegar
1 cup sugar	1 tbsp. ground allspice
6 whole cloves	1 tbsp. ground cinnamon
½ tsp. cayenne pepper	

Wash and stem 2 quarts of fully ripened berries, Place in a saucepan, add 3 cups cider vinegar, and cook until fruit softens. Remove from the heat and run through a food mill to remove the seeds and skins.

Put the juicy pulp in a saucepan, add in the sugar, spices, and mix thoroughly. Simmer over low heat until the sauce thickens. Stir occasionally. Pour the mixture into hot, sterile jars, seal, and label.

HOBBLEBUSH-GINGER SAUCE

3 cups ripe fruit	¼ tsp. ground ginger
¼ cup sugar	⅛ tsp. salt
1 cup boiling water	¼ cup honey

Wash and stem the ripe fruit, place in a saucepan, and cook over a moderate heat until fruit juices run. Remove and run the juicy pulp through a food mill, to remove the seeds and skins. Place in a saucepan, blend in the sugar, honey, salt, and ground ginger. Slowly add the water and bring to a boil, stirring constantly. Cook for 5 minutes.

Pour into hot, sterile jars, seal, and label. Goes well with meat dishes as a garnish.

DRIED HOBBLEBUSH BERRIES

Collect as many berries as needed, wash, and stem. Place the fruit on a cookie sheet and place in a warm shed or garage, out of the sunlight. Allow to remain until thoroughly dry. May take two or more days. Drying in a 160-degree oven will take but 3 to 4 hours. When dry, place the dried fruit in locking plastic bags and store in a dry dark place. Rehydrate when ready to use.

HOBBLEBUSH JUICE

2 qts. ripe fruit	1 cup water
1 cup lemon juice	sugar to taste

Add 2 quarts of fully ripened hobblebush berries to a saucepan. Cook the fruit for 5 to 6 minutes, then crush completely with a potato masher. Add 1 cup of water and cook at a simmer for 5 minutes.

Remove the juicy pulp, run through a few layers of cheesecloth. Collect the juice, add the lemon juice and sugar to taste. Mix thoroughly. Serve chilled—or frozen, and served as a hobblebush ice.

HONEY LOCUST
Gleditsia tricanthos

A LARGE TREE, THE HONEY LOCUST attains heights of 100 feet or more. It has a growth range from New England south to Florida and west to Texas. This very popular ornamental tree is often planted along highways and is used in landscaping public and industrial sites. It survives conventional air pollution quite well.

This particular locust species has quite sizable thorns along the trunk to the smaller branches. The leaves are twice compounded and 4 to 8 inches long. The leaflets are in pairs, up to 1½ inches long, with blunt ends and a shiny dark green on top and a yellow underside. The edges have inconspicuous, rounded teeth.

The flowers are small and greenish-white and appear in narrow clusters. They are 2 inches long and generally appear in the late spring. The flower clusters yield a purple-brown, twisted pod that grows up to 15 inches long. It is filled with large, flat seeds. The pods are thin, flat, somewhat curved, and filled with a sweet, greenish-yellow pulp that can be eaten raw or cooked. The pods turn first to a maroon then to a brown color when completely ripened.

HONEY LOCUST JELLY

> 4 cups ripe pulp
> sugar to taste
> 3 oz. liquid pectin

Gather 20 or so fully ripened pods. Slice the pods open and scrape out the sweetish pulp. Place in a saucepan with ½ cup of water. Bring to a boil, then simmer for 15 minutes. Strain the juicy pulp through a jelly bag. Depending on its sweetness, add sugar to taste, about 1 cup.

Mix thoroughly, bring to a boil until the sugar dissolves. Add the pectin and boil for 1 full minute. Skim the foam, pour into hot, sterile jars, seal, and label. Goes well on biscuits.

SPICED HONEY LOCUST SAUCE

> 4 cups pulp
> ¾ cup vinegar
> ⅓ cup water
> 3 cups sugar
>
> 1 tbsp. ground cinnamon
> ½ tbsp. allspice
> 6 whole cloves

Scrape out the sweet pulp of 20 or more ripe pods. Recover 4 cups of pulp, place in a saucepan, add water, vinegar of choice, sugar, and spices. Mix thoroughly, bring to a boil, and simmer for 30 minutes, stirring occasionally.

Pour the hot mixture through a food mill, pour into hot, sterile jars, seal, and label. Goes well with meats.

DRIED HONEY LOCUST

The large, flat seeds can also be harvested, dried, or roasted, then ground to a fine pulp. The pulp makes an excellent soup base. Save the seeds when preparing the honey locust jelly or any sauce. Place the seeds on a cookie sheet and dry in the hot direct sun. Takes but a few hours. Place the dry seeds in locking plastic bags and store in a dark, dry place. Grind the seeds when you are ready to make a fine hot soup in the winter months.

HONEY LOCUST LEATHER

2 cups pulp
2 tsp. lemon juice
$\frac{1}{2}$ cup sugar or corn syrup

You will need about 20 ripe seed pods. Scrape out the sweet pulp and obtain 2 full cups. Combine with the lemon juice and sugar or corn syrup. Place in a blender for a short whirl.

Cover a cookie sheet with plastic wrap, evenly spread the puree across the sheet and allow to dry in bright sunlight. Cover with cheesecloth to keep away the hungry insects. Dry in a 140-degree oven for 2 to 3 hours, When dry, roll and place in a locking plastic bag and store in a dark place. When ready to use, garnish with a chopped raisin and nut topping. Good camping food.

HONEY LOCUST GINGER SAUCE

2 cups sweet pulp
$\frac{1}{4}$ cup corn syrup
1 cup boiling water
1 tsp. vinegar
$\frac{1}{4}$ tsp. ground ginger
$\frac{1}{8}$ tsp. salt
$\frac{1}{4}$ cup honey

Blend the sweet pulp, corn syrup, honey, ginger, salt, vinegar, and boiling water. Stirring constantly, bring to a boil for 5 minutes. Remove and pour into hot, sterile jars, seal, and label. Goes well with chicken fixings.

HONEY LOCUST HOT SAUCE

2 cups pulp	3 cups minced onions
1 hot red pepper	2 cups cider vinegar
½ tsp. salt	1 tsp. celery seed
2 tbsp. brown sugar	1 tsp. hot mustard
½ tsp. chili powder	

Place the sweet pulp in a saucepan and bring to a boil. Add in the minced onions, minced hot red pepper, salt, vinegar, celery seed, and favorite hot mustard. Mix thoroughly and simmer for 5 minutes, then stir in the brown sugar. Simmer for another 5 minutes.

Pour the mixture into hot, sterile jars, seal, and label. Makes up to 2 pints. Flavor improves if allowed to sit for at least 1 month, then served with shrimp or other seafood.

IRISH MOSS
Chondrus crispus

KNOWN LOCALLY BY MANY NAMES, including carrageen, salt rock moss, and rock moss. An alga, it attains lengths of 1 to 2 feet and can be found growing in very large clumps. It commonly grows along the shallow shores of the Atlantic, usually on tidal rocks. It has a range from Newfoundland south to the Carolinas.

The fronds range in size from 6 to 24 inches, with thick stems. They are leathery, smooth, and colored olive or black. They can be gathered at any time of the year. Rather bland when eaten raw, but the flavor is greatly enhanced by cooking. The cooked fronds will yield large amounts of gelatin, which is quite nutritious.

IRISH MOSS JELLY

3 lbs. fresh alga	1 cup sugar per cup juice
juice of 1 lemon	2 qts. water

Collect about 3 pounds of fresh Irish moss alga. Rinse in fresh water to remove all traces of salt. Chop the fronds into small 1- to-2- inch pieces and place in a saucepan with 2 quarts of boiling water. Cook until the water begins to thicken. Remove from the heat, then strain and measure the juice. To each cup of juice add 1 cup of sugar. Mix in a saucepan, add the lemon juice, and bring to a boil. Stir constantly. Boil for 1 full minute. Pour the mixture into hot, sterile jars, seal, and label.

MANZANITA
Arctostaphylos manzanita

CONSIDERED AN EVERGREEN SHRUB, manzanita will attain heights of up to 10 feet. Usually it can be found growing from mountainous areas of Oregon south to southern California. It is also planted as an ornamental shrub in much of the eastern United States, where it has escaped to the wilds in many places.

The shrub thrives in wet, humid areas. It is an erect and somewhat brittle-looking plant. The leaves are evergreen, smooth, oblong, and small, with no teeth. The branches are covered with a fine hairy fuzz. Flowers are white and appear in dense clusters that yield reddish-brown berries. The berries are somewhat pulpy and acrid when eaten raw, but cooking greatly improves this. Only use fully ripened and fleshy berries—do not use dehydrated fruit.

MANZANITA JELLY

2 qts. ripe berries
3 oz. liquid pectin
1½ cups sugar per cup juice

Collect 2 full quarts of ripe berries and wash thoroughly to remove the grime. Place in a saucepan, add 1 cup of cold water, and bring to a boil. Simmer for 15 minutes. Strain the mixture through a jelly bag.

Recover and measure the juice, add 1½ cups of sugar to each cup of juice. Bring to a boil for 1 full minute, then add in the liquid pectin and boil for 2 full minutes. Skim the colorful foam, pour into hot, sterile jars, seal, and label.

MANZANITA JAM

2 qts. ripe fruit	1 cup water
3 oz. liquid pectin	1½ cups sugar per cup juice

Collect 2 quarts of fully ripened berries, discarding fried fruit. Wash thoroughly and place in a saucepan with 1 cup of cold water, bring to a boil, then simmer for 15 minutes. Remove from the heat and strain through a food mill, removing the skins and seeds.

Measure, add 1½ cups sugar or corn syrup to each cup of juicy pulp, and bring to a boil. Add in the liquid pectin, boil for 1 full minute, stirring constantly. Skim the colorful foam, pour into hot, sterile jars, seal, and label.

MANZANITA CONSERVE

4 cups ripe fruit	1½ cups water
10 cups sugar	¼ lb. chopped raisins
1 chopped orange	½ cup chopped nut meats

Wash and stem 4 cups fully ripened berries. Add to a saucepan with the water. Cook until the berries have softened and the juice runs freely. Add the raisins, chopped nut meats, diced orange, and sugar.

Mix the ingredients thoroughly and cook the mixture about 25 to 30 minutes or until thickening takes place. Skim off the foam, pour into hot, sterile jars, seal, and label. Goes well with biscuits.

MANZANITA CIDER

1 qt. ripe berries
1 qt. cold water

Wash and stem 1 full quart of ripe berries, place in a saucepan, add in the water, bring to a boil and simmer until berries soften and the juice runs. Crush with a potato masher and continue to simmer for 5 minutes.

Remove from the heat, strain through a jelly bag. Recover the juice, add a little sugar if you desire, and serve chilled. The juice is acid, as is apple cider, but very spicy and quite pleasant.

MANZANITA SALSA

2 cups ripe berries	1 small apple, diced
1 tbsp. honey	1 tbsp. lemon juice
1/4 cup minced onion	1 tsp. vinegar

Place the ripe berries into a saucepan and bring to a boil. Cook for 2 to 3 minutes. Remove from the heat, add in the remaining ingredients, and bring to a boil. Remove from the heat and serve chilled. Can be poured into hot, sterile jar(s) and refrigerated, to be used at a later time. Excellent dip for parties.

MANZANITA CHOWCHOW (RELISH)

2 cups ripe berries	1/2 diced sweet pepper
1/2 cup sugar	1 cup diced onion
1/2 tsp. salt	1/2 tsp. turmeric
2 tsp. celery seed	1/4 tsp. dry mustard
1/2 cup vinegar	

Wash the berries, place in a saucepan, and crush the fruit. Add in the spices and other ingredients and bring to a boil. Simmer for 20 minutes, stirring occasionally to prevent the bottom from burning.

Pour into hot, sterile jars, seal, and label. Makes an excellent condiment.

DRIED MANZANITA

Collect all the ripe berries you need. Wash and stem. This fruit may be dried whole but is best when diced. Place on a flat surface and dry in bright sunlight. These pulpy berries may take 2 to 3 days to fully dry. The process can be shortened by drying in a 145-degree oven or dehydrator.

When completely dry, place the fruit in a plastic locking bag and store in a dark, dry place. When ready to use, rehydrate with warm water. The berries do not have a pleasant taste when dried and eaten raw. Only use when cooked.

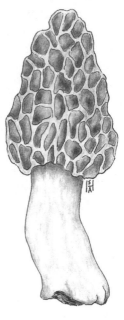

MOREL
Morchella spp.

THIS ODDLY SHAPED EDIBLE MUSHROOM IS found growing throughout most of the United States. It is erect, 6 to 8 inches in height, hollow, pale, and somewhat brittle and moist to the touch. It grows directly on the ground. Thrives in woodland areas that have recently been burned over. Can be found from May through to early July. Does not grow in large numbers, except directly after a long period of rain.

When harvesting, examine the fungi carefully, as they generally are infested with small insects. Many folks are turned away by the morel's unusual appearance. This is not the typical umbrella-shaped mushroom, but it is very edible and considered to be higher in nutritional value than most fungi. When washed thoroughly and thinly sliced, morels are excellent fried in butter or olive oil.

DRIED MORELS

Harvest as many morels as you need or can find. Wash thoroughly, examine for insects, thinly slice, and place on a tray or cookie sheet. Place in hot sunlight and dry. Should take but 1 day. When dried, place in a locking plastic bag and store in a dark, dry place.

Drying in a 140-degree oven or dehydrator may take only a few hours. They can be stored for several months, as long as they are kept dry. When ready to use, rehydrate using boiling water, for about 2 minutes.

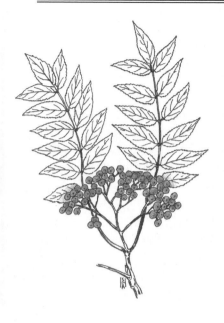

MOUNTAIN ASH
Sorbus spp.

THERE ARE THREE WELL-KNOWN species of mountain ash: American mountain ash (*Sorbus americana*), mountain ash (*S. scopulina*), and European mountain ash (*S. aucuparia*). *S. americana* ranges from Labrador south along eastern Canada and the United States to the Carolinas. *S. scopulina* ranges from Labrador and Alaska south to Pennsylvania and Utah. *S. aucuparia* is a transplanted native of Europe. It is widely planted throughout North America since it is a winter-hardy plant and has successfully escaped to the wilds.

A small tree, the mountain ash has twigs that are fuzzy, compound leaves and flowers appear are in round-topped clusters. The leaves have 9 to 15 leaflets and turn reddish in the autumn. The fruit is a berry, ½ inch wide and quite waxy. The fruit is found in heavy, drooping clusters. It is bright red in the American ash and orange in the European ash when mature, and it has a very unpleasant odor. Before using, the fruit should be carefully cleaned in hot water to remove the sticky substances and attached debris.

European mountain ash is easily located along highways and streets, as it is not harmed by most auto pollution or insects. All mountain ash fruit contains high concentrations of natural pectin.

MOUNTAIN ASH JELLY

2 lbs. ripe berries
2 cups water
1 cup sugar per cup juice

Select 2 pounds of fully ripened fruit, clean by rinsing in hot water. Remove blossom and stems. Place in a saucepan, add 2 cups cold water, bring to a fast boil, then simmer for 15 minutes or until fruit softens. Remove from heat and crush the cooked fruit with a potato masher. Cook another 5 minutes. Strain through a jelly bag.

Measure the juice, place in a saucepan, and add 1 cup of sugar per cup of juice. Bring to a boil for 1 full minute, stirring constantly. Remove from heat, pour into hot, sterile jars, seal, and label. Good on toast!

MOUNTAIN ASH JAM

2 lbs. ripe fruit
1 cup sugar per cup pulp

Select 2 pounds of fully ripened fruit. Wash thoroughly in hot water and remove the blossoms and stems. Place the fruit in a saucepan, mash with a potato masher, and cook the sauce for 15 minutes. Remove from the heat and pour the juicy pulp through a food mill. This will remove the seeds and skins.

Place the juicy orange sauce in a saucepan and add 1 cup of sugar to each cup of sauce. Mix well, bring to a boil, stirring constantly for 1 full minute. Pour into hot, sterile jelly jars, seal, and label.

MOUNTAIN ASH MARMALADE

3 lbs. ripe fruit	1 orange
2 tbsp. lemon juice	6 cups sugar

Wash the fruit in hot water. Remove the stems and blossom ends. Chop the fruit into small sections, place in a saucepan, add the lemon juice, 1 orange diced, skin and all. Mix thoroughly. Bring to a boil, remove, then add 6 cups of sugar and mix thoroughly. Bring to a boil for 2 minutes. Pour or spoon the mixture into hot, sterile jars, seal, and label.

MOUNTAIN ASH LEATHER

2 cups ripe berries	2 tsp. lemon juice
½ cup corn syrup	pinch ground cinnamon

Wash 2 full cups of berries in hot water. Remove the stem and blossom ends. Toss into a blender and produce a puree. Add in the lemon juice and corn syrup. Mix thoroughly.

Using a plastic wrap, cover a cookie sheet, spread the puree evenly across the plastic sheet. Place in a 160-degree oven and dry. When dry, roll the leather and place in a plastic locking bag and store in a dry, dark place. Use your favorite garnish when ready to use.

DRIED MOUNTAIN ASH

Collect as many berries as you need, wash in hot water, stem, and remove the blossom ends. Either use whole or diced, then spread on a flat tray and dry in bright sunlight. May take 1 to 2 days. Store in plastic locking bags in a dark, dry place.

MOUNTAIN ASH COOKING SAUCE

1 cup ripe berries	pinch salt
¼ cup minced onions	pinch sage
3 tbsp. white wine vinegar	1 tbsp. brown sugar
1 tsp. of soy sauce	

Wash the fruit, in hot water removing stems and blossom ends. Cook in a little water until fruit pops. Run through a food mill and place in a saucepan. Bring to a boil, then add in the remaining ingredients. Boil for 2 to 3 minutes. Pour into hot, sterile jars, seal, and label. When ready to use, blend in ¼ cup heavy cream and bring to a fast boil. Cover skillet chicken with sauce for a delicious treat.

MOUNTAIN ASH BUTTER

3 lbs. ripe fruit	½ tsp. cinnamon
1 cup vinegar	½ tsp. of allspice
6 cups sugar	

Wash, stem, and remove blossom in hot water. Bring to a boil and cook for 15 minutes at a simmer. Run through a food mill. Bring to a boil, add in the sugar, vinegar, and mix thoroughly. Spread the mix across a cookie sheet and bake at 250 degrees for 4 hours. Remove and spoon into hot, sterile jars, seal, and label. Goes well on toast.

MULBERRY
Morus spp.

THERE ARE SEVERAL SPECIES OF MUL-berry found throughout the United States. The red mulberry *(Morus rubra)* is perhaps the most common, being found in the eastern United States. It grows as a small tree to a height of 50 feet. The leaves are sim-ple, alternate on the stem, and have variable shapes, similar to the sass-afras. Some of the leaves may con-tain as many as five lobes.

Bright red berries are produced in July, depending on local condi-tions, then turn black, resembling the blackberry. The berry is made up of numerous drupelets, forming a fleshy fruit that is about 1 inch in length and ½ inch wide. The fruit is tasty when fully ripe; whereas the green, unripened fruit is bitter. The ripe berries can be used for sauces, jellies, jams, tarts, or pies or just eaten raw by the handful—a delicious treat!

White mulberry *(M. alba)* is similar to red mulberry with a fruit that is almost white and somewhat sweeter when ripe. In some instances, black mulberry *(M. nigra)* can be found in the wilds of the southeast-ern United States. Its black-colored fruit is sweet and prized for cultivation.

MULBERRY JELLY

2 qts. ripe fruit
1 to 2 cups sugar
3 oz. liquid pectin

Wash 2 quarts fully ripened mulberries. Remove the short stem. Place into saucepan, add a little cooking water, and bring to a boil. Simmer for 15 minutes. Crush the fruit with a potato masher. Strain the cooked sauce through a jelly bag.

Recover the juice and measure. If you prefer jellies that are tart, only add 1 cup of sugar to each cup of juice. Add 1½ to 2 cups of sugar if you desire a sweeter jelly. Mix thoroughly and bring to a boil for 1 full minute.

Add 3 ounces of pectin, mix well, and bring to a boil for 1 full minute. Skim the colorful foam, pour into hot, sterile jars, seal, and label. Excellent garnish for leathers and muffins.

MULBERRY JAM

2 lbs. ripe fruit
1 to 2 cups sugar or honey
3 oz. liquid pectin

Wash and stem 2 pounds of ripe fruit. Add to a saucepan with a little water and bring to a boil. Simmer for 20 minutes, keeping the pot covered. Remove from the pot and strain through a food mill, removing the skins and seeds.

Recover and measure the juicy pulp, adding 1 to 2 cups of sugar, depending on your sweet tooth. Mix thoroughly, bring to a boil for 1 minute. Add the pectin, mix thoroughly, and boil for 1 full minute. Skim the foam, pour into hot, sterile jars, seal, and label.

MULBERRY PRESERVES

2 qts. ripe fruit	1 cup water
1 cup sugar per cup fruit	2 juice oranges

Wash and stem, and place in a saucepan. Bring to a boil, then simmer for 10 minutes.

Add in the sugar and bring to a boil. Cook until the mixture becomes thick. Select the oranges, dice, skins and all, then add to the mulberry sauce. Bring the mixture to a boil, then simmer for 5 minutes. Remove from the heat, pour into hot, sterile jars, seal, and label. Goes well with ice cream and can serve as a topping for cakes.

MULBERRY LEATHER

2 cups ripe fruit
2 tsp. lemon or lime juice
1½ cups corn syrup

Wash 2 full cups of ripe berries. Toss into a blender and produce a puree. Add in the lemon or lime juice and sugar. Mix thoroughly.

Using a plastic wrap, cover a cookie sheet, spread the thick sauce evenly on the sheet. Place in a 140-degree oven and dry. When dry, remove and roll, then store in a plastic, locking bag. Use your favorite garnish when ready to use.

MULBERRY CONSERVE

4 cups ripe fruit	1½ cups water
¼ lb. seedless raisins	½ cup chopped nut meats
1 chopped orange	10 cups sugar

Wash and stem the ripe fruit, then place in a saucepan, add the water, and bring to a boil. Simmer for 10 minutes. Crush the fruit with a potato masher, add the chopped raisins, chopped orange (with the seeds removed), and sugar. Mix thoroughly, bring to a boil for 20 minutes, and then add the finely chopped nut meats. Simmer for an additional 10 minutes. Stir constantly. Remove from the heat, skim the foam, pour into hot, sterile jars, seal, and label.

MULBERRY RUM SAUCE

½ cup fruit juice	½ cup favorite rum
½ cup sugar	¼ cup water
⅓ cup orange juice	drop of vanilla extract

Combine the fruit juice and water. Bring to a boil for 1 full minute. Cool for a few minutes, then add in the orange juice, favorite rum, drop of vanilla extract, sugar and bring to a boil for 2 full minutes. Pour into hot, sterile jars, seal, and label. Makes an excellent garnish for cakes and puddings.

DRIED MULBERRIES

If you would like to use mulberries during the cold winter months in sauces and other recipes, then gather as much fruit as needed. Wash and stem carefully, avoid breaking or crushing the fruit.

Spread on a cookie sheet, place in a warm, dark place, and dry. Do not attempt to dry in an oven! May take 2 days to dry using the natural method. Rehydrate with warm water when ready to use.

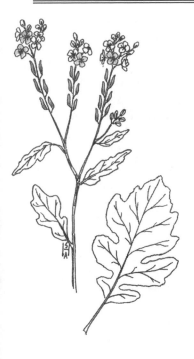

MUSTARD
Brassica spp.

SEVERAL MEMBERS OF THE MUSTARD family are commonly found wild edibles but also may be grown commercially. Black mustard (*Brassica nigra*), found throughout much of temperate North America, is grown commercially for the glucoside found in the seeds, which yields the volatile oil that gives table mustard its flavor. White mustard (*B. alba*) is also raised commercially and is the source of the famous mustard plaster. It is also used as a counterirritant.

The mustards are common in waste places and fields. Their height can vary from 2 to 10 feet, but 2 to 3 feet is more common. Most have slender, ascending, dark-brown seed pods that end in a conspicuous point and contain numerous small, dark seeds.

The flowers are yellow, four-petaled, small, and clustered at the ends of spikes. They bloom from July through August, with the seeds available in late summer. Most of the mustards have broad, deeply lobed lower leaves. The edges of the lobes tend to be toothed. The plant is generally fund in large stands, spreading across open fields as a weed.

DRIED MUSTARD SEED

Gather as many seed pods as needed. Remove the seeds and dry in an oven for 2 to 3 hours at 145 degrees. When dry, place in a locking plastic bag and store in a dry, dark place. Canning jars may also be used.

To make prepared mustard or mustard sauce, as it is sometimes known, use 2 to 3 tbsp. of ground mustard seed. Place in a small saucepan, add in enough cider vinegar to make a paste. When ready blend in some turmeric, pinch of salt, pepper, and blend. Store in a sterile jar and place in the refrigerator to keep cool. Experimentation with the ingredients will produce wonderful, tasty variations.

ONION MUSTARD

1 cup fine ground mustard seed	1 tsp. whole mustard seed
white vinegar	garlic clove
½ tsp. sugar	1 tsp. olive oil
	1 tsp. lemon juice

Combine enough ground mustard seed and white vinegar to form a loose paste. Add in the olive oil, ground garlic clove, lemon juice, and sugar.

Place in a blender and mix. Refrigerate as the mix will not keep well in a warm room.

SPICY MUSTARD

1 cup fine ground mustard seed	salt and pepper to taste
white vinegar	1 tsp. olive oil
3 peppercorns	1 tsp. mustard seed

Blend the fine ground mustard seed with enough white vinegar to form a loose paste. Place in a blender and add in the rest of the ingredients. Mix thoroughly. Adjust the white vinegar to suit your taste and consistency. Goes well with cold cut meats and hot dogs.

DILL MUSTARD

1 cup fine ground mustard seed	1 tbsp. olive oil
cider vinegar	pinch salt and pepper
1 tsp. ground dry dill seed	1 tsp. sugar
	1 tsp. whole mustard seed

Blend the fine ground whole mustard seed with enough cider vinegar to form a loose paste. Combine the remaining ingredients and mix well. Excellent basting sauce for meats, especially pan-fried chicken.

CHILI MUSTARD

1 cup fine ground mustard seed	salt and pepper to taste
white vinegar	1 tsp. sugar
1 tsp. chili powder	1 tsp. oil
1 tsp. onion flakes	1 tsp. whole mustard seed

Blend fine ground whole mustard seeds with a suitable amount of white vinegar to form a loose paste. Add in the chili powder and remaining ingredients, mix thoroughly, refrigerate, and serve when ready. Excellent with luncheon meats and hot dogs.

HONEY MUSTARD

1 cup fine ground mustard
    seed
white vinegar
1 tbsp. honey
1 tsp. soy oil
1 ground clove
1 tsp. corn syrup

salt to taste
1 tsp. lemon juice
1 tsp. dried onion flakes
$\frac{1}{2}$ tsp. ground ginger
pinch of turmeric
1 tbsp. whole mustard seed

Place all ingredients in a blender and mix until smooth. Adjust the amount of vinegar to produce a smooth paste. Goes well as a basting sauce for chicken and pork dishes.

COOKING MUSTARD SAUCE

1 cup ground mustard seed
white vinegar
pinch of turmeric
1 tbsp. olive oil

salt to taste
tomato catsup
$\frac{1}{2}$ tsp. ground ginger
1 tbsp. honey

Smother pan-fried chicken or any meat that is being roasted, especially ham. Save enough to cover when being served.

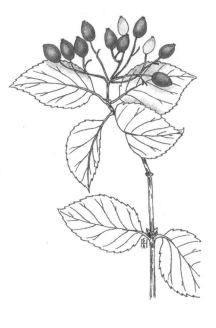

NANNYBERRY
Viburnum lentago

A TALL SHRUB, NANNYBERRY IS usually round-topped with many crooked branches. It attains heights of 10 to 20 feet and is common in wooded areas, along stream banks, and in wet thickets. It has a range from the Hudson Bay south to Pennsylvania and along the Appalachian Mountains south to Georgia. It can be found growing as far west as Iowa and Missouri.

The leaves have a deep, lustrous green color that is lighter underneath; they are oval-shaped with edges of fine teeth. The flowers are very small and white and grow in large clusters that may range up to 6 to 8 inches across. The flowers appear in June, yielding dark-blue fruit that is covered with a yeast bloom.

The fruit is oval, ½ inch in diameter, and upwards of 1 inch in length. It is edible raw and the pulp is quite tasty and sweet. The berries hang in rather large clusters and can often be found on the branch during the winter months. The dried fruit of fall can be rehydrated and used as easily as the summer fruit. One of the common names is wild raisin, for this reason.

NANNYBERRY JELLY

> 4 qts. ripe fruit
> ½ cup sugar per cup juice
> 3 oz. liquid pectin

Wash and stem the fruit. Place in a saucepan and cook over a moderate heat until the fruit pops. Remove and pour the juicy sauce through a jelly bag.

Measure the juice and add ½ cup of sugar to each cup of juice. Place over a high heat, bring to a boil until the sugar dissolves. Add 3 ounces of liquid pectin and boil for 1 full minute. Skim the colorful foam, pour into hot, sterile jars, seal, and label. Goes well on toast and waffles.

SPICED NANNYBERRY JELLY

> 4 cups ripe fruit
> 1 tbsp. ground cinnamon
> 1 tsp. ground allspice
> 5 cups sugar
>
> ½ cup water
> ¾ cup cider vinegar
> 6 whole cloves

Wash and stem the fully ripened fruit, place in a saucepan with the water, cider vinegar, spices, and sugar. Mix thoroughly. Place over a low heat and cook for 30 minutes.

Pour the mixture through a jelly bag. Recover the sauce, pour into a saucepan, and add in the liquid pectin. Bring to a boil for 1 full minute, skim the foam, pour into hot, sterile jars, seal, and label.

NANNYBERRY JAM

4 qts. ripe fruit
3 oz. liquid pectin
½ cup sugar per cup sauce

Wash and stem the fruit, place in a saucepan, and cook over a moderate heat for 10 minutes. Crush with a potato masher. Strain the pulpy sauce through a food mill, removing the skins and seeds.

Add in the liquid pectin, bring to a boil for 1 full minute. Stir constantly. Pour into hot, sterile jars, seal, and label.

NANNYBERRY LEATHER

2 cups ripe fruit
½ cup corn syrup

2 tsp. lemon juice
pinch ground cloves

Wash and stem the fruit, and place in a blender. Produce a colorful puree. Add 2 teaspoons of lemon juice, ground cloves, and corn syrup. Mix thoroughly.

Using plastic wrap, cover a cookie sheet, spread the puree evenly across the sheet. Place in oven at 145 degrees and dry. When dry, roll and store in locking plastic bag. Garnish when ready to serve.

DRIED NANNYBERRIES

Select ripe fruit, wash, and stem, then place on a cookie sheet or tray and place in warm, dark area and allow to dry.

Drying may take 2 to 3 days, When dry, store in locking plastic bags and keep in a dry, dark place. The dried fruit will resemble raisins. Rehydrate when ready to use.

NANNYBERRY RUM SAUCE

½ cup fruit juice	½ cup rum
½ cup sugar	1 drop vanilla extract
¼ cup water	⅓ cup orange juice
pinch ground cinnamon	

Combine the nannyberry fruit juice and water, bring to a boil for 1 full minute. Cool for a few minutes, then add in the orange juice, rum, vanilla extract, and ground cinnamon. Mix well and bring to a boil. Pour into hot, sterile jar(s), seal, and label. Goes well over cakes and muffins. Adds good color and taste to gourmet meals.

NANNYBERRY GINGER SAUCE

4 cups juicy pulp	¼ tsp. ground ginger
¼ cup sugar	⅛ tsp. salt
2 cups boiling water	¼ cup honey

Blend the sugar, honey, ginger, salt in a saucepan. Slowly add the water, stirring constantly. Bring to a boil and cook for 5 minutes over a moderate heat. Excellent garnish for custards, cakes, and pot roasts.

NANNYBERRY SAUCE

4 cups juicy pulp	2 cups sugar
1 grated orange rind	2 cups water

Place two cups of water, the grated rind of 1 orange, and 2 cups of granulated sugar into a saucepan; mix thoroughly and cook over moderate heat for 5 minutes.

Next add, washed and stemmed, 4 cups of fully ripened berries. Cook until the berries pop. When cooking is complete, place the hot sauce in a food mill and strain out the seeds. Place the sauce in a bowl and chill in the refrigerator. Serve chilled.

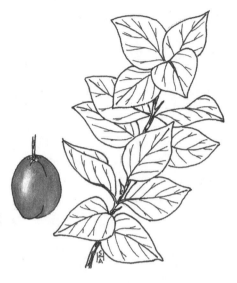

NATAL PLUM
Carissa spp.

THIS DELIGHTFUL BUSH IS OFTEN known as the carissa plum bush. A native of the semitropics, it was introduced to the United States from India. It survives in frost-free areas such as Florida, but it is banned in California and Arizona. There are several species, from the dwarf carissa (*Carissa bonsai*) to the larger boxwood variety (*C. grandifolia*). The latter is used as an ornamental for hedges or in flower boxes.

The waxy leaves are dark green, glossy, thick, oval, and blunt-tipped, with untoothed edges. They usually crowd on the stems in clusters. The flowers resemble large, fragrant, white stars and have a long, trumpetlike base. They yield a 1-inch round or oval fruit. The acidic fruit changes from bright green to red and contains a milky white juice. Both stages of the fruit may be present on the shrub at the same time.

The juice changes to a bright color when sugar is added. There is also a color change when honey is used instead of sugar. The ripe fruit makes excellent jellies, jams, sauces, or wines and can also be served fresh. Natal plum is an excellent source of vitamin C.

NATAL PLUM JELLY

1 lb. ripe fruit

1 cup of water

¹/₂ cup sugar per cup juice

3 oz. liquid pectin

Wash and stem the ripe fruit, place in a saucepan, and cook with the water, over a moderate heat for 15 minutes. Run the juicy pulp through a jelly bag.

Measure and add in the sugar or honey. Bring to a boil, then add in the liquid pectin and hold at a full boil for 1 minute. Stir constantly. Skim the foam, pour into hot, sterile jars, seal, and label. Goes well with biscuits and muffins.

NATAL PLUM JAM

1 qt. ripe fruit

¹/₂ cup sugar per cup sauce

3 oz. liquid pectin

Wash and stem the ripe fruit, then cook in a saucepan for 15 minutes, over a moderate heat. Remove from the heat and run through a food mill. Collect and measure juicy pulp, add in the sugar, and mix thoroughly.

Bring to a boil, then add in the liquid pectin and hold at a boil for 1 full minute. Skim the foam, pour into hot, sterile jars, seal, and label. Enhances toast with a delightful flavor and color.

NATAL PLUM PRESERVES

    2 qts. ripe plums
    ½ cup water
    6 cups sugar or honey

Wash and stem the ripe plums. Place in a saucepan, add in the water and sugar. Cook at a boil until the sugar dissolves. Reduce the heat and simmer until syrup gives a jelly test. Spoon the fruit and sauce into hot, sterile jars, seal, and label.

NATAL PLUM COOKING SAUCE

    1 cup diced plums   ¼ cup minced onions
    3 tbsp. white wine vinegar   1 tbsp. brown sugar
    pinch salt   pinch sage

Place the washed and stemmed fruit in a saucepan and cook over a moderate heat until the fruit pops. Run through a food mill, removing the skins.

    Combine the ingredients in a saucepan and cook at a boil for 2 minutes. Skim the foam and pour into hot, sterile jars, seal, and label. Good with skillet-cooked chicken, chops, or barbecue beef. Makes a good barbecue sauce.

NATAL PLUM FRUIT SALSA

    2 cups diced plums   1 small apple, diced
    1 tbsp. honey   1 tbsp. lemon juice
    pinch ground cinnamon

Combine the ingredients in a bowl and mix well. Store in refrigerator until ready to use. Goes well with chips.

NATAL PLUM LEATHER

2 cups ripe plums	2 tsp. lemon juice
½ cup corn syrup	pinch ground cloves

Wash and stem 2 full cups of ripe plums. Place in blender and puree. Place the puree in a bowl, add in the ingredients, and mix thoroughly.

Using a plastic wrap, cover a cookie sheet and spread the puree across the surface, evenly. Place in a 145-degree oven and dry. May take 3 to 5 hours. Once dried, roll and place in a locking plastic bag and store in a dry, dark place. Garnish when ready to use.

DRIED NATAL PLUMS

Gather as many ripe plums as you need, wash, and stem. The entire fruit may be dried as is or diced. Place the fruit on a cookie sheet and place in a warm dry area.

Drying whole fruit may take 4 to 5 days, depending on the heat. Drying diced plums will take 1 to 2 days. Either whole or diced, drying in a 150-degree oven will take less time.

When the whole fruit is dry, it will resemble a prune.

FROZEN NATAL PLUMS

Harvest as many ripened plums as needed. Wash and stem. Remove the flesh, discarding the seed. Place the flesh in plastic bags, label, and place in freezer. Will keep for three to four months.

NUTGRASS
Cyperus spp.

LOCALLY THIS PLANT MAY BE known as meadow grass or coco grass (*Cyperus esculentus*). Usually found in sandy fields or along roadsides and the margins of wet areas, nutgrass has a range from Florida north to New England and west to Texas. A perennial, it bears a number of small underground tubers, hence the name.

The leaves are grasslike, with a midrib, and may be as long as the stem. There are 3 to 6 smaller leaves that form an involucre just below the flower cluster. The flowers are contained in an umbel composed of 5 to 6 rays that in turn may be subdivided once again. The spikelets are numerous, straw-colored, and flattened on the top. The flower umbels yield a cluster of seeds that can be collected, dried, ground to a pulp, and used as a tasty flour base.

The small nutlike tubers also serve as an excellent food source. They must be dug from the ground, as they remain behind when the plant is pulled up. They contain high concentrations of carbohydrates and some protein.

DRIED NUTGRASS TUBERS

Dig up as many of the tubers as needed. Wash and clean thoroughly, removing any imperfect spots. The tubers may be dried whole or diced. Whole tubers will take longer to dry than diced tubers. Spread on a tray or cookie sheet and dry in a warm, dark place. A garage will do nicely. Will take about 5 to 6 days to dry. Drying in an oven will take 2 days at 145 degrees. Can be used in place of potatoes. Has a delicious nutty flavor.

Finely ground, dried nutgrass tubers can be used to flavor coffee. Experimentation is required to determine the correct amount to suit your taste.

COOKED NUTGRASS TUBERS

Collect as many tubers as needed, wash, and scrub the skin. Place into boiling water and cook until soft. Serve as a table vegetable.

WILD ONION
Allium spp.

THERE ARE SEVERAL SPECIES OF ALLIUM THAT are commonly referred to as wild onion. Similar in appearance, all have a bulb that is 1 to 2 inches at the base, are linear, and have tubular or flat dark-green leaves with a height of up to 2 feet. Plants are generally found in small clusters or umbels. Bell-shaped flowers appear in July or August. The small petals are rose-colored or white.

Wild onions are found in large clusters spread over the ground, usually in open wet areas. They range from Nova Scotia south to Florida and west to the Rocky Mountains, New Mexico, South Dakota, and the Pacific coast.

Entire plant contains a strong onion odor and taste. Depending on individual preference, bulbs may have to be parboiled before eating. Bulbs and leaves can be eaten or used to flavor a large variety of foods.

PICKLED ONIONS

2 lbs. ½-inch onions	3 tbsp. cane sugar
3 cups water	1 tbsp. salt
3 cups white wine vinegar	pinch dry mustard
3 whole cloves	pinch allspice
3 bay leaves	pinch turmeric

Place cleaned onions in boiling water and allow to stand for 2 minutes. Remove, place in cold water, and peel. Scalding helps free the skin.

Combine remaining ingredients in a saucepan and bring to a boil. Simmer for 5 to 6 minutes.

Pack the hot onions in hot, sterile jars, seal, and label. Hot, pickled onions may be used immediately or stored in a cool, dark place. May keep 4 to 6 months. Wild onions have a flavor that remains throughout the pickling process. Stays on the tongue for a while!

WILD ONION RELISH

4 cups blanched onions	⅛ tsp. ground clove
½ cup honey	⅛ tsp. whole mustard seed
½ cup vinegar	⅛ tsp. ground allspice
1 cup seedless raisins	
4 tbsp. brown sugar	

Wash and blanch 4 cups of onions. Peel and dice. Place in a saucepan, add in all of the above ingredients, and bring to a boil. Cook until onion pieces are tender, stirring constantly. Simmer for ten minutes. Spoon into hot, sterile jars, seal, and label. Excellent garnish for hot dogs and hamburgers.

DRIED WILD ONIONS

Harvest as many onions as needed, but do not wash off the soil after pulling from the ground. Spread out on newspapers and allow to dry in warm but shady area. Bright sunlight will only cook the oils and destroy the onion. When the necks of the onions have dried, the plant is ready. Drying time depends on humidity and temperature. Drying may take 7 to 10 days. *Do not tie together and attempt to dry*: the onions will only get moldy.

Using clean, discarded panty hose, cut off length of leg, fill with bulbs, and hang in a well ventilated, dry area. Bulbs will keep for several months.

The flat or tubular leaves can be used as a seasoning. Collect and clean, then dice into ¼-inch sections. Dry as described above. When completely dry, store in an airtight, dry container. Crush if a powder is required. These dried leaves can be used as a savory garnish.

WILD ONION–MUSTARD SAUCE

1 cup thin white sauce	1 tsp. ground mustard
½ cup minced onions	salt and pepper to taste

Prepare a thin white sauce. Add in the ground mustard, minced onions, and salt and pepper to taste.

Place in a saucepan and bring to a boil for 1 full minute. Mix thoroughly. Remove from the heat, pour into a hot, sterile jar, seal, and label.

Excellent when used to flavor ham, chicken, or any meat loaf.

GLAZED WILD ONIONS

1 ¼ lbs. onions	3 tbsp. sugar
¼ cup butter	¼ tsp. salt
pinch pepper	1 tsp. corn syrup

Select the onions and wash thoroughly, removing the outer skins. Place in a saucepan and cover with boiling water, add in the salt, and boil gently until tender, about 12 to 15 minutes.

Combine the butter, salt, corn syrup, and sugar in a separate saucepan and heat slowly until butter melts. Drain the onions, place in the syrup, and continue to cook for 2 to 3 minutes. Turn the onions to evenly glaze the surfaces with the hot syrup.

When it appears that the onions are completely covered, remove and place in hot, sterile jars, cover with the syrup, seal, and label. They go well with any meat dish as a side serving.

WILD ONION SPREAD

3 cups diced onions	1 tbsp. chopped parsley
mayonnaise to blend	pinch allspice

Mix thoroughly in a bowl, then pour into a sterile jar. Keep in the refrigerator until ready for use. Use on bread, covering generously, and place in hot oven and toast. Serve with onion soup.

OREGON GRAPE
Berberis spp.

COMMONLY KNOWN AS THE HOLLY grape, the Oregon grape (*Berberis repens*) is an evergreen shrub that has leaves resembling holly leaves. A low-growing shrub, it seldom exceeds 4 feet in height. It can be found growing in the wilds from British Columbia south to California. It is commonly grown as an ornamental hedge shrub and has therefore escaped to the wilds in other parts of the United States.

The leaves are compound, holly-shaped, tough, and leathery, with spine-tipped edges and, usually, 5 to 9 leaflets. The leaves are quite glossy and very attractive. During the cold winter months, the shiny leaves take on a very attractive bronze color.

During the early spring the plant bears small short clusters of yellow flowers, usually at the tip of each of the branches. These brightly colored flowers yield edible blue berries; they resemble small grapes, hence the name. Although the fruit is somewhat pulpy, it can be made into excellent jellies and jams.

A related species, the dwarf Oregon grape (*M. aquifolium compacta*), is widely used as a small, ground-hugging, ornamental shrub. Its berries are also blue. Both shrubs contain fair amounts of pectin in the ripe fruit.

OREGON GRAPE JELLY

8 cups ripe fruit
1½ cups sugar per cup juice

Select only fully ripened fruit. Wash and stem 8 cups of fruit and place in a saucepan. Crush the fruit with a potato masher. Add a little cooking water, bring to a boil, and cook over a moderate heat for 10 minutes.

Strain the colorful juice through a jelly bag. To each cup of juice add the sugar, mix thoroughly, and bring to a boil. Boil until the sugar dissolves. Skim the colorful foam, pour into hot, sterile jars, seal, and label. Excellent garnish for toast!

SPICY OREGON GRAPE JELLY

4 cups ripe fruit	1 tbsp. ground cinnamon
¾ cup cider vinegar	½ tbsp. ground allspice
⅓ cup water	4 whole cloves
4 cups sugar	

Wash and clean 4 cups of fully ripened berries. Place in a saucepan, add the cold water, cider vinegar, sugar, and spices. Mix thoroughly, bring to a boil, then simmer for 30 minutes, stirring occasionally. Keep covered.

Remove the sauce from the heat and strain through a jelly bag. Bring the juice to a boil for 1 full minute. Skim the colorful foam, pour the sauce into hot, sterile jars, seal, and label. Will look just like grape jelly.

OREGON GRAPE JAM

3 lbs. ripe berries
2 cups water
1 cup sugar per cup sauce

Wash and stem 3 pounds of ripe fruit, place in a saucepan with the water, and cook until the fruit softens and the juice runs freely. Remove from the heat and press the juicy pulp through a food mill.

Recover the juicy pulp, measure, and add 1 cup of sugar to each cup of juice. Mix thoroughly, bring to a boil, and hold there for 15 minutes. Stir constantly.

Remove from the heat, skim the blue foam, pour into hot, sterile jars, seal, and label. Excellent garnish for fruit leathers.

OREGON GRAPE PRESERVES

2 qts. ripe fruit
6 cups sugar or honey
½ cup water

Place the ripe berries, water, and sugar into a saucepan and cook until the sugar dissolves. Continue to cook at a boil for 10 minutes. Reduce heat and cook at a simmer until syrup gives a positive jelly test.

Spoon the mix into hot, sterile jars, seal, and label.

OREGON GRAPE COOKING SAUCE

1 cup ripe berries
3 tbsp. white wine vinegar
pinch sage
¼ cup minced onions

1 tbsp. brown sugar
pinch salt
¼ cup heavy cream

Place the ripe berries in a saucepan and cook until the fruit pops. Run the juicy mess through a food mill, removing the skins and seeds. Combine the other ingredients, except the heavy cream, and boil the juicy pulp for 2 minutes, then run through a jelly bag.

Pour the hot sauce into hot, sterile jars, seal, and label.

Blend in ¼ cup of heavy cream, bring to a boil, when ready to use. Goes well as a cooking sauce for chicken and fish.

OREGON GRAPE LEATHER

> 2 cups fruit puree
> 2 tsp. lemon or lime juice
> ½ cup corn syrup

Wash and stem the berries. Toss into a blender, producing a fruit puree. Add in the corn syrup, lemon or lime juice. Mix thoroughly.

Using plastic wrap, cover a cookie sheet and spread the puree evenly. Place in a 145-degree oven and dry. When dry, roll and place in locking plastic bag, then store in a dry, dark place. Garnish when ready to eat.

OSWEGO TEA
Monarda didyma

THIS SCENTED NATIVE OF NORTH America can be found growing from Nova Scotia south to Florida and west to the Plains states. A dozen or so species can be found throughout the eastern United States.

Attains heights of up to 3 feet, with an erect, four-sided stem typical of the mint family. Leaves are paper-thin, up to 6 inches long, dark green, and opposite one another on the stem. Flowers appear at the terminal stem. They are a brilliant scarlet color.

Known by many local names, including wild bergamot and bee balm. Often used to make a strong, flavorsome tea.

DRIED OSWEGO TEA

Identify the plants you wish to collect the day before. Select the stems you need, and pick just after the dew evaporates. Wash the stem, to remove any grime, in a little warm water. You may dry the plant stems as whole or cut into small pieces.

If you dry the stems, tie 3 or 4 in a small bundle and hang in a warm, dark place, upside down. Leave there until plants become brittle-dry. Either hang in a dry, dark place or place into a large storage bag and keep dry.

Cutting the stems into smaller sections will speed up the drying process by several hours or days. Dry in the shade and when dry, place in locking plastic bags and store in a dry, dark place.

OSWEGO TEA

A tablespoon of the dried leaves and stems placed in a cup of boiling water will yield an excellent but strong tea. Add in a little sugar or honey if you have a cold.

The dried leaves and stems of oswego tea can be added to other commercial teas to flavor.

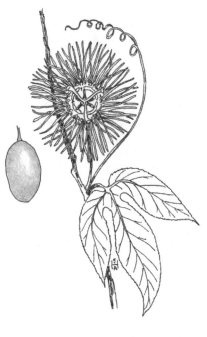

PASSION FLOWER
Passiflora spp.

THIS TRAILING OR CLIMBING PEREN-
nial vine can be found growing in
open, dry, vacant areas and old
fields and farmlands, as well as
along roadsides and forest or field
edges. Passion flower (*Passiflora
incarnata*) ranges in growth
throughout Florida north to southern Virginia and west to Texas.

The often-lobed leaves alternate on the vine. The flowers are
showy, 1½ to 2 inches wide and white with a purple-pink crown.
They yield a large berry, which is edible. The fruit is egg-shaped,
turns yellow in color when mature, and may be up to 2 inches in
length.

Common names include May pop, wild lemon vine, and apricot
vine. Purple granadilla *(P. edulus)* also yields a fruit, which is edible,
dark purple in color, and up to 3½ inches long.

The vine usually covers considerable ground, ranging from 20 to
50 feet across.

PASSION FLOWER JELLY

> 8 cups ripe fruit
> 3 oz. liquid pectin
> 1 cup sugar per cup juice

Select ripe fruit, wash, and stem. Place in a saucepan with a little water and bring to a boil. Cook over a moderate heat for 15 minutes. Strain the mixture through a jelly bag and collect the juice. Measure and add 1 cup sugar to each cup of juice.

Place in a saucepan and bring to a boil for 1 full minute. Cook over a moderate heat until the sugar dissolves.

Add in the liquid pectin, mix, and bring to a boil for 1 full minute. Skim the colorful foam and pour the sauce into hot, sterile jars, seal, and label. Goes well as a garnish for cakes and cupcakes.

PASSION FLOWER JAM

> 2 lbs. ripe fruit
> 1 cup sugar per cup sauce
> ½ tsp. lemon juice
>
> 2 cups water
> 3 oz. pectin

Wash and stem the ripe fruit, place in a saucepan with the water, and cook until the fruit softens and the juice runs freely. Remove from the heat and press the juicy pulp through a food mill, removing the seeds and skins.

Recover the juicy pulp, measure and add 2 cups of sugar or honey to each cup of juice. Mix thoroughly, bring to a boil, and hold there for 15 minutes, stirring constantly, dissolving the sugar.

Remove and skim the foam, pour into hot, sterile jars, seal, and label.

PASSION FLOWER RUM SAUCE

$\frac{1}{2}$ cup fruit juice	$\frac{1}{2}$ cup favorite rum
$\frac{1}{2}$ cup corn syrup	1 drop vanilla extract
$\frac{1}{4}$ cup water	$\frac{1}{3}$ cup lemon or lime juice

Combine the passion flower fruit juice and water. Bring to a boil for 1 full minute. Add in the remaining ingredients and boil for 1 minute. Mix thoroughly.

Skim the foam, pour into hot, sterile jars, seal, and label.

Makes an excellent garnish for desserts and cakes.

DRIED PASSION FLOWER

Dry either the entire fruit pod or cut into small sections. Wash thoroughly, place the whole fruit on a tray, and dry in the bright sunlight until the fruit shrivels and is crunchy. This may take 2 to 3 days. Store in plastic bags in a dry, cool place.

Cutting the fruit into smaller section, drying in the sun will take 1 to 2 days. Store in plastic bags. Rehydrates quickly in warm water.

SWEET AND SOUR PASSION FLOWER SAUCE

1 cup ripe fruit	2 tsp. lemon juice
$\frac{1}{2}$ cup water	1 tbsp. butter
2 tbsp. sugar	1 tsp. soy sauce
$\frac{3}{4}$ tsp. corn starch	$\frac{1}{4}$ tsp. salt
$\frac{1}{2}$ tsp. ginger	

Place the ripe fruit in a saucepan with a little water and cook until the fruit juice runs free. Run the juicy pulp through a food mill and place in a saucepan. Combine the corn starch, sugar, soy sauce, ground ginger, and salt, stirring constantly. Cook until the mess thickens.

Once the sauce has thickened, add in the lemon juice and butter. Mix thoroughly. Cook for 1 full minute at a boil. Pour the mixture into hot, sterile jars, seal, and label. Excellent cooking sauce for fish, noodles, pork, and chicken.

PASSION FRUIT BRANDY SAUCE

1 cup fruit sauce
2 tbsp. brandy
1 cup sugar or corn syrup

Cook enough passion flower fruit to obtain 1 cup of juicy pulp. When cooked, run the mixture through a food mill, removing the seeds and skins.

Combine the sugar and your favorite brandy, mix well and bring to a boil. Be certain to taste the brandy to make sure it is good quality.

Pour the hot sauce into hot, sterile jars, seal, and label. Goes well as a topping with desserts, cakes, and other pastries. Adds flavor to pork and chicken dishes.

PASSION FLOWER COOLER

Collect as much ripened fruit as you wish. Wash and clean and remove stems. Place in a blender, with a little water, and produce a thick puree.

Remove from the blender and run the mess through a sieve, removing the seeds and large portions of the pulp.

Add in a little sugar and stir well. Place the mixture in the refrigerator and chill. Serve in glasses with ice cubes and that little umbrella.

PAPAW
Asimina spp.

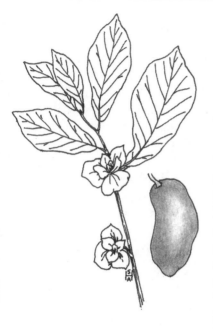

THE PAPAW (*ASIMINA TRILOBA*) CAN attain heights of up to 50 feet, but it is more often found growing as a large shrub in the wilds or as an ornamental. It is relatively common along stream edges and in wet thickets. The papaw ranges from southern Canada south to Florida and Texas. There are about seven related species in the eastern and southeastern United States.

The leaves are large, 10 to 12 inches long, and oblong with pointed tips. The young stem growth is covered with a fine fuzz. The fruit is large, fleshy, up to 8 inches in length, and 2 to 3 inches thick. It is brown, grows in small clusters, and is very sweet when ripe—the pulp can be sickeningly sweet! The fruit is abundant, available in late September or early October, and is best after it has been nipped by a good frost. A single fruit may weigh upwards of a pound.

The sweet pulp has a sepia or dull yellow color and can easily be removed by scraping the inside of the fruit hull. Be prepared to dislike this fruit: for as many as there are that like it, there are equally as many who dislike it.

PAPAW JELLY

3 lbs. ripe fruit pulp	½ cup water
½ cup sugar per cup juice	6 oz. liquid pectin

Select about 4 pounds fully ripened papaws. Skin the fruit and remove the seeds. Scrape and remove 3 pounds of the sweet yellow-brown pulp. Place in a saucepan with ½ cup water and bring to a boil. Simmer for 15 minutes, covered. Remove from the heat and strain through a jelly bag.

To each cup of recovered juice add ½ cup sugar and bring to a boil for 1 full minute. Add in the 6 ounces of liquid pectin, mix thoroughly, bring to a hard boil for 1 minute. Remove from the heat, skim, pour into hot, sterile jars, seal, and label.

SPICED PAPAW JAM

3 lbs. ripe fruit	6 whole cloves
¾ cup cider vinegar	1 tsp. allspice
6 oz. liquid pectin	1 tbsp. cinnamon
6 cups sugar	

Select about 4 pounds of fully ripened papaws. Remove the pulp and recover 3 pounds. Place in a saucepan with just a little cooking water, bring to a slow boil, then simmer for 10 minutes. Remove and run through a food mill, removing the seeds.

Place the juicy pulp in a saucepan, add the cider vinegar, water, sugar, and the ground spices. Mix thoroughly and cook over a low heat for 30 minutes, stirring occasionally. Do not allow the mixture to burn.

Strain the sauce through a fine sieve, add 6 ounces of liquid pectin, and bring to a boil for 1 full minute. Skim, pour into hot, sterile jars, seal, and label.

PAPAW LEATHER

2 cups papaw puree
2 tsp. lemon juice
½ cup corn syrup

Harvest enough fruit to produce 2 cups puree. Scrape the juicy pulp from the fruit and using a blender produce a golden-brown puree. Add in the lemon juice and sugar and blend. Using plastic wrap, cover a cookie sheet and spread the puree evenly across the surface.

Dry in bright sunlight as long as possible or in a 140-degree oven. Once dried, roll the puree and store in a plastic locking bag. When ready to use, cover with a delightful garnish.

SPICY PAPAW SAUCE

2 cups puree
1 grated orange rind
2 cups water

2 cups sugar
½ tsp. ground cinnamon
pinch ground cloves

Combine the grated rind of 1 orange, 2 cups water, and 2 cups sugar in a saucepan. Mix and cook over a moderate heat for 10 minutes. Add the 2 cups of fruit puree and spices. Cook for 5 minutes, stirring frequently.

Spoon the mixture into hot, sterile jars, seal, and label. Goes well as a basting for chicken and pork dishes.

PAPAW CURRY SAUCE

½ cup fruit puree	2 tbsp. butter
1 cup beef stock	3 tbsp. flour
½ tsp. salt	pinch pepper
1 tbsp. minced onion	1 tsp. curry powder

Make up a typical brown sauce by melting the butter and mixing in the flour; cook over a low heat until brown. Slowly add in the pepper and the fruit puree. Bring to a boil and cook for 5 minutes.

Add in the beef stock, salt, onion, curry powder and boil for 1 full minute. Enhances the flavor of fowl, pork, and veggie dishes.

PAPAW BUTTER

6 cups fruit puree	½ tsp. ground cinnamon
1 cup cider vinegar	½ tsp. ground allspice
6 cups sugar	

Place the puree into a saucepan, add the sugar, cider vinegar and mix thoroughly. Spoon the mixture into a baking pan and bake in 250-degree oven for 4 hours. When the juice can no longer be separated, the butter is finished. Spoon into hot, sterile jars, seal, and label. Excellent garnish for toast and fruit leathers.

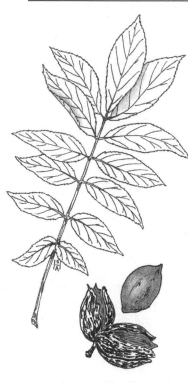

PECAN
Carya illinoensis

A TALL, STATELY TREE, OFTEN REACH-
ing heights of up to 170 to 190 feet.
Thrives in rich bottomlands such as
old river flood plains. Many folks
plant the pecan as a means of harvesting the nut and selling it.

Considered a tree of the South, as
it requires 150 or more warm growing
days to yield a bountiful supply of
nuts. Ranges from Georgia west to
Texas and, in the central United
States, north to Indiana.

The leaves are long, with 9 to 17
smooth-edged leaflets. The nuts range in size from 1 to 2 inches and
are thin-husked and thin-shelled. Nut meats are large, with four sections. The fruit ripens in late September, usually in great abundance,
depending on the age of the tree. Large numbers of nuts are produced
each year. Nut meats are known to have 70 percent fat content.

DRIED PECANS

Collect as many nuts as you need. Place the nuts on an open surface
and allow to remain for several days. This drying time will allow the
husk to dry out. When ready, remove the thick husks. You may
require a good pair of leather gloves to accomplish this process. The
husks will stain your hands with a yellow dye that is difficult to
remove.

Dry the nuts while in their shells. This may take a full 6 to 7 days. Place in a warm, dry, shaded area. If placed in the sun the oils inside will cook. Fill a net bag and hang to dry until ready for use.

Crack the shells and dry the nut meats in a warm, shady area until dry. Store in plastic locking bags. Drying may take 2 days.

Dried, ground pecans can be stored and used during the cold, winter months as toppings for desserts and baked goods. The dried nuts can be used to make that delicious pecan pie from Grandma's recipe.

PECAN-MAPLE SAUCE

¼ cup chopped pecan meats   ¼ cup water
½ lb. maple sugar   dash of salt
⅛ tsp. vanilla

Place the maple sugar, water, salt, and vanilla in a saucepan. Boil the mixture to 230 degrees, using a good candy thermometer to determine the temperature. Remove from the heat and add in the pecans. Serve hot as a topping for vanilla ice cream.

PEPPERMINT
Mentha piperita

LONG USED AS A MEDICINAL PLANT, peppermint has been used to quell such chronic disorders as colic, nausea, and headaches. Peppermint tea is still a popular remedy for the common cold and is regularly used as a flavoring for some cough syrups. It is also used in soaps, candies, and perfumes.

Peppermint is a member of the mint family. It can be found growing at the edges of marshlands and streams and in various wastelands. It grows to a height of 3 feet, with erect stems that are somewhat branched and crowded. The leaves are opposite one another on the stem, 3 inches long, oblate, slightly fuzzy, and dark green. Oil glands cause spots to form on the leaf surfaces.

The flowers appear in thick spikes, usually purple in color, sometimes white or pink. The leaves can be used fresh or dried.

PEPPERMINT JELLY

fresh peppermint leaves	4 ½ cups sugar
1 tbsp. lemon juice	3 oz. liquid pectin

Collect a few handsful of fresh peppermint leaves. Wash thoroughly, then crush between your hands to break the surface of the leaves. Place the leaves in 2 quarts of boiling water. This will yield a strong peppermint tea. Boil for 10 minutes. Measure out 4 cups of the infusion, place in a saucepan, add 1 tbsp. of fresh lemon juice, and bring to a boil.

Remove from the heat, add the liquid pectin, sugar, bring to a boil once again. Add in a small amount of red food coloring (for the peppermint), mix, and pour into hot, sterile jars, seal, and label.

PEPPERMINT–CRAB APPLE JELLY

4 cups peppermint tea	10 partially ripened crab
3 ½ cups sugar	apples
3 oz. pectin	

Prepare a strong peppermint tea from freshly picked leaves. Measure out 4 cups of the hot beverage.

Peel 10 or so partially ripened crab apples. Cook the peels in a little water at a boil for 10 minutes.

Combine the hot brew and the juice from the apple peels in a saucepan. Add 3 ½ cups of sugar, mix thoroughly. Bring to a boil for 1 full minute, skim the surface, and pour into hot, sterile jars, seal, and label. The color will resemble that of apple juice.

PEPPERMINT SAUCE

1 cup peppermint leaves	honey to taste
1 cup vinegar	$\frac{1}{2}$ tsp. salt

Finely ground or shredded leaves are added to the vinegar (malt vinegar is preferred) and the salt. Mix thoroughly and simmer for 15 minutes. Remove from the heat, cover, and allow to stand for 25 to 30 minutes. This will allow the flavor time to concentrate.

Strain the mixture carefully. Add enough honey to thicken the mixture to your taste. Usually 2 to 3 ounces should be suitable. You may wish to add red food coloring as the sauce lacks color. This delightful tasting sauce goes well with lamb or poultry dishes. A delight when served with Cornish hen.

DRIED PEPPERMINT

Select the plants you wish to harvest the day before. Pick just after the morning dew has disappeared. Wash thoroughly, but not in hot water. Shake with care to remove as much of the water as possible. Make bundles of stems with the leaves, six stems will do. Tie together and hang in a warm, dry place such as your garage. Do not dry in direct sunlight! Allow to hang until the leaves become crisp. The dried stems can be stored as is in a dry, dark place.

Cut the stems and leaves into small pieces and spread them across a tray or cookie sheet. Place in a warm, dark place and allow to dry. These smaller sections will dry much faster than the stems. Place the dried section in locking plastic bags and store in a dark, dry place. Can be used to make jellies and delightful teas during the bleak months of winter!

PEPPERMINT ICE CREAM TOPPING

¼ cup sugar
¼ cup water
2 drops red coloring
2 tsp. cornstarch

⅛ tsp. grated lemon rind
¼ cup concentrated
  peppermint tea
3 tbsp. honey

Combine the sugar and cornstarch, add in the water, peppermint tea, and blend, until smooth. Heat until boiling, stir constantly. Boil slowly for 1 full minute or until thick. Remove from the heat, add in the rind, red food coloring, and honey. Stir well and allow to cool. Makes about 1 cup of delightful sauce. Serve as a garnish over ice cream or puddings. Refrigerate.

PEPPERMINT–WILD CHERRY SAUCE

1 cup strong peppermint brew
½ lb. pitted cherries
2 tbsp. cornstarch

½ cup sugar
4 tbsp. lemon juice

Combine the wild cherry sauce with the strong peppermint tea, stir in the sugar. Heat to just below boiling point for 10 minutes.

Combine the cornstarch with a tablespoon of water, stir into the fruit mixture, and cook over a low heat until the mixture thickens. Excellent garnish for ice cream and pastries.

PERSIMMON
Diospyros spp.

A NATIVE FRUIT, PERSIMMON (*Diospyros virginiana*) was praised by many of the early North American settlers and explorers. De Soto made note of it in his journals in 1557.

The persimmon is colored yellow-red when ripe and may range in size from 1 to 3 inches in diameter. It is very bitter or astringent when eaten green; the unripe fruit contains high concentrations of tannin, which are reduced considerably as it ripens. For best results, use only fully ripened fruit.

A medium-size tree, it is usually found in the eastern United States and is quite common in southern Iowa and Nebraska. The leaves are oval or elliptical, about 2 to 6 inches long, pointed, and rounded at the base. The top surface is shiny and dark green, whereas the underside is lighter in color and may be smooth or fuzzy.

The male and female flowers on different trees in the spring are ⅜ to ¾ inch long, white, and in the axil of the leaf. The fruits appear from September through November.

There are 160 species in the genus located throughout the temperate zones of the world, but they are found mostly in Asia. Chapote (*D. texana*) has a growth range from Texas west to southern California. The fruits of both species can be eaten when ripe, but they are best when preserved. *D. virginiana* is orange-red when ripe, and *D. texana* is blue-black.

PERSIMMON JELLY

3 lbs. ripe fruit	1 cup sugar per cup juice
¼ cup water	6 oz. liquid pectin

Stem and wash the fruit, then cut into halves and remove the seeds. Crush the juicy pulp and strain through a food mill. Add ½ cup of water, mix thoroughly. Pass through a jelly bag and recover the juice.

Place the juice in a saucepan, add in the sugar for each cup of juice, mix thoroughly, and bring to a boil. Add in the liquid pectin and bring to a boil for 1 full minute. Skim the foam, pour into hot, sterile jars, seal, and label. Excellent on biscuits.

PERSIMMON JAM

3 lbs. ripe fruit	1 cup sugar per cup juicy pulp
¼ cup water	6 oz. liquid pectin

Clean and stem the fruit, cut into halves, removing the large seeds. Crush the fruit with a masher, then run through a food mill. Recover the juicy pulp and place in a saucepan.

Add 1 cup of sugar per cup of juicy pulp. Bring to a boil, then add in the pectin, stir, and boil for 1 full minute. Pour into hot, sterile jars, seal, and label. Excellent garnish for fruit leathers.

PICKLED PERSIMMONS

3 lbs. ripe fruit	6 cups sugar
¾ cup cider vinegar	1½ cups water
4 tbsp. whole cloves	½ stick cinnamon

Wash the ripened fruit but do not remove the stems. Make a syrup of the sugar, cider vinegar, water and bring to a boil. Add the spices, fruit. Mix thoroughly and bring to a boil. Cook until the fruit is tender.

Pack the fruit into hot, sterile jars and cover with the syrup. Seal and label the jars. Do not serve for about 1 month. This will allow the spices a chance to work.

PERSIMMON SAUCE

3 lbs. ripe fruit   1 grated orange rind
2 cups sugar   2 cups water
1 drop vanilla extract

Place the water, grated rind of 1 orange, and sugar into a saucepan. Mix thoroughly and cook over a moderate heat for 5 minutes. Add the persimmon fruit and cook until the fruit softens. Run through a food mill and recover the sauce. Pour into hot, sterile jars, seal, and label. Serve chilled for best flavor.

SPICED PERSIMMON BUTTER

5 lbs. ripe fruit   6 cups sugar
1 cup cider vinegar   ½ tsp. ground cinnamon
½ tsp. ground allspice   1 drop of vanilla extract

Wash, stem, and remove the flower ends of the fruit. Cut the persimmons into quarters, place into a saucepan, add a little cooking water, and bring to a boil. Allow to simmer until the fruit becomes soft. Crush with a potato masher and strain through a food mill, removing the skin and seeds. Place the juicy pulp into a saucepan, add the sugar and cider vinegar, and mix thoroughly. Stir in the spices and spoon the spicy pulp into a baking pan. Place in a 250-degree oven for 4 hours. Occasionally stir the mix. When juice can no longer be separated from the pulp, the butter is ready. You may serve warm or spoon into hot, sterile jars, seal, and label. The amount of sugar depends on your sweet tooth.

PERSIMMON CONSERVE

2 lbs. ripe fruit   1½ cups seedless raisins
½ lemon   1½ oranges
4 cups sugar   1 cup minced nuts
pinch allspice   pinch ground cloves

Wash and stem the fruit, cut into quarters, and remove the seeds. Slice the lemon and oranges into very thin sections and dice. Mince the raisins and the nut meats. Combine all ingredients in a saucepan with the sugar and cook over a low heat for about 1 hour. Stir occasionally to prevent burning.

Pour into hot, sterile jars, seal, and label.

PINYON PINE
Pinus spp.

CONSIDERED A SMALL TREE, THE pinyon pine (*Pinus cembroides*) can be 30 to 40 feet tall. The branches are almost horizontal and droop in older trees. The leaves are clusters of 2 to 3 needles that are dark green in color, an inch or so long, and quite brittle. The younger branches are tan or yellow-brown. The cones are almost without stems, yellowish, and about 2 inches long. The seeds, or "nuts," are about ½ inch long and are sweet-tasting and delicious when roasted.

Pinyon pine ranges from Colorado south to Mexico. Some varieties are planted as ornamentals as far north as New York State. It thrives on dry hillsides where there is just enough water to support vegetation. The seeds have long been a food staple of Native Americans that live in the area.

DRIED PINYON PINE SEEDS

The cones are gathered and then roasted quickly in an open fire to free the seeds. The seeds are then beaten from the cones. Once freed, the seeds can be eaten as is or ground into a meal, which when mixed with a little water, makes an excellent pan-fried sweet bread. One-half cup of seeds yields 260 calories and 12 grams of protein.

The freed seeds can be rubbed between gloved hands to remove the small wing. Place the cleaned seeds on a cookie sheet and dry in bright sunlight. Allow to dry one full day. When ready, place the seeds in locking plastic bags and store in a dark, dry area.

During the winter months, the small seeds can be roasted and served as a garnish, or eaten as is.

Finely chopped seeds can be stored, after being dried in locking plastic bags. When ready they may be used to flavor coffee.

SALTED PINYON PINE NUTS

Once you have cleaned the nuts, place in a shallow pan and lightly salt. Place the mixture in an oven at 140 degrees and heat for 1 hour. Remove, allow to cool, and store in plastic bags.

WILD PLUM
Prunus spp.

THERE ARE SEVERAL SPECIES OF wild plums that can be found throughout most of the United States and Canada. The red plum (*Prunus americana*) and the Chickasaw plum (*P. angustifolia*) are perhaps the most common. They grow as small coarse shrubs to a height of 20 feet or more and range from southern New England south to Florida and west to Colorado. The size of the fruit depends on the locale, being much larger in the Ohio River Valley. They are found growing in thickets and along stream and forest edges.

The most famous of the wild plums is the so-called beach plum (*P. maritima*), which has a magical sound to its name and a unique flavor. It is usually found along the eastern coastlines and inland as an ornamental shrub. Cape Cod is quite famous for its beach plum jelly.

The wild goose plum (*P. hortulana*) grows in lowlands, whereas the Canada plum (*P. nigra*) is more common at elevations of 2,000 to 4,000 feet. The Klamath plum (*P. subcordata*), also known locally as the western plum, can be found growing throughout Washington, Oregon, and California, especially along the coastal areas. Porter's plum or Allegheny sloe (*P. alleghaniensis*), a spreading, ground-hugging shrub, can be found growing from New England south to the mountains of Pennsylvania. Hog Plum (*P. umbellata*) ranges throughout the coastal pine areas of Florida.

The fruit of the wild plum, when ripe, has a flavor that is superior to that of the commercially grown varieties. The ripe fruit yields 30 calories and 200 IU of vitamin A.

WILD PLUM JELLY

5 lbs. ripe plums	1 cup water
7 cups sugar	3 oz. liquid pectin

Select 5 pounds of any of the wild plums, include some partially ripened fruit for flavor and pectin. Place in a saucepan and crush the fruit with a potato masher. Do not remove the pits or peels. Add 1 cup of cold tap water, bring the mixture to a boil. Simmer, covered, for 15 minutes. Place in a jelly bag and remove the juice.

Measure the juice; you should recover about five cups. Add 7 cups of sugar and bring the mixture to a boil. Add 3 ounces of liquid pectin and once again bring to a boil. Hold at a boil for 1 full minute, stirring constantly. Skim the colorful foam, pour into hot, sterile jars, seal, and label.

Save the plum pulp, which can be used to make an excellent plum butter.

WILD PLUM JAM

3 lbs. ripe plums
4 cups sugar
3 oz. liquid pectin

Wash and stem the fruit, adding in some partially ripe fruit. Place in a saucepan and crush with a potato masher. Bring the mess to a boil, then simmer for 10 minutes. Remove from the heat, then pour the mixture through a food mill, removing the seeds and skins.

Place the hot juicy pulp in a saucepan, add the sugar, and bring to a boil. Cook until the mixture thickens. You may reduce the cooking time by adding in 3 ounces of liquid pectin. Once completed, pour into hot, sterile jars, seal, and label. Excellent garnish for muffins and toast!

WILD PLUM SAUCE

4 cups ripe plums	1 grated orange rind
2 cups water	2 cups sugar
1/8 tsp. ground cinnamon	

Place 2 cups of water, the grated orange rind, and sugar in a saucepan, mix thoroughly, and cook over a moderate heat for 5 minutes.

Next add washed plums and cook until the fruit softens. Crush with a potato masher, add in the ground cinnamon, and cook for 5 minutes. Place in a food mill and strain out the seeds and skins. Place the hot sauce in hot, sterile jars, seal, and label. Serve chilled with meat dishes. Plum sauce and goose is famous.

WILD PLUM GINGER SAUCE

4 cups ripe plums	1/4 tsp. ground ginger
1/4 cup sugar	1/8 tsp. salt
1 cup boiling water	1/4 cup honey
3 whole cloves	

With a little water, cook the ripe plums until the skins break open. Crush with a potato masher. Strain through a food mill and place in a saucepan.

Blend in the sugar, honey, ginger, salt, and whole cloves with the juicy sauce. Slowly add the cup of boiling water, bring to a boil, and cook for 5 minutes. Pour the mix into hot, sterile jars, seal, and label. Excellent garnish for wild fowl, especially duck.

WILD PLUM PRESERVES

5 lbs. ripe plums	1 cup of water
1 cup sugar per cup fruit	2 juice oranges
pinch ground cloves	pinch allspice

Wash and cut into halves about 5 pounds of firm fully ripened wild plums. Remove the pits. Place the cut fruit into a saucepan, add in the water, and to each cup of fruit add 1 cup of sugar, then add the seasonings. Mix well and bring to a boil, then simmer for 5 minutes. Remove from the heat, pour into hot, sterile jars, seal, and label.

DRIED WILD PLUMS

The ripe fruit can be harvested and dried in bright sunshine and will keep in a dry place for several months.

Harvest as much fruit as you can, wash, and stem, removing the grime. The whole fruit can be spread on a tray and placed in bright, hot sunlight and allowed to dry. This process may take several days. Remember, the large seed will still be in place. The result, depending on the color of the plum, will resemble a dried prune. If you wish and have the time, make a cut into the side of the fruit and remove the seed. If the fruit is ripe the seed can easily be removed.

Cut the ripe fruit into sections, removing the seed. Place the sections on a cookie sheet or tray and dry in the bright sunlight. Drying make take 2 to 3 days. Speed up the process by drying in a 140-degree oven.

Place the dried plums or sections in a locking plastic bag and store in a dry, dark place. The dried fruit can be rehydrated using warm water.

WILD PLUM LEATHER

4 cups ripe fruit
2 tsp. lemon juice
½ cup sugar

Cut the ripe plums into sections, removing the seeds. Place the cut pieces into a blender and produce a puree. Add in the lemon juice and sugar and mix thoroughly.

Using a plastic wrap, cover a cookie sheet and spread the puree evenly across the surface. Place in bright sunlight and dry. Cover with cheesecloth to keep away the pesky insects. Dry in a 145-degree oven for less drying time.

When dry, roll the puree and store in a locking plastic bag. Garnish when ready to serve.

WILD PLUM BRANDY SAUCE

2 cups plum puree	1 cup sugar or honey
4 tbsp. your favorite brandy	pinch ground cloves

Combine the plum puree with the sugar and brandy. Mix thoroughly and bring to a quick boil. Serve hot or pour into hot, sterile jars, seal, and label. Excellent garnish for pastries.

WILD PLUM CURRY SAUCE

½ cup chopped ripe fruit	2 tbsp. butter
1 cup beef stock	3 tbsp. flour
½ tsp. salt	pinch pepper
2 tbsp. minced onion	1 tsp. curry powder

Make up a brown sauce by melting butter in a saucepan, add in the flour, and cook over a low heat until brown. Slowly add in the seasonings, beef stock, salt, butter, flour, pepper, and minced onions. Cook at a boil for 5 minutes, stirring constantly.

When ready, serve hot with poultry, meat, or vegetable dishes. You can also pour, when hot, into a hot, sterile jar, seal, and label.

WILD PLUM CONSERVE

1 qt. chopped ripe fruit
4 cups sugar
2 cups seedless raisins
pinch ground cloves

1 cup water
1 cup orange pulp
pinch cinnamon

Remove the skins and seeds from the ripe fruit and dice. Place into a saucepan with 1 cup of water. Cook for 15 minutes over a moderate heat, stirring occasionally.

Force the mix through a food mill. Place in a saucepan, add in the seedless raisins, orange pulp, and the sugar, then cook over a moderate heat for 40 minutes, stirring frequently.

Remove and pour the conserve into hot, sterile jars, seal, and label. Allow at least 1 month before serving. This will enhance the flavor.

PRICKLY PEAR CACTUS
Opuntia spp.

PRICKLY PEAR CACTUS IS FOUND IN the southwestern United States and from Cape Cod south to Florida, where it can be found in patches of considerable abundance. It thrives in loose, sandy, dry soils.

The leaves (pads) are pear-shaped, hence the name. The yellow flowers yield a fruit that is red, about 3 inches long, rounded, and oblong. It is edible raw or cooked.

There are over 200 species of this cactus genus scattered throughout much of the warm, dry areas of the country. Usually found as a small, shrublike plant, it may reach a height of 10 feet. The fruit is covered with fine bristles that are easily rubbed off with a pair of leather gloves.

PRICKLY PEAR JELLY

3 lbs. ripe fruit	1 cup water
7 cups sugar	3 oz. pectin

Collect enough fruit to yield 4 cups fruit pulp. Split the fruit lengthwise and remove the juicy pulp. Place the pulp into a saucepan and add in the water. Bring to a boil and continue to cook over a moderate heat for 10 minutes.

Run the juicy sauce through a jelly bag and collect the juice. Place in a saucepan and add in the sugar. Mix thoroughly and cook over a moderate heat until the juice begins to thicken. Add in the liquid pectin, mix well, and hold at a boil for 1 full minute.

Skim the foam, pour into hot, sterile jars, seal, and label. Leaves a very colorful jelly.

PRICKLY PEAR JAM

4 cups fruit pulp
4 cups sugar

Cut the side of the fruit and scrape out the juicy fruit. Place in a saucepan with a cup of water and cook over a moderate heat for 10 minutes. Run the mix through a food mill and place in a saucepan.

Add in the sugar and cook over a moderate heat for 10 minutes, or until juice thickens. Add 3 ounces of liquid pectin if in a hurry. Pour the mix into hot, sterile jars, seal, and label.

PRICKLY PEAR LEATHER

2 cups puree
2 tsp. lemon juice
½ cup sugar or corn syrup

Collect enough juicy pulp to make up 2 cups. Place in a blender and mix. Add in the lemon juice and sugar or corn syrup. Mix thoroughly.

Using a plastic wrap, cover the surface of a cookie sheet and spread the puree evenly across the surface. Place in a 145-degree oven and dry. Do not place in bright sunshine to dry, as it will destroy the puree.

When dry, roll the puree and store in locking plastic bag. Garnish when ready to use.

PRICKLY PEAR SAUCE

6 cups fruit pulp	½ cup lemon juice
1 cup sugar or corn syrup	⅛ tsp. plain gelatin
½ cup water	pinch of ground cinnamon

Collect 6 cups of the juicy pulp and place in a saucepan. Mix in the sugar and lemon juice. Then, mix in slowly the gelatin and water. Cook over a low heat until the sauce thickens. Pour into hot, sterile jar(s), seal, and label. Can be served hot as a side dish or as a garnish for pastries.

PRICKLY PEAR CREOLE SAUCE

1 cup puree	dash basil and salt
1 onion, minced	pinch ground peppercorn
1 bell pepper, minced	pinch ground red pepper

Combine the ingredients and allow to stand for 30 minutes. Bring to a quick boil and hold for 2 minutes. Pour into hot, sterile jars, seal, and label.

Serve hot with steaks, casseroles, fish, or chops.

PRICKLY PEAR ORANGE SAUCE

6 cups fruit pulp	1 cup sugar
1 thin sliced orange	½ cup Sauterne (wine)
pinch ground cloves	

Remove enough juicy pulp to collect 6 cups of pulp. Place in a saucepan with a little cooking water. Cook over a moderate heat for 10 minutes. Run through a food mill and collect the juicy pulp. Mix in the thinly sliced orange pieces. Add the sugar and cover with the Sauterne. Allow the mixture to stand for 45 minutes, then pour into hot, sterile jars, seal, and label. Goes well with wild meats of any kind.

SPICY PRICKLY PEAR SAUCE

2 cups pulp	1 cup sugar
1 small minced onion	pinch salt
¼ cup cider vinegar	pinch dry mustard
pinch allspice	

Cook the juicy pulp for 5 minutes over a moderate heat. Remove from the heat and run through a food mill or sieve.

Add the sugar, salt, dry mustard, and allspice. Bring the mixture to a boil and simmer for 1 hour. Pour into hot, sterile jars, seal, and label. Serve as a hot or cold garnish with any meat dish.

WILD RAISIN
Viburnum spp.

THE WILD RAISIN (*VIBURNUM cassinoides*) is one of the many species of the viburnum shrubs that produces edible berries. Wild raisin, or withe rod, is usually found in wet areas such as swamps, thickets, and woodland edges. A small shrub, it can attain heights of 12 to 15 feet. It occurs from Newfoundland south to Maryland, then further south to Alabama along the Appalachian uplands and west to the Ohio Valley.

The leaves are simple, ovate, and blunt-tipped. They have small-toothed edges and fuzzy undersides. The white flowers grow in large clusters that may be up to 10 inches wide. The flower clusters yield heavy, drooping clusters of berries that change color from white to pink to blue-black. The berry clusters may be so full that they droop as much as 3 feet. The berries are a drupe of one seed covered with a sweet pulp.

You may find, in your foraging, berries in all stages of ripening: pink through dried. The dried fruit resembles raisins, hence the name. The berries are sweet and tasty and can be eaten raw or cooked into jellies, sauces, or pies.

WILD RAISIN JELLY

2 qts. ripe fruit	½ cup lemon juice
6 cups sugar	6 oz. pectin

Wash and stem 3 pounds of ripe fruit. Do not use any dried fruit. Place in a saucepan and crush. Place the juicy mess over a moderate heat and cook for 15 minutes. Strain the sauce through a jelly bag and recover 3 cups of juice. Place into a saucepan. Add the lemon juice and mix thoroughly.

Add the sugar and boil until sugar is completely dissolved. Add the liquid pectin and bring to a boil for 1 full minute. Skim the foam, pour into hot, sterile jars, seal, and label. Excellent garnish for toast and pancakes.

WILD RAISIN–APPLE JELLY

2 qts. ripe berries	4 med. cooking apples
2 qts. water	1 cup sugar per cup juice
1 tbsp. lemon juice	pinch ground cinnamon

Crush 2 quarts of ripe wild raisins, cleaned and stemmed. Place the fruit in a saucepan.

Wash, stem, and remove the flower remnants of 4 medium cooking apples. Cut the apples into quarters, add to the berries, and mash. Add 2 quarts of water and cook at a simmer for 20 minutes. Stir occasionally to prevent burning.

Strain the mixture through a jelly bag. Measure the juice, place in a saucepan, and add 1 cup of sugar per cup of juice. Stir in the lemon juice and bring the mixture to a boil for 1 full minute. Lower the heat and cook until the sauce passes the "sheet test." Then pour into hot, sterile jars, seal, and label. Try this on hot English muffins.

WILD RAISIN LEATHER

2 cups wild raisin puree	2 tsp. lemon juice
½ cup corn syrup	pinch allspice

Gather enough ripe wild raisin berries to produce 2 cups of fruit puree. Add in the lemon juice, sugar, allspice and toss into a blender and mix thoroughly.

Using a plastic wrap, cover a cookie sheet and spread the puree evenly across the sheet. Place in a 140-degree oven and dry for at least 6 to 8 hours. Do several leathers at the same time to save energy.

When dry, roll and place in a locking plastic bag and store in a dry, dark place. When ready to use, garnish with a jam or jelly or crushed nut meats.

DRIED WILD RAISIN

Collect only fully ripened fruit, include the already dried fruit if you wish. Wash and stem the fruit, then spread across a cookie sheet or tray. Dry in direct sunlight until fruit resembles a raisin. Drying time may take 2 to 3 days. Remember there is a large seed still in the fruit. When dry, place the fruit in locking plastic bags and store in a dark, dry place. Use warm water when ready to rehydrate the fruit.

SWEET AND SOUR WILD RAISIN SAUCE

1 cup wild raisin puree	1½ tsp. lemon juice
½ cup water	1 tsp. butter
2 tbsp. sugar	1 tsp. soy sauce
¾ tsp. corn starch	¼ tsp. salt
pinch dry mustard	

Combine the puree, corn starch, sugar, and salt and pour in ½ cup boiling water. Cook over a moderate heat until sauce thickens, stirring constantly.

Add in the remaining ingredients and cook for 23 minutes longer. When ready, pour into hot, sterile jars, seal, and label.

Makes an excellent cooking sauce for stir-fry. Makes one pint of sauce.

WILD RAISIN AMARETTO SAUCE

2 cups wild raisin puree	1 tbsp. lemon juice
½ cup sugar	¼ cup favorite Amaretto
pinch of nutmeg	

Combine the fruit puree and sugar in a saucepan. Cook over low heat for 10 minutes. Cool slightly, add in the lemon juice, favorite Amaretto, nutmeg, and blend. Reheat to a boil and pour into hot, sterile jar(s), seal, and label. Makes an excellent sauce for coating cakes and other tasty desserts. Store for at least 2 to 3 months to enhance flavor.

RASPBERRY
Rubus spp.

THE FRUIT OF TWO WELL-KNOWN species of raspberries, red raspberry *(Rubus strigosus)* and the familiar black raspberry *(R. occidentalis)*, can be found between July and September. Considered native shrubs from the Carolinas northward to Newfoundland, they can be found growing upwards to elevations of 2,000 feet.

The red raspberry is common to sandy soils and burnt-over lands. The canes usually grow to upwards to 4 to 6 feet and in somewhat thick stands. The plants bear leaves that are compound, with 3 to 5 leaflets, toothed edges, and light-green surfaces. The canes only bear fruit in the second year of growth.

The black raspberry, also known as black cap, has a much wider range of growth and usually bears more fruit. About ½ cup of freshly picked wild raspberries will yield 3.5 calories and 80 IU of vitamin A, with 16 mg of vitamin C. It is therefore desirable to use the fruit for preserves as soon as possible, in order to preserve the flavor and nutrition.

RED RASPBERRY JELLY

3 qts. ripe berries
7½ cups sugar
6 oz. liquid pectin

Red raspberry jelly is rare since it requires many berries in order to produce a small batch. Collect 3 quarts of fully ripened raspberries. Crush the berries in a saucepan, extract the juice with a jelly bag.

Measure 4 cups of the colorful red juice. Add the sugar and mix well. Bring the mixture to a boil, add the liquid pectin. Bring to a boil for 1 full minute, stirring constantly. Remove from the heat, skim off any foam, pour into hot, sterile jelly jars, seal, and label.

Black raspberries, when used in place of red raspberries, yield a spectacular color.

RASPBERRY–CRAB APPLE JELLY

2 qts. ripe berries
⅛ cup water
pinch nutmeg

1 cup sliced semiripe crab apples
¾ cup sugar per cup juice

Wash and stem 2 quarts of either red or black raspberries. Place in a saucepan with the water and cook over a moderate heat until soft.

In a separate saucepan, place 1 cup of sliced semiripened crab apples. Include the cores and peels. Cook until soft and juicy.

Combine the fruits and strain through a jelly bag. Measure the clear juice, place into a saucepan, and add ¾ cup sugar for each cup of juice. Bring to a boil and cook for 5 minutes. Remove from the heat, skim the foam, pour into hot, sterile jars, seal, and label. Great garnish on waffles or muffins.

RASPBERRY-CURRANT JELLY

1 qt. ripe currants

1 qt. ripe raspberries

¾ cup sugar per cup juice

3 oz. liquid pectin

Add 1 quart of stemmed and washed currants to a saucepan. Red currants are preferred. Crush the bottom layer of berries. This provides a little cooking juice. Add 1 quart of red or black raspberries. Red is preferred because the red color matches the red currants. Cook over a low heat for 5 minutes or until the fruit softens and the skins are colorless. Once enough juice appears, pour the batch through a jelly bag.

To each cup of measured juice add ¾ cup of granulated sugar, bring to a boil. Add 3 ounces of liquid pectin and bring to a boil. Hold at a boil for 1 full minute, stirring constantly. Remove the foam, ladle into hot, sterile jelly jars, seal, and label. Excellent garnish for fruit leathers and pastries.

RASPBERRY JAM

2 qts. ripe berries

6 oz. liquid pectin

½ cup sugar per cup crushed fruit

Wash, crush, and measure the fruit. Add sugar, depending on your taste for raspberries. Add an average of ½ to ¾ cup of sugar to each cup of crushed fruit.

Place the mixture over a moderate heat and cook for 2 minutes, then bring to a boil. Add in the liquid pectin and boil for 1 full minute, stirring constantly. Skim the colorful foam, pour into hot, sterile jars, seal, and label. There will be seeds in your jam, but it is excellent on toast, biscuits, and pancakes.

RASPBERRY-STRAWBERRY JAM

1 qt. ripe raspberries	6 cups sugar
1 qt. ripe strawberries	6 oz. liquid pectin

Select 1 quart each of fully ripened red raspberries and strawberries. Wash and stem. Mash the berries in a saucepan, using a potato masher. You should recover about 6 cups of mashed berries. Add 6 cups of sugar, mix thoroughly, and bring the mixture to a boil.

Add in the liquid pectin and bring to a boil for 1 full minute.

Remove from the heat, skim the foam, pour into hot, sterile jars, seal, and label.

If wild strawberries are not available, certainly use commercially grown berries; but, alas the flavor is not the same! Use as a garnish for any fruit leather or pancakes.

RASPBERRY COOKING SAUCE

1 cup ripe berries	pinch sage
1/2 cup minced onions	1 tbsp. brown sugar
3 tbsp. white wine vinegar	1/4 cup heavy cream
pinch salt	

Place clean berries into a saucepan, cook over a moderate heat until fruit pops and the juices flow freely. Run through a food mill, removing the seeds and skins.

In a saucepan combine all of the above ingredients, except the heavy cream, and boil for 2 minutes. Pour into hot, sterile jars, seal, and label.

When ready to use, blend in 1/4 cup of heavy cream and bring to a boil. Cover skillet-cooked chicken or fish with the thick sauce.

RASPBERRY PRESERVES

ripe berries
sugar

Collect as many ripe berries as needed. Wash and place the ripe fruit into hot, sterile jars and fill with sugar to the top. Cover but do not seal tightly. Place in a refrigerator and allow 2 to 3 days. Replace any sugar that settles. When ready, seal tightly and store in a dark, dry place. Allow several months to produce an abundance of thick syrup. Serve whole on waffles or pancakes.

RASPBERRY FRUIT SALSA

2 cups ripe berries
1 small apple, diced

1 tbsp. honey or corn syrup
1 tbsp. lime juice

Combine the ingredients in a bowl and mix well. Refrigerate until ready to use.

RASPBERRY-BRANDY SAUCE

2 cups ripe berries
2 tbsp. brandy

1 cup sugar
pinch allspice

Place the washed fruit in a saucepan. Add in your favorite brandy and sugar. Mash the mixture and bring to a quick boil. Pour into hot, sterile jar(s), seal, and label. Goes well with wild fowl dishes. Either cook with it or use as a garnish when the dish is served.

RASPBERRY DRESSING

2 cups raspberry juice
2 tbsp. whole raspberries
1 tsp. lemon juice
pinch nutmeg

½ cup corn syrup
½ cup red wine
2 tbsp. soybean oil

Gather enough ripe raspberries to produce two full cups of fruit juice. Cook the berries in a saucepan until the juice runs free. Drain through a sieve to remove some of the pulp and seeds. Place the fruit juice in a saucepan and add in the remaining ingredients, as well as the whole ripe fruit. Mix well. Gently mash the few whole berries. Bring the mess to a quick boil and stir constantly.

Pour the mixture into hot, sterile jar(s), seal, and label. Should be stored in the refrigerator until ready to use. Goes well as a cooking sauce for wild fowl dishes.

RASPBERRY CONSERVE

2 qts. ripe berries
¾ tsp. ground cinnamon
3 tbsp. lemon juice

2 juice oranges
3 cups sugar

Slice 2 oranges into very thin sections, removing the seeds. Cook the sections in a little water until tender.

Clean the raspberries and crush the fruit in a saucepan. Do not use a blender as it will pulverize the seeds. Strain the pulpy mess through a strainer or a food mill, removing the seeds. Add the juicy pulp to the cooked oranges and mix well.

Add ¾ teaspoon of ground cinnamon, 3 tablespoons of lemon juice, and 3 cups sugar. Mix thoroughly and simmer over a low heat until sauce thickens. Allow to cool a few minutes then spoon the conserve into hot, sterile jars, seal, and label.

RASPBERRY JUICE

Add 2 quarts of ripe raspberries to a saucepan and cook for 5 to 6 minutes, then crush the fruit completely. Add 1 cup of water and simmer for 5 minutes. Remove the juicy pulp, run through a few layers of cheesecloth. Collect the juice, add in the lemon juice, and mix. Serve chilled; it can also be frozen.

RED HUCKLEBERRY
Vaccinium parvifolium

A SHRUB THAT RANGES IN HEIGHT TO 10 feet. The leaves are somewhat rounded and light green in color. Usually found growing under other trees.

The flowers are urn-shaped and may range in color from white to yellow to pink. Small berries, which are bright red in color, ripen in August. The bush is generally laden with many berries. The fruit is somewhat sour to the taste when eaten raw but greatly improves when cooked into jellies and jams.

Generally considered a western United States plant, ranges in growth from coastal areas of Alaska south to Washington, Oregon, and northern California. You may even find people who purchase these colorful shrubs and grow them as ornamental shrubs.

RED HUCKLEBERRY JELLY

9 cups ripe berries	3 oz. liquid pectin
½ cup water	¾ cup sugar per cup juice

Wash and stem 9 cups of ripe and partially ripened fruit. Place in a saucepan and crush. Add the water and cook over a medium heat for 3 to 4 minutes, then simmer for 5 minutes. Remove and drain the juicy pulp through a jelly bag and recover the juice.

Add ¾ cup of sugar to each cup of recovered juice, and mix well in a saucepan. Bring the mixture to a boil, add in the pectin, and hold at a boil for 1 full minute, stirring constantly. Drain off the colorful red foam, pour into hot, sterile jar(s), seal, and label. Enhances the flavor of toasts and waffles.

RED HUCKLEBERRY JAM

9 cups ripe berries	**½ cup water**
¾ cup sugar per cup sauce	**3 oz. liquid pectin**

Wash and stem 9 cups fully ripened berries. Crush in a deep saucepan, add the water, and cook over moderate heat for 5 minutes. Measure the sauce and add ¾ cup of sugar to each cup of juicy pulp. Mix well and bring to a boil. Add in the liquid pectin and bring to a boil for 1 full minute. Skim the colorful foam, pour into hot, sterile jars, seal, and label.

RED HUCKLEBERRY–MAPLE SYRUP SAUCE

4 cups ripe berries
¾ cup maple syrup

Wash and stem 4 cups ripe berries. Crush the berries in a saucepan and cook over a moderate heat for 5 minutes. Remove from the heat, add ¾ cup of maple syrup, and mix thoroughly. If you do not have maple syrup, then use corn syrup. Place over a moderate heat until thoroughly mixed. Remove from the heat and serve while hot. Terrific when used as a topping for ice cream. The same effect can be achieved if you use blueberry jam in place of the fresh berries.

RED HUCKLEBERRY PRESERVES

ripe berries
sugar

Wash and stem the ripe berries and place in hot, sterile jars. Add in enough sugar to completely cover the ripe fruit. Place in a refrigerator for a few hours and allow the sugar to settle. Fill in the spaces created by settling. Seal and label. Place in a dry, dark place as storage. The berries will be whole and tasty. Can be used to make tarts and pies. Serve as a garnish for pancakes.

SPICY RED HUCKLEBERRY SAUCE

1 qt. ripe berries	1 grated orange rind
2 cups sugar	pinch ground cloves

Combine the grated rind of a fresh orange, water, and sugar in a saucepan, mix, and cook over a moderate heat for 10 minutes. Add the ripe berries and cook until the fruit pops. Now add the pinch of ground cloves and cook for 5 minutes. Stir frequently.

Spoon the mixture into hot, sterile jars, seal, and label. Serve chilled. This is a delightful red-colored, spicy sauce and is best served as a flavoring with meat.

RED HUCKLEBERRY CONSERVE

4 cups ripe berries	1½ cups water
¼ lb. seedless raisins	½ cup chopped nut meats
1 chopped orange	8 cups sugar

Clean 4 cups of fully ripened berries. Add to a saucepan with 1½ cups water. Cook until the berries pop. Stir occasionally. Add ¼ pound of chopped seedless raisins, ½ cup of chopped nut meats (walnuts are best), 1 finely chopped orange, and 8 cups of sugar. Mix well and stir constantly. Cook the mixture for 20 to 30 minutes. Skim the foam, spoon into hot, sterile jars, seal, and label.

DRIED RED HUCKLEBERRIES

Harvest as many ripe huckleberries as you need, wash thoroughly, and stem. Place the whole fruit on a tray or cookie sheet and place in bright sunlight. Allow to dry for 2 to 3 days. The dried fruit should be crisp and shriveled. The whole fruit can be rehydrated using warm water, but will not resume its original, plump shape.

Ripe berries diced into small sections and placed on trays or cookie sheets will dry in a single day. Can also be rehydrated using warm water.

The dried whole fruit can be added to trail gorp for delicious snacks.

WILD ROSE
Rosa spp.

CONSIDERED BOTANICALLY TO be a shrub. There are many different species of wild rose, all of which produce beautiful and aromatic flowers. The flowers yield fruits (the "hips") that vary in color from orange to red, when ripe, and resemble small apples. The fruits also vary in size from ¼ inch to 3 inches in diameter. They may be eaten raw or used for sauces, jellies, and jams. The inside section of the hip is pulpy and filled with fibers that are quite bitter.

Roses are commonly found in open rocky places. They range from the Arctic, Newfoundland, and Alaska south throughout most of the United States. The leaves are generally compound with 3 or more leaflets, saw-toothed edges, and a somewhat oblong shape. The stems generally have spines of some type, either all along the cane or scattered.

Smooth rose (*Rosa blanda*) blooms early in June and is common from New Brunswick south to New Jersey. Wrinkled rose or beach rose (*R. rugosa*) yields a plum-size fruit, usually during August and September. Rose hips should be prepared as soon after picking as possible to ensure maximum flavor.

ROSE HIP JELLY

3 lbs. ripe rose hips	2 cups water
6 cups sugar	6 oz. liquid pectin

If the rose hips have small spines on them, remove before cooking by rubbing them off. Wash the hips, remove the "tails," and place into a saucepan. Add the water, bring to a boil, and cook over a moderate heat for 15 minutes. You may speed up the process by crushing the hips. Pour the sauce through a jelly bag and recover 5 cups of juice.

Add the juice to a saucepan, add 6 cups sugar, mix thoroughly, and bring to a boil. Add the liquid pectin, bring to a boil for 1 full minute, and remove from the heat. Skim the foam, pour into hot, sterile jars, seal, and label. The color of the jelly will be a delicate pink.

ROSE PETAL–CRAB APPLE JELLY

1-pint jar rose petals	1 qt. ripe crab apples
1½ cups sugar per cup juice	6 oz. liquid pectin

Fill a pint jar completely with fresh picked wild rose petals. Cover the blossoms with boiling water and cover. Keep out of bright sunshine. Allow to sit for 24 hours. This will leach the color and flavor oils from the petals. The next day strain the infusion, removing the petals.

Wash and remove the stems and flower remnants from the ripened crab apples. Cook in a little water until soft. Mash the apples, freeing the juice. Simmer for 15 minutes. Strain through a jelly bag, but do not squeeze.

Combine the rose petal juice, crab apple juice, sugar, mix thoroughly, and bring to a boil until the sugar has dissolved. Add in the liquid pectin, hold at a boil for 1 full minute, then remove from the heat. Skim the surface, pour into hot, sterile jars, seal, and label. The color will be a dark pink.

Rose petal jelly is easily made—leave out the crab apples and substitute 1 teaspoon of lemon juice. Adjust the liquid pectin and you can produce a delicately flavored and colored jelly.

ROSE HIP RELISH

4 cups ripe hips	6 cups sugar
¼ cup water	6 whole cloves
¼ cup cider vinegar	1 tsp. ground cinnamon
2 oz. liquid pectin	pinch allspice

Wash and clean the hips, removing any debris, including the flower ends. Crush the fruit in a saucepan. Add the spices, water, and cider vinegar. Bring the mixture to a boil, stirring constantly. Place over a low heat and simmer for 10 minutes. Keep the pan covered.

Recover 4 cups of the hot sauce, place in a saucepan, add the sugar, and mix well. Bring to a boil, then add the pectin, stirring constantly, for 1 full minute. Allow to sit and cool for 3 to 5 minutes. This will prevent the fruit pulp from floating to the top. Skim the colorful foam, pour into hot, sterile jars, seal, and label. Serve as a garnish to pork dishes.

ROSE PETAL-CRANBERRY JELLY

1 pint rose petals	1 cup water
2 cups cranberries	4 cups sugar

Fill a pint jar with freshly picked and washed wild rose petals. Cover the blossoms with boiling water and keep covered. Keep out of bright sunlight. Allow the infusion to sit overnight for 24 hours. Next day strain the infusion, removing the petals.

Place wild bog cranberries in 1 cup of water and boil for 20 minutes, until the juice runs freely. Strain through a jelly bag. Combine the rose infusion and cranberry juice, bring to a boil until the sugar completely dissolves. Skim the foam, pour into hot, sterile jars, seal, and label. Adjust the sugar to suit your taste.

DRIED ROSE HIPS

Collect as many ripe rose hips as you think you will need. The more the better during those cold, winter months. Wash and remove the flower remnants. Place as is on a cookie sheet(s) and dry in direct sunlight until hips are crisp or brittle.

When dry, place in locking plastic bags and store in a dry, dark place. Can easily be rehydrated for use using warm water. Does not work well in gorp.

Finely chopped rose hips can be dried very quickly in direct sunlight. Place the dried hips in locking plastic bags and store in a dry, dark area. Keep out of direct sunlight as the light will bleach the color from the diced hips.

SALAL
Gaultheria shallon

A SMALL SHRUB, 2 TO 3 FEET IN height, salal has evergreen leaves, rounded or heart-shaped, and dark green in color. The small, stubby branches are usually covered with a fine fuzz.

The flowers appear in slender clusters, upwards of 6 inches long, at the tip of the branches. They are white with triangular lobes and yield a small berry that is black in color when fully ripened, hairy, and hard. These small berries are not very palatable when eaten raw, but cooking certainly improves the flavor. They are available in the fall of the year.

Native to western North America, salal ranges from Alaska south to southern California. It grows in dry soils but does best where the air is quite humid. It is widely used as an ornamental evergreen shrub throughout much of the United States.

SALAL JELLY

1 qt. ripe berries	½ cup water
1 cup sugar per cup juice	3 oz. liquid pectin

Wash and stem the ripe berries, place in a saucepan, add in the water, and bring to a boil. Simmer for 10 minutes or until the juice flows from the berries. Remove and strain through a jelly bag or cheese-cloth.

Recover the juice. Measure, place in a saucepan, and add 1 cup of sugar per cup of juice. Mix thoroughly and bring to a boil. Add in the liquid pectin and boil for 1 full minute. Skim the foam, pour into hot, sterile jars, seal, and label. Excellent garnish for fruit leathers.

SPICED SALAL JELLY

6 cups ripe berries	½ cup water
1 cup cider vinegar	6 cups sugar
6 oz. liquid pectin	1 tbsp. ground cinnamon
1 tsp. allspice	6 whole cloves

Wash and stem the fruit, place in a saucepan with water, cider vine-gar, spices, and sugar. Mix thoroughly, then place over a low heat and cook for 20 minutes, stirring constantly to prevent bottom burn. Remove from the heat and run through a jelly bag.

Bring the spicy juice to a boil, add the liquid pectin, and hold at a boil for 1 full minute. Skim the foam, pour into hot, sterile jars, seal, and label. Enhances toast and biscuits.

SALAL TEA

2 cups fresh leaves
2 qts. water
sugar to taste

Collect fresh leaves, wash, then dry. When dry, crush. The oil content within the leaves will remain. This provides the aroma and flavor. Add the leaves to the water, bring to a boil, then allow to steep for 10 minutes. Strain the tea and sweeten with sugar or honey. Excellent brew. Dried leaves from the summer can also be used.

SALAL LEATHER

2 cups salal puree
2 tsp. lemon juice
$\frac{1}{2}$ cup sugar or corn syrup

Wash and stem enough ripe berries to produce 2 cups puree. Add in the lemon juice and sugar and mix thoroughly. Using a plastic wrap, cover a cookie sheet and spread the puree evenly across the surface. Place in a 145-degree oven and dry. When dry, after about 4 to 5 hours, roll and store in a locking plastic bag. Store in a dark, dry place. When ready to use, garnish with nuts or your favorite jam or jelly.

SALAL AMARETTO SAUCE

2 cups ripe berries   1 tbsp. lemon juice
$\frac{1}{2}$ cup sugar or honey $\frac{1}{4}$ cup Amaretto

Combine the berries and the sugar in a saucepan. Cook on a low heat for 10 minutes. Cool slightly and place in a blender with the lemon juice and Amaretto. Puree.

Pour into hot, sterile jars, seal, and label. An excellent garnish to pour over cakes, cupcakes, and other desserts.

SALAL RUM SAUCE

$\frac{1}{2}$ cup fruit juice $\frac{1}{2}$ cup rum
$\frac{1}{2}$ cup sugar $\frac{1}{4}$ cup water
$\frac{1}{3}$ cup orange juice   1 drop vanilla extract

Bring to a boil enough ripened berries to yield $\frac{1}{2}$ cup of juice. Strain through some cheesecloth, add water, and bring to a boil for 1 full minute. Cool for a few minutes and add in the orange juice, favorite rum, and 1 drop of vanilla extract. Bring to a quick boil, pour into a hot, sterile jar, seal, and label.

Use as a delightful garnish for fruit dishes and cakes.

DRIED SALAL

The leaves and berries can be dried and used at a later time. Collect as many berries and leaves as you wish. Wash the berries and leaves, removing the grime and insects.

Place the washed berries on a cookie sheet and dry in bright sunshine. This may take 3 to 4 days. When dry, place the fruit in locking, plastic bags and store in a dark, dry place. Rehydrate with warm water when ready to use.

Place the washed leaves on a cookie sheet and dry in a warm, dark place. Sunshine will destroy the oils in the leaves.

When crunchy, place in locking plastic bags. Store in a dark, dry place. Makes excellent tea in the winter.

SALMONBERRRY
Rubus spectabilis

THIS MOST COLORFUL MEMBER OF THE raspberry family is a woody shrub that ranges in height up to 8 feet. The long-branched canes are covered with many small prickles. The leaves are generally found as three-toothed leaflets.

Generally grows in large thickets in moist areas, along wooded margins, on hillsides, and especially in burned-over areas. Ranges in growth along the Pacific Coast from Alaska south to California.

Beautiful rose- or purple-colored flowers will yield salmon-yellow or bright red berries in late August. The entire plant resembles a very large raspberry plant. The fruit can be eaten raw or made into colorful and tasty preserves. The leaves of the plant can be used to make a delightful tea.

SALMONBERRY JELLY

> 3 qts. ripe berries
> 7½ cups sugar
> 6 oz. liquid pectin

Wash the fruit completely, place in a saucepan, and crush. Cook the juicy pulp at a simmer for 10 minutes. Pass the cooked juice through a jelly bag or cheesecloth and strain out the pulp and seeds.

Measure out 4 cups of the colorful juice. Add the sugar and mix well. Bring the mixture to a boil, add in the liquid pectin, and hold at a hard boil for 1 full minute, stirring constantly. Skim the colorful foam, pour into hot, sterile jars, seal, and label. Great taste on waffles and pancakes.

SALMONBERRY JAM

2 qts. ripe fruit
$\frac{1}{2}$ cup sugar per cup crushed fruit
6 oz. liquid pectin

Wash, crush, and collect the juicy pulp. Run through a food mill to remove the seeds. Add the sugar, according to your taste, place in a saucepan, and cook for 2 minutes over a moderate heat. Then, boil for 1 full minute. Add in the pectin and bring to a boil. Stir constantly. Skim the foam, pour into hot, sterile jars, seal, and label.

SALMONBERRY FRUIT SALSA

2 cups fresh berries
1 small, diced apple
1 tbsp. honey or corn syrup

1 tbsp. of lemon or lime
juice

Wash the fruit and place in a saucepan. Wash, core, and stem the small apple, then dice into small pieces. Combine with the ripe berries, then add in the honey or corn syrup, lemon juice and mix well. Be careful not to bruise the fruit.

Makes an excellent party salsa.

SALMONBERRY PRESERVES

ripe fruit
sugar as needed

Collect as many berries as needed. Wash thoroughly and fill hot, sterile jars to the top. Next, add in the sugar until all the spaces are filled. When ready, place in a refrigerator and allow the sugar to settle. Refill sugar to the top of the jar. Seal and store in a dark, dry place. Allow several months for the sugar to work its magic. The sugar will preserve the fruit whole. Makes an excellent garnish on pancakes and waffles.

DRIED SALMONBERRY LEAVES

Collect and wash as many leaves as you wish. Place them on a tray or cookie sheet and dry in a warm, dark place. Drying in the bright sun will destroy the volatile oils in the leaves. When crunchy dry, place in locking, plastic bags and store in a dark, dry place. Makes excellent tea in the winter months.

SALMONBERRY–FRUIT HONEY COMPOTE

1 cup salmonberries	¼ cup seedless raisins
¼ cup lemon juice	4 medium apples
¼ cup honey	1 cup seeded prunes
¼ cup minced nuts	1 cup whole cranberries
1 cup blueberries	1 tbsp. lemon rind

Grate the lemon rind, squeeze the juice, and measure. Grate the apples, skin and all, then add to the lemon juice. Place the fruit in a bowl and add in the lemon juice. Mix in the honey and place in a refrigerator and allow to stand for 24 hours. Stir in the minced nuts and serve. If you wish, place the mix into freezer bags and keep in a freezer until ready to use. When ready to serve add a little rum or brandy to the juice.

SALMONBERRY CONSERVE

4 cups ripe fruit	1½ cups water
¼ lb. seedless raisins	1 chopped orange
½ cup minced nut meats	10 cups sugar

Wash 4 cups fully ripened fruit. Place in a saucepan with the water and bring to a boil. Simmer for 10 minutes. Crush the fruit and add in the chopped seedless raisins, chopped orange, with the seeds removed, and 10 cups of sugar.

Mix the sauce thoroughly. Bring to a boil, cook for 20 minutes, and then add the finely chopped nut meats. Simmer the mixture for 10 minutes. Stir constantly. Remove from the heat, skim the foam, pour into hot, sterile jars, seal, and label.

SALMONBERRY FRUIT SALSA

2 cups berries	1 small apple, diced
1 tbsp. honey	1 tbsp. lemon juice
½ cup raisins	

Soak ½ cup seedless raisins until plump. Combine with the remaining ingredients and mix well. Freeze and use at a later time or refrigerate and serve chilled.

SAPPHIREBERRY
Symplocos paniculata

A LARGE, WIDE-SPREADING, DENSE shrub, sapphireberry is used in ornamental plantings where large growth is desired. It has escaped to the roadsides, thickets, and woodland margins of the U.S. Although not too common, it can be found in semirural areas, where parks are located, and along interstates and other highways. It has a growth range from New England south to Florida and west to Iowa.

The plant is well named, for the small berries are sapphire-blue in color. It is usually difficult to obtain enough of these colorful berries, although the shrub bears an abundance, because birds eat them as soon as they ripen. The berries normally remain on the bush for about 1 week.

The flowers are small, grow in fuzzy clusters, and are very aromatic. The leaves are dark green in color, oblong, pointed at the ends, and smooth-edged.

SAPPHIREBERRY JELLY

1 qt. ripe berries	½ cup water
1 cup sugar per cup juice	3 oz. liquid pectin

Stem and wash the fully ripened berries. Place in a saucepan, add the water, and bring to a boil. Simmer for 5 minutes, then mash the fruit. Cook for another 5 minutes, then strain the juicy pulp through a jelly bag.

Recover the blue-green juice, add 1 cup of sugar to each cup of juice. Mix well and bring to a boil. Cook for 3 to 5 minutes, until the sugar dissolves. Add in the liquid pectin and bring to a full boil for 1 minute. Skim the colorful foam, pour into hot, sterile jars, seal, and label.

SAPPHIREBERRY JAM

1 qt. ripe berries	½ cup water
1 cup sugar per cup juice	3 oz. liquid pectin

Stem and wash 1 quart of ripe berries, place in a saucepan, mash, and add the water. Bring to a boil. Simmer the fruit for 5 minutes.

Train the juicy pulp through a food mill, measure the juicy pulp, and add in 1 cup of sugar to each cup of juicy pulp. Add in the liquid pectin and bring to a boil for 1 full minute. Skim the foam, pour into hot, sterile jars, seal, and label. Makes an excellent garnish for fruit leathers.

SPICY SAPPHIREBERRY SAUCE

6 cups ripe berries	½ cup water
1 cup cider vinegar	6 cups sugar
1 tbsp. cinnamon	6 whole cloves
1 tsp. ground allspice	6 oz. liquid pectin

Wash and stem 6 cups ripe berries, place in a saucepan with water, vinegar, ground cinnamon, ground allspice, whole cloves, and sugar. Mix thoroughly, then place over a low heat and cook for 20 minutes, stirring constantly.

Remove from heat and pour through a jelly bag, recovering the juice. Bring the juice to a boil, add the liquid pectin, and hold at a boil for 1 full minute. Remove the foam, pour into hot, sterile jars, seal, and label.

SAPPHIREBERRY RUM SAUCE

1 cup sapphireberry juice	½ cup rum
½ cup sugar	¼ cup water
⅓ cup orange juice	1 drop vanilla extract
pinch ground cloves	

Combine the fruit juice and water in a saucepan and bring to a boil for 1 full minute. Cool for a few minutes, then add in the orange juice, seasonings, and your favorite rum. Mix thoroughly and hold at a boil for 1 full minute. Pour into hot, sterile jars, seal, and label. Excellent garnish for cakes, muffins, and ice cream.

SAPPHIREBERRY PRESERVES

ripe fruit
water
sugar

Harvest as many ripe berries as you need. Wash and stem. Place in a little water and cook over a moderate heat for 3 to 5 minutes. Pour off the water and place the fruit in hot, sterile jars, add in the sugar, cover in the spaces between the fruit completely. Place the jars in the refrigerator and allow to sit until the sugar settles. Then refill the jars to the top. Seal and label. Allow the whole fruit to sit for a few months and the sugar to become liquid.

Serve as a side dish or as a garnish to pancakes or waffles.

SAPPHIREBERRY CONSERVE

4 cups ripe fruit	1 1/2 cups water
1/4 lb. seedless raisins	1 chopped orange
1/2 cup minced nut meats	10 cups sugar
pinch ground cinnamon	pinch salt

Wash and stem the fully ripened fruit. Place in a saucepan, add the water, and bring to a boil, then simmer for 10 minutes. Crush the berries, add in the chopped seedless raisins, chopped orange, with the seeds removed, and the sugar. Mix thoroughly and bring to a boil, cook for 20 minutes. Add in the minced nut meats and simmer for an additional 10 minutes. Stir constantly. Remove from the heat, skim the surface, pour into hot, sterile jars, seal, and label.

DRIED SAPPHIREBERRIES

Collect as many berries as you can, wash, and stem. Place them on a cookie sheet and dry in bright sunshine. This may take 3 to 4 days. Dry in a 140-degree oven to do so in one day. Place the dried fruit in locking plastic bags and store in a dark place.

SEA GRAPE
Cocolobis floridana

THIS VINE IS A HIGH CLIMBER and grows along the lengths of some tall trees, bearing fruit all the way. It has broad, ovate leaves with tapered tips. At times, especially in coastal areas, you may find this vine acting more like a shrub but still bearing an abundance of fruit. The fruits are small, nearly 1 inch in diameter, and grow in loose clusters. They are sweet and can be eaten raw.

Sea grape ranges from coastal Virginia south to Florida and west to Texas. Grows in wet soils along stream edges and in thickets. Several different varieties exist throughout the southeastern United States. The only difference in taste is tied to acid content; some are sweet, while others are very acidic. All are edible and make for excellent wild fare.

SEA GRAPE JELLY

5 lbs. sea grapes	½ cup water
8 cups sugar	2 oz. liquid pectin

Stem and clean the wild sea grapes. Using a ratio of 3 pounds partially ripened sea grapes and 2 pounds fully ripened sea grapes, place in a saucepan and crush. Add ½ cup water and bring to a boil. Cover and simmer for 15 minutes.

Strain the cooked fruit through a food mill, then through a jelly bag. Save the juicy pulp to make sea grape butter. Place the juice in a saucepan, add the sugar, and bring to a boil. Add 2 ounces of liquid pectin and again boil for 1 full minute. Skim off the delightful foam, pour into hot, sterile jars, seal, and label. Serve as a garnish on pancakes and waffles.

SEA GRAPE JAM

3 lbs. ripe grapes	½ cup water
1 cup sugar per cup pulp	3 oz. liquid pectin

Stem and wash partially and fully ripened sea grapes. Crush a few at a time in a saucepan. Add the water and bring the mix to a boil. Simmer the sauce for 10 minutes.

Strain the mixture through a food mill, measure the juicy pulp, and add 1 cup of sugar to each cup of juicy pulp. Boil for 1 minute, then add the liquid pectin, and boil for 1 full minute. Skim the colorful foam, pour into hot, sterile jars, seal, and label. Serve on hot toast and biscuits.

SEA GRAPE CONSERVE

3 qts. sea grapes	1 cup water
4 cups sugar	1 cup orange pulp
2 cups chopped seedless raisins	pinch allspice
½ tsp. ground cinnamon	pinch ground cloves

Stem and wash the fully ripened fruit, peel the skins, and place them in a saucepan, with a cup of water. Cook over a moderate heat for 15 minutes. Remove the mixture and press through a food mill or sieve.

Combine the two juices, sugar, orange pulp, seedless raisins, seasonings, and cook over a medium heat for 40 minutes, stirring frequently. Skim the foam and pour into hot, sterile jars, seal, and label. Allow at least 1 month to age before serving. Makes an excellent side dish or garnish for meat dishes.

DRIED SEA GRAPES

Gather as many sea grapes as you need, wash, and stem. Discard any imperfect fruit. Place on trays or cookie sheets and lay out in direct sunlight. Allow the grapes to remain in the sunlight until they shrivel. Yes, they will look just like raisins. When ready, place in locking plastic bags and store in a dark, dry place. Can be used as you would raisins. Just remember there are seeds, unless you take the time to remove the seeds before drying. If deseeded they make an excellent addition to trail mix.

SPICED SEA GRAPE BUTTER

5 lbs. ripe sea grapes	½ tsp. ground cinnamon
1 cup cider vinegar	½ tsp. ground allspice
6 cups sugar	pinch ground cloves

Wash, stem, and crush the ripened fruit in a saucepan. Add a little cooking water and bring to a boil. Allow to simmer until the fruit softens and the juice runs freely. Strain through a food mill, removing the seeds and skins.

Place the pulp in a saucepan, add the sugar, vinegar, and mix thoroughly. Blend in the spices, then spoon the mix into a baking pan. Place in a 250-degree oven and bake for 4 hours. When the juice can no longer be separated from the butter, it is finished. Remove and spoon into hot, sterile jars, seal, and label. Goes well on plain bread or rolls.

SPICED SEA GRAPE PRESERVES

ripe sea grapes	water
sugar	ground cinnamon
ground nutmeg	ground cloves

Gather as many ripe sea grapes as needed, wash, and stem. Cut and remove the seeds, keeping the grapes as whole as possible.

Mix the seasoning with the sugar as to your taste. Place the grapes in hot, sterile jars, fill all the spaces between the grapes with the sugar-spice mix. Cover and place in the refrigerator until all the sugar settles. Cover and allow to sit for 6 months. This will enable the sugar to work. Serve as a side dish.

SERVICEBERRY
Amelanchier spp.

THERE ARE SOME 20 DIFFERENT species of serviceberry located throughout the northern U.S., with *Amelanchier canadensis* and *A. alnifolia* as the two most common. Serviceberries are usually found on a large bush, 20 to 30 feet in height. The leaves are oval-shaped, with finely serrated edges. All serviceberries produce large clusters of sweet berries, red to purple in color and ranging up to ½ inch in size.

Serviceberries tend to resemble blueberries and generally grow in much the same area. They can be used as you would blueberries. The fruit has an excellent flavor when picked fresh but tends to change flavor as it dries. The berries can still be used if you find them dried on the bush, as they often can be found in late fall, but they should be rehydrated before use. One cup of ripe berries will yield about 90 calories.

The various serviceberries range throughout most of North America, from Alaska south to California, Newfoundland south to Georgia. They thrive in a variety of conditions and can be found at altitudes of 4,000 feet or more.

SERVICEBERRY JELLY

9 cups ripe berries	½ cup water
¾ cup sugar per cup juice	3 oz. liquid pectin

Stem and wash the ripe fruit, place in a saucepan, crush, and add the water. Simmer the fruit for about 10 to 15 minutes. Strain the cooked fruit through a jelly bag.

Recover the fruit juice, measure, and place in a saucepan. Add ¾ cup of sugar to each cup of juice. Mix well, place over a high heat, bring to a boil. Add in the liquid pectin and bring to a boil for 1 full minute. Skim the foam, pour into hot, sterile jars, seal, and label. Makes an excellent garnish for toast, biscuits, and waffles.

SERVICEBERRY–BLACK CHERRY JELLY

1 qt. ripe berries	½ cup water
2 lbs. ripe cherries	1 cup sugar per cup juice
6 oz. liquid pectin	

Wash and stem the ripe serviceberries, place in a saucepan, and crush. Wash and stem the wild black cherries, place in a separate saucepan, crush, but do not break the hard rounded stones or pits.

Combine the juicy pulp of the two fruits, add the cold water, place over a high heat, and bring to a boil. Keep covered and allow to simmer for 10 minutes. Remove and press the mixture through a jelly bag. Do not squeeze.

Measure the recovered juice, place in a saucepan, add 1 cup sugar to each cup of juice. Mix thoroughly and cook over a moderate heat until the sugar has dissolved. Bring to a boil, add the liquid pectin, and hold at a boil for 1 full minute. Remove the foam, pour into hot, sterile jars, seal, and label. Goes well with meat dishes and toast.

SERVICEBERRY JAM

10 cups ripe fruit   ½ cup water
¾ cup sugar per cup juice   6 oz. liquid pectin

Wash and stem the ripe berries, place in a saucepan, and crush. Add the water and cook over moderate heat for 5 to 6 minutes. Measure the juicy pulp and add ¾ cup sugar to each cup of pulp.

Place over a low heat and cook for a few minutes or until the sugar dissolves. Bring to a boil, add in the liquid pectin, and hold at a boil for 1 full minute. Skim the foam, pour into hot, sterile jars, seal, and label. Excellent garnish for waffles and pancakes.

SERVICEBERRY PRESERVES

ripe fruit
sugar

Gather as many fully ripened berries as you need, wash, and stem. Scald in a saucepan with a little water for 1 to 2 minutes. Pour the berries into hot, sterile jars and fill to the top with sugar. Place in a refrigerator and wait for the sugar to settle downward through the spaces. Refill to the top, seal, and label. Allow a few months for the sugar to work.

When ready you may use this canned fruit for pies, turnovers, muffins, and sauces.

SERVICEBERRY RELISH

4 cups ripe berries   ¼ cup water
¼ cup cider vinegar   6 cups sugar
1 tsp. ground cinnamon   6 whole cloves
2 oz. liquid pectin

Wash and stem 4 cups ripe berries, place in a saucepan, and crush. Add the spices, water, and vinegar. Bring the mixture to a boil, stirring constantly. Place over a low heat and simmer for 10 minutes. Keep the pan covered.

Recover 4 cups of the hot sauce, place in a saucepan, add the sugar, mix well, and bring to a boil. Add the liquid pectin and bring to a boil for 1 full minute. Skim the foam, and allow to sit for 3 to 5 minutes. This will prevent the fruit pulp from floating to the top. Spoon the mix into hot, sterile jars, seal, and label.

SERVICEBERRY SAUCE

4 cups ripe fruit	1 grated orange rind
2 cups water	2 cups sugar
pinch ground cinnamon	

Place 2 cups cold water, the fresh grated orange rind, and 2 cups sugar in a saucepan. Mix well and cook over a moderate heat for 5 minutes. Add 4 cups washed and stemmed serviceberries. Cook until the fruit pops, about 5 minutes. Place the sauce in a refrigerator and serve chilled. This sauce has a high concentration of natural pectin, and therefore can be preserved in hot, sterile jars.

SERVICEBERRY-BRANDY CONSERVE

2 qts. ripe berries	3 tbsp. lemon juice
2 juice oranges	4 cups sugar
¾ tsp. ground cinnamon	⅓ cup brandy

Slice 2 juice oranges into very thin sections, removing the seeds. Cook the slices in a little water until tender.

Clean and stem the berries, place in a saucepan, and crush. Strain the juicy pulp through a food mill or a strainer. Add the juicy pulp to the cooked oranges and mix well. Add the cinnamon, lemon juice, sugar, and brandy. Mix well and bring to a boil, then simmer until mixture thickens. Remove from the heat, pour into hot, sterile jars, seal, and label. Excellent garnish for deserts, especially custards.

SERVICEBERRY-MAPLE SUGAR SAUCE

4 cups ripe berries
¾ cup maple syrup

Wash and stem 4 cups fully ripened berries, place in a saucepan, and crush. Cook over a moderate heat for 5 minutes. Remove from the heat and add ¾ cup of maple syrup. Mix thoroughly. (You may use corn syrup if maple syrup is not available.)

Remove from the heat and serve while hot. Terrific topping for ice cream. You may also, while the sauce is hot, pour it into hot, sterile jars, seal, and label.

SERVICEBERRY LEATHER

2 cups ripe berries
2 tsp. lemon juice
½ cup sugar, honey, or corn syrup

Wash and stem 2 cups fully ripened berries. Place in a blender and produce a colorful puree. Add in the lemon juice and sugar and mix thoroughly.

Using a plastic wrap, cover a cookie sheet and spread the puree evenly. Dry in a 140-degree oven 6 to 8 hours. When dry, roll and place in a locking plastic bag and store in a dry, dark place. Serve with a garnish when ready. Good nibbling food for young folk.

DRIED SERVICEBERRIES

Gather as many ripe berries as needed. Wash and stem, discarding imperfect fruit. Spread on a cookie sheet or tray and allow to dry in bright sunlight until fruit wrinkles. Will look like small prunes. When dried, place in locking plastic bags and store in a dark, dry place. Rehydrate when ready to use or use as is in gorp.

SPICED SERVICEBERRY CONSERVE

4 cups ripe fruit	1½ cups water
¼ lb. seedless raisins	½ cup chopped nut meats
1 orange	6 cups sugar
pinch of mace, allspice	

Wash and stem the ripe fruit, add to a saucepan with the water. Cook until the berries soften and juice runs freely. Stir to keep the bottom berries from burning.

Add the chopped raisins, chopped nut meats, chopped orange (rind and pulp), spices, and 6 cups sugar. Mix thoroughly and cook for 25 minutes.

Skim the colorful foam, pour into hot, sterile jars, seal, and label.

SNOWBERRY
Symphoricarpos albus

THIS SMALL PLANT TAKES ITS name from the bright white berry that it bears on its slender branches. It has small branches that trail along the ground, and it is usually found growing in thick mats. The woody stems are short, with an abundance of small, ovate leaves ½ to 1 inch in length.

Ranges from Labrador west to British Columbia and south to Pennsylvania. Areas of growth range from conifer forests and mixed woodlands to boggy wetlands.

The white flowers yield, a white, fleshy, juicy, but acidic berry. The berries and leaves are highly aromatic, with a wintergreen flavor. Have patience in collecting this delicate fruit—it is sparse but well worth the effort.

SNOWBERRY JELLY

1 qt. of fruit	2 handsful fresh picked
1 cup water	leaves
3 oz. liquid pectin	1 cup sugar per cup juice

Wash and bruise 2 handsful of fresh picked leaves. Place in a saucepan with the water and bring to a boil Allow to steep 15 to 20 minutes. This will extract much of the wintergreen flavor. Strain the hot tea, discard the leaf residue.

Wash and stem the ripe fruit, eliminate overripe fruit as it lacks flavor. Place the berries and the hot tea in a saucepan. Crush the fruit and bring to a boil. Allow to simmer for 5 minutes. Remove from the heat and pour through a jelly bag. Recover the aromatic juice, measure, and into a saucepan add 1 cup of sugar to each cup of hot juice. Mix thoroughly and bring to a boil.

Add 3 ounces of liquid pectin and hold at a boil for 1 full minute, stirring constantly.

Skim the foam, pour into hot, sterile jars, seal, and label. This jelly will have a delightful wintergreen flavor but the color will be a light brown. If you wish, add a few drops of vegetable coloring to give it a better appearance.

DRIED SNOWBERRY LEAVES

Gather as many leaves as needed, wash, and remove any undesirable or discolored leaves. Place on a tray or cookie sheet. Place in a warm, dark place and allow 2 to 3 days to dry properly. Do not dry in bright sunlight as it will destroy the flavored oils.

When dry, place in locking plastic bags and store in a dark place. Makes an excellent hot tea, especially good for the winter months.

SNOWBERRY-BLACKBERRY LEATHER

2 handsful fresh leaves	2 cups blackberries
1/2 cup corn syrup or honey	1 cup water

Wash and bruise two handsful fresh snowberry leaves. Discard any imperfect leaves. Place in a saucepan with 1 cup water and bring to a boil. Allow to steep for 15 to 20 minutes. Strain the tea, discarding the leaf residue.

Mash the blackberries in a saucepan and strain through a food mill to remove the seeds and skins. Combine the snowberry tea and blackberry sauce in a saucepan and add in the sugar. Mix well.

Cover a cookie sheet or tray with a plastic wrap, then spread the juicy mix evenly across the surface. Place in a 140-degree oven and dry for 6 to 8 hours. When dry, roll and place in a locking plastic bag and store in a dry, dark place. Garnish when ready to serve.

SPICED SNOWBERRY JELLY

2 handsful fresh leaves
1 cup sugar per cup juice
1 cup ripe fruit
pinch ground cloves

1 cup cold water
3 oz. liquid pectin
pinch ground cinnamon

Wash and bruise 2 handsful of fresh leaves. Place into a saucepan with the water and bring to a boil. Allow to steep for 15 to 20 minutes. This will extract much of the wintergreen flavor. Strain the hot tea, discarding the leaf residue.

Wash and stem 1 cup ripe berries, eliminate overripe fruit as it lacks flavor. Place the berries and the cup of hot snowberry tea into a saucepan. Crush the fruit and bring to a boil. Allow to simmer for 5 minutes. Remove from the heat and pour through a jelly bag. Recover the aromatic juice, measure, and add to a saucepan with 1 cup of sugar to each cup of hot juice. Mix thoroughly and bring to a boil. Add in the spices and boil for 1 minute. Add the liquid pectin and hold for a boil for 1 full minute. Skim the foam. If you wish add in a food color as the brown color may not be suitable. Pour into hot, sterile jars, seal, and label.

SNOWBERRY DRESSING

1 cup fruit juice
½ cup soybean oil
½ cup corn syrup

1 cup ripe fruit
½ cup red wine

Combine the above ingredients in a blender and thoroughly mix. Place in a freezer bag and store in the refrigerator until ready to use. Serves as an excellent garnish for meat dishes.

SPEARMINT
Mentha spicata

THIS WELL-KNOWN MEMBER OF THE mint family is known by many local common names. It was brought to North America by European settlers for their herb gardens. It is still used today as a medicinal herb.

This aromatic plant can be found growing in wetlands, along stream edges, and within the margins of wet forests. It ranges from Nova Scotia south to Florida, west to Washington State, and south to California.

Typical of the mints, it has a square, smooth, branched stem. The leaves are opposite one another on the stem and have toothed margins. The light purple flowers are whorled, with two or more spikes of flowers on each plant.

The volatile oils that make up the pungent taste and odor are l-carvone and dihydrocarveol. They are easily destroyed if dried in sunlight.

DRIED SPEARMINT LEAVES

Identify the plants to be harvested the day before picking. Just after the dew has evaporated the next day, harvest what you need. Do not harvest the entire plant, allow it to survive.

Cut the entire stem, wash, and tie in small bundles. Allow to dry upside down in a warm area but away from bright sunlight. This may take the entire week.

Cut the crunchy stems and leaves into pieces and place in a locking plastic bag. Store in a dark, dry place until ready to use. The leaves can be used to make tea or a flavorful jelly.

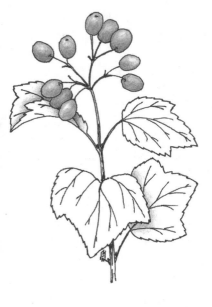

SQUASHBERRY
Viburnum edule

THIS SPRAWLING SHRUB RANGES IN height from 2 to 5 feet. The leaves are opposite one another on the stem and feature uneven lobes and irregularly toothed edges.

Squashberries grow in thickets, in cool, moist soils, and at the edges of woods, open fields, and rivers. They can be found growing from Labrador west to Alaska and south to Oregon and New York.

A large cluster of white flowers blooms from May through early August. The fruit is a round berry ranging in color from yellow to red. The ripened fruit can be found at the end of the stem from August to October, if the birds have not eaten it first.

The fruit can be eaten raw or cooked in jellies, pies, and sauces; it is rich in vitamin C and sweet-tasting.

SQUASHBERRY JELLY

> 4 qts. ripe fruit
> ½ cup sugar per cup juice
> 3 oz. liquid pectin

Wash and stem the ripe fruit, place in a saucepan, and cook over moderate heat until the fruit pops and the juice runs free. Remove and run through a jelly bag.

Measure the juice and add ½ cup sugar to each cup of juice. Bring to a boil and cook until the sugar completely dissolves.

Add the liquid pectin and boil for 1 full minute. Skim the foam, pour into hot jars, seal, and label. Excellent garnish for cakes and muffins.

SPICED SQUASHBERRY JELLY

4 cups ripe fruit	½ cup water
¾ cup cider vinegar	1 tbsp. ground cinnamon
1 tsp. ground allspice	6 whole cloves
5 cups sugar	

Wash and stem the fruit, place in a saucepan with the water, cider vinegar, spices, and sugar. Mix the ingredients thoroughly and place over a low heat and cook for 30 minutes.

Pour the cooked sauce through a jelly bag, recover the sauce, and pour into hot, sterile jars, seal, and label.

SQUASHBERRY JAM

4 qts. ripe fruit	½ cup sugar per cup juice
3 oz. liquid pectin	pinch ground cinnamon

Wash and stem the fully ripened berries, place in a saucepan, and cook over a moderate heat for 10 minutes. Then mash the fruit. Strain the juicy pulp through a food mill or sieve to remove the seeds and skins.

Measure the juicy pulp, add ½ cup sugar to each cup of juicy pulp and bring to a boil. Add the liquid pectin and boil for 1 full minute. Skim the colorful foam, pour into hot, sterile jars, seal, and label. Try this on toast.

SQUASHBERRY SAUCE

4 cups ripe fruit	1 grated orange rind
2 cups water	2 cups sugar

Place 2 cups of water, the grated rind of 1 orange, and 2 cups of sugar into a saucepan, mix thoroughly, and cook over a moderate heat for 5 minutes.

Add the washed and stemmed fully ripened berries to a saucepan and cook until the berries pop. When cooking is complete, place the sauce in a food mill and strain out the seeds. Combine the cooked orange rind mixture and mix well. Place the sauce in a bowl and chill before serving. While still hot, pour into hot, sterile jars, seal, and label. Goes well with meat dishes, especially lamb or pork.

SQUASHBERRY-GINGER SAUCE

2 cups fruit puree	¼ tsp. ground ginger
¼ cup sugar	pinch salt
1 cup boiling water	¼ cup honey

Blend the fruit puree, honey, ground ginger, salt, sugar in a saucepan and slowly add in the boiling water. Stir constantly and bring to a boil and cook for 5 minutes.

Serve chilled. While hot, pour into hot, sterile jar(s), seal, and label. Makes an excellent cooking sauce or garnish for poultry dishes, especially wild fowl.

SQUASHBERRY CONSERVE

4 cups ripe berries	1½ cups water
¼ lb. minced seedless raisins	8 cups sugar
½ cup chopped nut meats	1 chopped orange
pinch of ground cinnamon	pinch ground cloves

Wash and stem the fruit, add to a saucepan with the water, and cook until the berries pop. Stir occasionally. Run through a food mill to remove the seeds and skins.

Add in the minced raisins, nut meats, chopped orange, and sugar. Mix well and stir constantly. Cook the mixture 20 to 30 minutes. Then, skim the foam, pour into hot, sterile jars, seal, and label.

DRIED SQUASHBERRIES

Harvest as many of the ripe berries as needed, wash, and stem. Place the berries on a cookie sheet and dry in bright sunlight. This may take 2 to 3 days. When dry, place the fruit in locking plastic bags and store in a dark, dry pace. Rehydrate when ready to use. Remember that there are large seeds in this fruit. Makes excellent sauce when rehydrated.

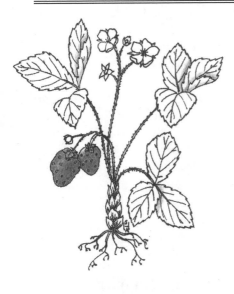

WILD STRAWBERRY
Fragaria spp.

THERE ARE MANY WILD FRUITS that are much easier to gather than the wild strawberry, but none that has its exotic taste and aroma.

There are several species of the wild strawberry; among the more common is the wood strawberry (*Fragaria vesca*) and the bog strawberry (*F. canadensis*). All produce a similarly sized berry: small, unlike the commercial varieties.

The wild strawberry ranges from Florida northward to New Brunswick and Nova Scotia and west to Iowa. The plant is easily recognized by its compound leaves. Composed of 3 broad leaflets, they are quite saw-toothed along the edges. A low ground plant, the strawberry sends out runners, which establish new plants. This type of reproduction produces thick growths of plants. They appear to do best in shaded, sandy, and somewhat moist soils.

The white flowers yield a red, pulpy, and quite juicy fruit. The berries do not keep very well and easily bruise as they are picked. Both the fruit and the leaves contain vitamin C; about ½ cup of fruit yields 44 mg.

WILD STRAWBERRY JELLY (UNCOOKED)

1½ qts. ripe fruit	4 cups sugar
2 tbsp. cold water	3 oz. liquid pectin

Select and wash 1½ quarts of fully ripened fruit. Place in a saucepan and crush with a potato masher or crush in a blender. Place the juicy pulp in a jelly bag and recover the juice.

Measure out 1¾ cups of strawberry juice into a saucepan, add 4 cups of sugar and mix thoroughly. Allow to stand for 10 minutes. Add 2 tablespoons of cold tap water, 3 ounces of pectin and mix well. Stir constantly for 5 minutes.

Pour directly into freezer containers, seal, and allow to sit at room temperature overnight. Freeze or use immediately.

WILD STRAWBERRY JELLY (COOKED)

1 qt. ripe berries	1 cup water
2 cups sugar	3 oz. liquid pectin

Remove stems and blossoms and place in a saucepan. Add in the water and bring to a boil. Cook for 2 to 3 minutes. Strain the cooked sauce through a jelly bag and recover 2 cups of juice.

Combine the 2 cups sugar, liquid pectin, and the juice. Bring to a boil for 1 full minute. Skim the foam, pour into hot, sterile jars, seal, and label.

STRAWBERRY JAM

2 cups ripe fruit	½ tsp. lemon juice
3 cups sugar	3 oz. liquid pectin

Pick, stem, remove blossoms, and wash. Place into a saucepan, add in the lemon juice, and bring to a boil. Add the sugar and cook at a boil for 1 minute. Add in the pectin and cook at a boil for 1 minute. Skim the foam, pour into hot, sterile jars, seal, and label.

STRAWBERRY PRESERVES

2 ½ cups fruit
3 ½ cups sugar
½ tsp. lemon juice

Wash, stem, and remove the flower blossoms, then pack in the bottom of a saucepan, covering each layer with sugar. Bring the mixture to a quick boil. Remove from the heat, set aside to cool at room temperature for 3 to 4 hours. Keep covered.

Place the fruit over high heat, bring to a boil for a full 2 minutes. Stir gently. Remove from the heat and gently spoon into hot, sterile jars, seal, and label. Be certain you cover the fruit with the thick sugar sauce or the fruit will dehydrate in the jars.

SUNSHINE STRAWBERRY PRESERVES

1 qt. ripe berries
sugar

Wash and remove the blossom ends, then place a layer of berries into a saucepan, cover freely with sugar. Cover each layer with an equal amount of sugar. Cover and allow to stand for ½ hour. Bring to a quick boil, then simmer for 10 minutes. Pour the berries into a bake pan of some type and loosely cover with clear plastic sheeting of some type. Place the covered berries out into bright sunlight for 1 to 2 days, until the juice forms and thickens. When ready, spoon the berries into hot, sterile jars, cover with the syrup, seal, and label. Serve as a side dish or as a garnish for pastries and waffles or pancakes.

PICKLED STRAWBERRIES

1 qt. ripe berries	½ cup white vinegar
1 cup sugar	pinch ground cinnamon
pinch ground cloves	

You may use wild or cultivated strawberries. Clean the berries. Use 1 full quart. Place the fruit in a saucepan, cover each layer with a little ground cinnamon and ground cloves.

In a separate saucepan bring the white vinegar and sugar to a boil. Pour the syrup over the berries, cover, and allow to stand overnight.

The next day, drain the syrup and bring to a boil. If wild strawberries are used, combine the hot syrup and the berries and bring to a boil for 10 minutes.

If cultivated berries are used, pour the hot syrup over the fruit, cover, and allow to stand for a second night. Next day, drain the syrup, bring to a boil, then pour over the berries. Boil the fruit for 20 minutes in the syrup.

When ready, spoon the cooked fruit into hot, sterile jars, cover the fruit with the hot syrup, seal, and label.

WILD STRAWBERRY SAUCE

4 cups ripe berries	1 grated orange rind
2 cups water	2 cups sugar

Wash and remove the blossom ends of the fruit, place in a saucepan, and crush. Cook for 5 minutes over moderate heat.

Place the water, grated rind of 1 orange, and 2 cups sugar in a separate saucepan and cook for 5 minutes. Stir to prevent burning.

Combine and cook for another 5 minutes. Mix well. When ready, serve chilled; or, pour into hot, sterile jar(s), seal, and label. Serve with ice cream or as pastry topping.

WILD STRAWBERRY–MAPLE SYRUP SAUCE

4 cups ripe berries
¾ cup maple syrup

Wash and remove the blossoms of the wild berries and place in a saucepan and crush. Cook over a moderate heat for 5 minutes. Remove and add in ¾ cup maple syrup and mix thoroughly. If you do not have maple syrup you may substitute corn syrup. Place over a moderate heat until thoroughly blended.

Serve hot or pour directly into hot, sterile jars, seal, and label. Makes an excellent topping for ice cream and pastries.

DRIED STRAWBERRIES

Collect as many wild strawberries as needed, or as you can find. Wash and remove the blossom ends. Leave the fruit whole, thereby losing none of the juices.

Place the whole fruit on trays or cookie sheets and allow to dry in bright sunlight. This process may take 2 to 3 days. When dry, place the crunchy fruit in locking plastic bags and store in a dark, dry place. Rehydrate with warm water when ready to use. Great when added to a gorp mix.

WILD STRAWBERRY CONSERVE

4 cups ripe fruit
¼ lb. minced seedless raisins
½ cup minced nut meats
pinch ground cinnamon

1½ cups water
1 chopped orange
10 cups sugar

Wash and remove the blossom ends of the fruit. Place in a saucepan, add the water, and bring to a boil. Simmer for 10 minutes. Crush the fruit, add the minced raisins, chopped orange, and sugar. Mix well. Bring to a boil, cook for 20 minutes, and add the minced nut meats.

Simmer for an extra 10 minutes. Stir constantly. Remove and pour into hot, sterile jars, seal, and label.

WILD STRAWBERRY–BLACKBERRY BRANDY SAUCE

2 cups ripe fruit
3 tbsp. blackberry brandy
2 cups sugar

Clean the ripe fruit and place in a saucepan with a little water. Bring to a quick boil. Add in the sugar and your favorite blackberry brandy. Crush the strawberries and stir the mixture thoroughly. Cook for 5 minutes then pour into hot, sterile jars, seal, and label. Serve hot over ice cream or pastries, especially cakes.

WILD STRAWBERRY LEATHER

2 cups ripe fruit puree
½ cup honey or corn
    syrup

2 tsp. lemon juice
pinch ground cinnamon

Wash and clean the ripe berries and crush in a saucepan. Run the mess through a food mill and collect the juicy pulp. Place the pulp in a saucepan, add in the lemon juice and honey, and mix thoroughly.

Using a plastic wrap, cover a cookie sheet and evenly spread the sauce on the sheet. Place in a 140-degree oven for 6 to 8 hours to dry. When dry, roll and place in a locking plastic bag. Store in a dark, dry place. Garnish when ready to serve.

SUMAC
Rhus spp.

COMMONLY KNOWN AS THE LEMON-
ade tree, as the red berry clusters are
used to make a very pleasing but
tart drink. Smooth sumac *(Rhus
glabra)*, fragrant sumac *(R. canadensis)*, and red lemon berry *(R. inte-
grifolia)* are all large shrubs that produce large clusters of red berries
with a tart, lemon flavor.

The staghorn sumac *(R. typhina)* is perhaps the largest of the
genus, attaining heights of 20 to 30 feet The young twigs are covered
with a fine fuzz, whereas in other species the twigs are lacking. The
leaves all have 11 to 29 leaflets, are oblong, and are colored dark
green with pale undersides. Berries appear on the bush in early fall
and remain all year.

The shrub grows in soils that are sandy and dry. Ranges from Georgia north to Nova Scotia. Can be found growing near roadsides, forest
edges, abandoned fields, and thickets.

The noxious sumac species should not be mistaken for the edible
ones. They are: poison sumac *(R. vernix)*, poison ivy *(R. toxicoden-
dion)*, and poison oak *(R. quercifolia)*. All have clusters of green-white
berries.

SUMAC JELLY

4 cups ripe berries
1 cup sugar per cup juice
3 oz. liquid pectin

Wash and remove all debris from the berries. Place into 2 cups boiling water and cook until the berries blanch clear. Drain the liquid through a jelly bag and measure. Place in a saucepan, add the sugar, and bring to a boil. Add in the liquid pectin and boil for 1 full minute. Pour into hot, sterile jars, seal, and label. Delightful with hot toast.

SUMAC TEA

Collect two cups of the dried berries, fresh on the shrub. Wash thoroughly and pat dry with a paper hand towel. Place into a saucepan of boiling water and allow to steep for several minutes. Can be served as a hot tea or as a chilled pink lemonade.

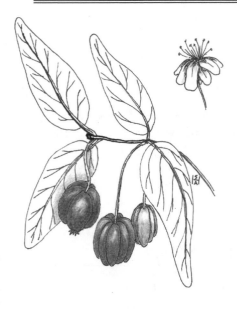

SURINAM CHERRY
Eugenia spp.

A MEMBER OF THE MYRTLE FAMILY, the surinam cherry escaped to the surrounding countryside after being brought to the United States from Brazil. This colorful ornamental grows throughout the semitropical areas of Florida and California. There are several species of the genus, including *Eugenia uniflora*, *E. paniculata australis*, and the smaller *E. smithi*.

The leaves are oblong, pointed, and often double-toothed. They alternate on the stem and appear dark green and leathery. The flowers are abundant, are usually pink or lilac-colored, and yield a fleshy fruit that is ½ to 1 inch in diameter. When the fruit is ripe, it turns a deep red. It is eaten raw or cooked. Be careful of the juices, as they stain clothing.

Surinam cherries are rich in vitamins A and C, as well as iron and calcium. The fruit is harvested year-round in frost-free areas. The main crop ripens in the early spring with a smaller crop of fruit produced in the fall.

SURINAM CHERRY JELLY

> 5 cups cherry juice
> 3 oz. liquid pectin
> 5 cups sugar

Collect enough ripe fruit to produce 5 cups juice. Remove the large seed or pit, place in a saucepan with a little water, and cook until the juice runs free. Collect the juice and run through a jelly bag, Measure out 5 cups and combine the sugar in a saucepan. Bring to a boil. Add in the liquid pectin and boil for 1 full minute. Pour into hot, sterile jars, seal, and label.

SPICED SURINAM CHERRY SAUCE

> 6 cups ripe fruit
> 5 cups sugar
> pinch ground cinnamon
> pinch allspice
>
> 3 oz. liquid pectin
> 1 tsp. lemon juice
> pinch ground cloves
> drop almond extract

Wash and stem the fruit and remove the large seed. Place in a saucepan with a little water and cook until the fruit softens and the juice runs free. Drain the colorful juice through a jelly bag.

Combine the hot juice with the spices, lemon juice, and sugar. Mix thoroughly and bring to a boil. Add in the liquid pectin and hold at a boil for 1 full minute. Blend in the drop of almond extract, pour into hot, sterile jars, seal, and label.

SURINAM CHERRY RUM COOKING SAUCE

> 1 cup ripe fruit
> ¼ cup minced onions
> 3 tbsp. white wine vinegar
> ½ cup rum
>
> pinch of salt
> pinch of sage
> 1 tbsp. brown sugar
> ¼ cup heavy cream

Wash and remove the large stone from the fruit, and place in a saucepan. Cook until the juice runs free. Remove and run the mess through a food mill. Combine the above ingredients (except the cream) and cook at a boil for 2 minutes. Pour into hot jars, seal, and label. Can be used as is in the cooking of poultry or pork dishes.

Can be stored until ready to use. When ready, blend in a ¼ cup heavy cream, bring to a boil, and cover skillet-cooked chicken or other fowl.

SURINAM CHERRY JAM

6 cups pitted cherries	3 oz. liquid pectin
6 cups sugar	5 drops lemon juice

Cook the cherries until the tissue softens and the juice run free. Put the mixture through a food mill. Place in a saucepan and add the sugar and lemon juice. Bring slowly to a boil, stirring frequently. Add the liquid pectin and boil for 1 full minute. Skim the colorful foam, pour into hot, sterile jars, seal, and label.

SURINAM CHERRY SALSA

2 cups diced cherries	1 small apple, diced
1 tbsp. honey	1 tbsp. lemon juice

Combine in a bowl, mix well, and refrigerate. Serve chilled. Can be frozen and kept for several months.

SURINAM CHERRY PRESERVES

pitted cherries
sugar

Wash and pit as many cherries as you need. Place in hot, sterile jars. Cover with sugar and allow to sit in a refrigerator for 5 to 6 hours. Refill the sugar that settled. Seal and label. Can be used as a side dish or as a garnish with poultry dishes. Try as a garnish with pancakes and waffles.

DRIED SURINAM CHERRIES

Wash and pit as many cherries as needed. Place on a tray or cookie sheet to dry. Diced fruit will dry much faster. Place in a warm but shaded area to dry. Will dry much faster if place in a 140-degree oven. If shade-dried, cover with cheesecloth to keep the hungry insects away. When dry and crunchy, place in locking plastic bags, and store in a dark, dry place. Goes great when making up gorp.

SURINAM CHERRY DRESSING

2 cups cherry juice
½ cup red wine
1 tsp. lemon juice
½ cup corn syrup
½ cup soybean oil
½ cup cider vinegar

Combine the above ingredients in a saucepan, mix thoroughly, bring to a quick boil, then pour into container and store in refrigerator until ready for use. Excellent garnish for salads. Can be used as a cooking flavor.

SWEET BAY
Persea borbonia

A MEMBER OF THE LAUREL FAMILY, sweet bay is considered to be both a small tree and a large shrub. It attains heights of 20 to 50 feet and has a growth range from Delaware south to Florida and west to Texas. It is usually found in wet areas such as marshes, stream edges, river embankments, and swamps.

A highly branched shrub, sweet bay has a noticeably reddish bark. The leaves are alternate, evergreen, leathery, and bright green above with pale green undersides. They are oblong with untoothed margins. Small, greenish flowers arise from the axils of the leaves. Blue, single-seeded berries are produced in late summer. They closely resemble the fruit of sassafras.

The entire shrub is aromatic and has been used for centuries as a seasoning. Sweet bay is sold in most stores and is commonly used in stuffings for fowl dishes.

SWEET BAY SEASONING

Wash the small, young fresh leaves and discard any that are discolored. Place in bright sunlight until completely dried. This may take up to 2 to 3 days.

A fruit-drying oven may speed up the process. Do not attempt to dry the leaves in a cooking oven as this only cooks the fragile leaves and destroys the natural oils.

The dried leaves can be used to flavor stews, gravies, relishes, pickled beets, spiced vinegar, marinades, and wild game. Store in sealed jars. Use either crushed, ground, or whole leaves.

SWEET BAY TEA

Place several clean, dried leaves into boiling water and allow to steep for several minutes. Has a pleasant aroma. Taste requires some getting used to.

THORNAPPLE
Crataegus spp.

SCATTERED THROUGHOUT THE EAST-ern portions of Canada and the United States are some 20 or more species of the so-called thornapple. There are hundreds of local names, such as hawthorn, haw apples, rose apple, and so on.

A small tree or large shrub, the thornapple attains heights of 15 to 20 feet. It is easily recognized because of the plentiful crooked thorns on its many branches. The leaves are simple and lobed, and the edges are highly serrated.

The fruit resembles a miniature apple, similar to a crab apple, ranging in size from ½ inch to 1 inch. The color varies from yellow to red and generally matures in September or early October. There are 1 to 5 nutlets as seeds, with a pulpy outer flesh that is quite flavorful when raw but much tastier when cooked. In some species the flesh is bitter and no amount of cooking seems to improve the palatability.

THORNAPPLE JELLY

5 lbs. ripe fruit	8 cups sugar
5 cups water	3 oz. liquid pectin

Select 5 pounds of ripe thornapples. If possible, it is advisable to have ½ pound of the fruit partially ripened to enhance the flavor and increase the amount of pectin.

Cut the fruit into thin pieces, place into a saucepan with the water, bring to a boil, then simmer for 10 minutes. Mash with a hand masher, then allow the pulp to simmer for another 5 minutes.

Remove from the heat and strain through a jelly bag. Gently squeeze out the juice; do not force any of the pulp through the cloth. Save the pulp to make a delicious thornapple butter. Measure the hot juice, recovering 8 cups. Place in a saucepan and combine 8 cups of sugar. Mix thoroughly and cook over a moderate heat for 3 minutes. Bring to a boil, add 3 oz. of liquid pectin, and hold at a boil for 1 full minute. Skim the foam, pour into hot, sterile jars, seal, and label. Great garnish for toast and biscuits.

SPICED THORNAPPLE JELLY

5 lbs. ripe fruit	8 whole cloves
8 cups sugar	1 tsp. ground allspice
5 cups water	2 2-inch cinnamon sticks
3 oz. liquid pectin	1-inch square whole ginger

Select 5 pounds of ripened thornapples. Remove the flower remnants and stems. Cut into thin slices. Place in a saucepan with the water and add the spices in a small cloth bag. Bring the mixture to a boil, then cook at a simmer for 10 minutes. Remove the juicy pulp through a jelly bag.

Place the hot juice in a saucepan, add the sugar, mix thoroughly, and bring to a boil. Hold at a boil for 3 minutes, stirring constantly to prevent bottom burn. Add the liquid pectin, hold at a boil for 1 full minute, skim the foam, pour into hot, sterile jars, seal, and label.

THORNAPPLE MARMALADE

2 qts. ripe fruit	2 medium oranges
1 medium lemon	1 cup water
8 cups sugar	3 oz. liquid pectin

Remove the skins from 2 medium oranges, preferably navel oranges, and 1 medium-size lemon. The skins should be peeled in quarters, removing most of the internal white pulp. Chop the rinds into small pieces. Place the chopped rinds into a saucepan, add 1 cup water, and bring to a boil. Simmer for 20 minutes, stirring occasionally.

Wash, stem, and remove the blossom remnants from 2 quarts of fully ripened thornapples. Place in a saucepan with the fruit rinds.

Add the sugar and bring to a boil. Mix thoroughly. Add the liquid pectin, bring to a boil for 1 full minute. Remove from the heat, skim the surface, pour into hot, sterile jars, seal, and label.

THORNAPPLE PICKLES

3 lbs. ripe fruit	6 cups sugar
¾ cup cider vinegar	1½ cups water
4 tbsp. whole cloves	½ stick cinnamon

Wash thoroughly, but do not remove the stems. Make up a syrup of 6 cups of sugar, cider vinegar, water and bring to a boil. Cook the syrup until thickening occurs. Add the spices, fruit, mix thoroughly, and bring to a boil. Cook until the fruit becomes tender.

Pack the whole fruit into hot, sterile jars, cover with the hot syrup, seal, and label. Do not serve for about a month. This will give the spices a chance to do their work.

SPICED THORNAPPLE BUTTER

5 lbs. ripe fruit	6 cups sugar
1 cup cider vinegar	½ tsp. ground cinnamon
½ tsp. ground allspice	

Wash, stem, and remove the flower ends of the ripe thornapples. Cut the little apples in quarters, place in a saucepan, add a little cooking water, and bring to a boil. Allow to simmer until fruit becomes soft. Crush and strain through a food mill. This will remove the skins and seeds. If you have leftover fruit pulp, use it in place of new pulp.

Place the pulp in a saucepan, add in the sugar, cider vinegar, and mix well. Add the spices, mix, and spoon the spicy pulp into a baking pan. Place in the oven and bake for 4 hours at 250 degrees. Occasionally stir the mixture. When the juice can no longer be separated from the pulp, the butter is finished.

Remove from the oven and spoon into hot, sterile jars, seal, and label, or use immediately.

THORNAPPLE MINT JELLY

2 cups thornapple juice	1½ cups sugar
2 cups boiling water	1 cup spearmint leaves

Use 1 cup fresh or dried tightly packed mint leaves. Peppermint leaves are not suitable. Place the leaves in a saucepan and pour the boiling water over them. Allow to steep for 1 hour. Press the juice from the leaves. Place the mint juice, apple juice, and sugar in a saucepan and bring to a boil. Continue to boil until mixture passes the jelly test.

Add a few drops of green vegetable coloring, pour into hot, sterile jars, seal, and label. Excellent garnish for lamb or pork dishes.

THORNAPPLE LEATHER

2 cups puree
1 tsp. lemon juice
½ cup corn syrup or maple syrup

Wash, stem, remove the flower ends, and cook enough thornapples to yield 2 cups of puree. After the fruit becomes soft, crush and run through a food mill, then place in a blender.

Add in the lemon juice and either corn syrup or maple syrup, if you have some. Mix thoroughly.

Using a plastic wrap, cover a cookie sheet, spread the mix evenly, and place in an oven at 140 degrees until dry. When dry, roll and place in a locking plastic bag and store. Garnish with jam or a topping when serving.

VIOLET
Viola spp.

MANY OF THE VIOLETS FOUND GROW-
ing in the wild are edible; others are
poisonous or fuzzy or bitter to eat. The
wild sweet violet (*Viola blanda*), also
known as white violet, is an outstand-
ing wild edible. A very attractive
flower, the violet can be found growing in a large variety of environments.
It thrives in cool, moist, shaded places
where competition is minimal.

Generally small plants of 6 to 10
inches, violets are highly branched
and slender, producing a great many horizontal runners. The heart-
shaped leaves are on long petioles and range from 3 to 4 inches in
width. They yield a fragrant flower that is quite edible.

The early blue violet, or Johnny-jump-up (*V. palmata*), has long
been called wild okra and is used to thicken soups. The roots and the
stem of the violet are edible and have served as a food source for several hundred years or more. The leaves are dried and used as a source
for an excellent tea. The flowers of all the violets can be used to make
fine jellies.

VIOLET JELLY

1 pint flowers
2 cups sugar per cup juice

juice of ½ lemon
3 oz. liquid pectin

Collect enough violet flowers to tightly fill a pint jar. Place in a saucepan and cover with boiling water and cover. Keep out of bright sunshine and other bright lights. Allow the mixture to sit for 24 hours. This will draw the color and sugar from the blossoms into the solution.

Strain the infusion through a jelly bag, removing the blossoms and other debris. Place the juice in a saucepan, add the lemon juice, and mix well. The lemon juice will greatly alter the color of the violet infusion. Bring the mixture to a boil for 1 minute. Add 2 cups sugar to each cup of the infusion and 3 oz. of liquid pectin. Hold at a hard boil for 1 full minute. Skim the surface, pour into hot, sterile jars, seal, and label.

VIOLET–CRAB APPLE JELLY

1 pint violet flowers
6 to 8 semiripe crab apples

3 oz. liquid pectin
2 cups sugar per cup juice

Fill a pint jar with as many violet flowers as you can. The more the stronger the flavor and color. Place in a saucepan and cover with boiling water, and cover. Allow to stand for 24 hours, drawing out the flavor, color, and sugar.

The next day, core and remove the blossom ends of 6 to 8 semiripe crab apples. Cut into quarters, place in a saucepan, and cook over a moderate heat until soft and the juices run, then crush.

Strain the crab apple sauce through a jelly bag. Combine the apple juice with the violet infusion. Bring the mixture to a boil for 1 full minute. Add 2 cups sugar to each cup of juice. Bring to a hard boil for 1 full minute.

Remove from the heat, skim the surface, pour into hot, sterile jars, seal, and label. Excellent garnish for lamb and pork dishes.

JOHNNY-JUMP-UP JELLY

1 cup flowers
1 cup sugar
peels of 3 to 4 crab apples

Johnny-jump-ups do not grow in great abundance. Collect 1 full cup of flowers, as stuffed as you can. Place the flowers into a heat resistant jar, cover with boiling water, cover, and place in a dark place, away from bright light. Allow to stand for 24 hours.

Next day strain the infusion, removing the debris.

Peel the partially ripened crab apples and cook the peelings in a little water for 10 minutes. Strain, recover the juice. This juice will contain a little pectin. Combine the two juices, bring to a boil for 1 full minute. Add 1 cup sugar, mix well, and boil for 1 full minute. Skim the surface, pour into hot, sterile jars, seal, and label.

VIOLET HERB JELLY

1 pint violet flowers
3 oz. liquid pectin

2 cups sugar per cup juice
1 cup peppermint leaves

Place the violet flowers into a heat resistant jar, cover with boiling water, and allow to stand in the dark for 24 hours. Strain, removing the debris.

Place the cup full of fresh or dried peppermint leaves in a saucepan and cover with boiling water. Allow to steep for 1 hour. Strain the debris.

Combine the two infusions in a saucepan and add the sugar. You may want to add in a green vegetable coloring for the mint. Bring to a boil, add in the liquid pectin, and hold at a boil for 1 full minute. Pour the mix into hot, sterile jar(s), seal, and label.

DRIED VIOLET FLOWERS AND LEAVES

The use of the roots reduces the number of violets growing in the area that you harvest. Leave them and harvest the flowers and leaves.

Wash well, removing as much debris and grime as possible. Place on a cookie sheet or tray and dry in a warm, dark area. Allow to dry for 1 to 2 days.

Store in locking plastic bags and keep in a dark, dry place. The leaves may be stored whole or crushed.

Either the dried flowers or the dried leaves can be used to make a delicious tea or jelly.

WALNUT
Juglans spp.

A TALL TREE REACHING HEIGHTS OF 150 feet or more. Leaves are compound, with 15 to 23 leaflets and downy undersides, and may range up to 28 to 30 inches. Can be found growing in lowland areas with rich soil.

Walnut trees range from southern New Hampshire south to Florida, west to Texas, and as far north as Minnesota. Usually can be found in large stands.

Nut is round, 1 to 2 inches in diameter, and very thick, with husks in four sections. Nut meats are divided into 2 sections.

DRIED WALNUTS

The husks are quite thick and should be removed when drying, as this will hasten the process. It is advisable to wear gloves—the husks contain natural dye that will stain human skin.

Place as many nuts as you need in a warm, dark place and allow to dry. This process may take 3 to 4 weeks.

Remove or break the thin shells, remove the nut meats, and spread on a cookie sheet or tray. Allow to dry in warm, shaded area. This process may take 2 to 3 days. You may speed up the process by drying in a 140-degree oven. Allow 6 to 8 hours.

Once dried, the nut meats can be eaten directly or stored. To store, place in plastic locking bags and keep in a dark, dry place.

Makes an excellent garnish or addition to trail foods such as gorp. They are wonderful during winter holiday seasons.

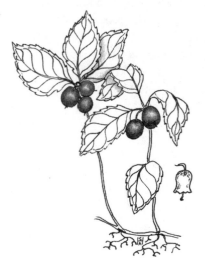

WINTERGREEN
Gaultheria procumbens

THIS LITTLE TREASURE IS KNOWN BY many local names, among them checkerberry, teaberry, and boxberry. It is common to shaded, moist woodlands. A small, shrubby plant, it attains heights of up to 3 to 6 inches and generally grows in thick ground plantings.

The leaves are evergreen, tasty, and aromatic, and they appear in clusters at the top of the stem, which rises from an underground rhizome. Their color is dark green or red with a lighter underside. The leaves contain oil of wintergreen, hence the flavor and aroma.

The white, bell-shaped flower yields a fleshy, berrylike fruit. The fruit can be found on the plant from August throughout the winter and spring months, unless the birds get there first. Wintergreen has a growth range from Georgia north to Newfoundland. The leaves and berries can be dried for later use.

WINTERGREEN JELLY

1 pt. fresh leaves	1 pt. ripe berries
1 qt. water	1 cup sugar per cup juice
3 oz. liquid pectin	green food coloring

Wash and discard any bad leaves, bruise all leaves, and place in a saucepan with 1 pint of water. Bring to a boil and simmer for 15 minutes. This will free the oil of wintergreen.

In a separate saucepan, combine 1 pint of ripe berries and 1 pint of water. Bring to a boil, simmer until berries soften, then crush. Drain the hot, juicy aromatic pulp through a jelly bag.

Strain the leaf infusion, combine with the berry juice and 1 cup of sugar to each cup of juice, in a saucepan. Bring to a boil, add the pectin, and hold at a boil for 1 full minute. Add green food coloring, pour into hot, sterile jars, seal, and label.

VINEGARS
and
OILS

FLAVORED VINEGARS

THE MAKING OF WILD HERBAL VINEGAR IS RELATIVELY EASY AND very rewarding. With a commercial vinegar and a select herb or herbs, you can produce a very satisfying and flavorful dressing.

The process is made easier if you start with a good cider vinegar or white vinegar. A good red or white wine may be used in place of vinegar. Select a plain or decorative jar for storage. Liqueur bottles or former vinegar bottles, when drained, washed, and dried, make excellent glass containers.

Gather enough herbs to fill the container(s). Around 3 to 4 sprigs should do very well indeed. Add in the selected vinegar to cover the herb and seal tightly. Place in a warm, sunny location (such as a window) and allow to sit for 2 to 3 weeks. Shake gently on a daily basis.

After three weeks, taste. If not suitable, add in a few more sprigs of the herb. When the taste is suitable, drain the vinegar, pour it into a decorative bottle, add in a fresh sprig or two of the herb, and seal.

There are many types of commercial vinegar available, including cider vinegar, distilled white vinegar, wine vinegar, red or white wine, balsamic vinegar, rice wine, and malt vinegar. Although vinegar will keep for a while without refrigeration, it will not remain usable after long periods of time.

BARBERRY VINEGAR

½ cup washed barberries
1 qt. cider vinegar
1 tsp. sugar

Place the ripe berries into a saucepan of boiling water for several seconds to destroy the bacteria. Remove and place in a quart glass or desired decorative container. Cover with desired vinegar. A red wine vinegar would enhance the flavor. Seal the bottle with hot sealing wax.

Place in sunlight for a week or so, then use on salads or as a cooking dressing. Label.

BARBERRY VINAIGRETTE

½ cup ripe berries	1 tbsp. olive oil
1½ pts. vinegar (warmed)	½ tsp. sugar
½ tsp. dry mustard	1 tsp. salt
⅛ tsp. black pepper	1 tsp. allspice
1 tsp. whole cloves	

Scald the ripe berries first. Combine all of the above ingredients and mix thoroughly. Pour the mixture into a hot, sterile jar or decorative bottle and seal. If decorative bottle is used, seal by dipping cap and bottle top into hot, sealing wax. Allow to sit for 1 week, then use as needed. Label.

BLACKBERRY VINEGAR

½ cup fruit	pinch allspice
1 qt. red wine vinegar	pinch salt
6 pepper corns	

Scald the ripe blackberries, remove, and place in a quart glass or decorative bottle. Cover with red wine vinegar. Seal with wax or a tight cover. Allow to stand for 1 week before using. Label.

BLACKBERRY VINAIGRETTE

½ cup ripe fruit
1½ pts. red wine vinegar
⅛ tsp. black pepper
1 tbsp. olive oil

½ tsp. sugar
½ tsp. salt
pinch allspice

Scald the berries, then remove and combine all ingredients and mix thoroughly. Pour into desired container and cap. Allow to sit in the light for 1 week before using. Label.

BLACK HAW VINEGAR

½ cup ripe berries
1 qt. cider vinegar (warmed)
8 peppercorns

1 tsp. sugar
pinch salt

Scald the haws for several seconds, then remove from the heat and combine all the remaining ingredients. Mix thoroughly. Pour into a sterile container or desired decorative bottle, then cap. Allow to sit for 1 week to age before using. Label.

BLUEBERRY VINEGAR

½ cup ripe berries
1 qt. cider vinegar
pinch dry mustard

1 tsp. sugar
pinch salt

Scald the ripe berries, remove from the heat, and combine all the above ingredients. Mix well. Pour into a desired glass container, then cap. Allow to sit for 1 week before using. Label.

BLUEBERRY VINAIGRETTE

½ cup ripe berries	½ tsp. salt
1½ cups cider vinegar	½ tsp. sugar
1 tbsp. oil	2 whole cloves

Scald the ripe fruit and combine all the above ingredients. Mix thoroughly. Pour the mixture into selected glass container, cap, and store for 1 week for aging. Label.

CANADA MAYFLOWER VINEGAR

½ cup ripe berries	pinch allspice
1 qt. cider vinegar	pinch salt
3 peppercorns	pinch ground dry mustard

Scald the fruit and combine all the above ingredients. Mix well. Pour the mixture into selected glass bottles, cap, and store for 1 week, allowing to age. Label.

CANADA MAYFLOWER VINAIGRETTE

½ cup ripe berries	pinch black pepper
1½ cups cider vinegar	½ tsp. salt
1 tbsp. oil	½ tsp. dry mustard
½ tsp. sugar	pinch tarragon powder

Scald the ripe berries and combine all of the above ingredients. Mix thoroughly and pour into a selected glass container, and cap. Allow to sit for 1 week before using. Label.

CRANBERRY (BOG) VINEGAR

$\frac{1}{2}$ cup ripe berries
1 qt. cider vinegar
1 tsp. lemon juice

Scald the ripe bog cranberries and combine with the lemon juice and cider. Mix well. Pour into a selected glass container, cap, and allow to sit for 1 week, before using. Label.

CRANBERRY (BOG) VINAIGRETTE

$\frac{1}{2}$ cup ripe berries
1$\frac{1}{2}$ cups cider vinegar
1 tsp. sugar
1 tbsp. oil

$\frac{1}{2}$ tsp. salt
pinch pepper
$\frac{1}{2}$ tsp. dry mustard
pinch paprika

Scald the ripe berries and combine with the remaining ingredients. Mix thoroughly. Pour into a selected glass container, cap, and allow to sit for 1 week to age. Label.

CRANBERRY (HIGHBUSH) VINEGAR

$\frac{1}{2}$ cup ripe berries
1 tsp. sugar
1$\frac{1}{2}$ cups balsamic vinegar (warmed)

Scald the ripe berries and combine with the remaining ingredients. Mix well and pour into a selected glass container and cap.

Allow to sit for 1 week before using. Label.

CRANBERRY (HIGHBUSH) VINAIGRETTE

½ cup ripe berries
1½ cups balsamic vinegar
1 tsp. sugar

½ tsp. salt
pinch pepper
1 tbsp. oil

Scald the ripe berries and mix with the remaining ingredients. Pour the mixture into selected glass containers, cap, and allow to sit for one week to mature. Label.

CURRANT VINEGAR

½ cup ripe currants
1½ cups warm vinegar

6 peppercorns
pinch salt

You may use any of the wild currants, red or black. Scald for a few seconds and combine with the other ingredients. Mix well and pour into selected glass bottles, cap. Allow to mature for 1 week before using. Label.

CURRANT VINAIGRETTE

½ cup ripe berries
1½ cups vinegar
1 tbsp. sugar
pinch dry mustard

pinch pepper
3 dried tarragon leaves or
    pinch tarragon

Use any of the currants, scald, and combine with the remaining ingredients. Mix well. Pour into a selected glass container, cap, and allow to sit for 1 week before using. Label.

FALSE SOLOMON'S SEAL VINEGAR

$1/2$ cup ripe berries
1 tsp. lemon juice
$1 1/2$ cups vinegar

Use only ripe berries, scald for a few seconds, then combine with the lemon juice and vinegar. Mix thoroughly.

Pour into a selected glass container, cap, and allow to sit for 1 week to age. Label.

FALSE SOLOMON'S SEAL VINAIGRETTE

$1/2$ cup ripe berries
$1 1/2$ cups vinegar
1 tsp. grated orange rind
1 tsp. sugar

pinch salt
pinch pepper
pinch dry mustard

Scald the ripe berries and combine with the remaining ingredients. Mix thoroughly. Pour into a selected glass container, cap, and allow to sit for a few days to age. Label.

FENNEL (WILD) VINEGAR

3 sprigs leaves
$1 1/2$ cups white vinegar

pinch salt
pinch pepper

Select either fresh or dried leaves. Carefully place the leaves in a selected glass container. Mix the salt and pepper with the vinegar and gently pour into a glass container with the ripe berries, and cap. Allow to sit and age for 2 to 3 days. Label.

FENNEL (WILD) VINAIGRETTE

3 sprigs leaves   1 tsp. oil
1½ cups white vinegar   pinch dry mustard
pinch salt   pinch pepper

Place the fresh or dried leaves carefully into the selected glass container. Combine the seasoning with the vinegar and pour into the glass container with the ripe berries. Cap and allow to sit for 2 to 3 days to age. Label.

GRAPE (WILD) VINEGAR

½ cup ripe grapes   pinch salt
1½ cups grape or cider vinegar 2 fresh grape leaves

Roll the 2 fresh grape leaves and slide into the glass container. Insert the whole ripe grapes. You will have to select those that will fit into the neck of the bottle. Combine the vinegar and seasonings, then add to the glass container. Cap and allow to sit in bright sunlight for 4 to 5 days to age properly. Label.

GRAPE (WILD) VINAIGRETTE

½ cup ripe grapes   pinch salt
1½ cups rice wine vinegar   1 tbsp. oil
1 tsp. sugar   pinch pepper
2 fresh grape leaves

Insert the fresh picked grape leaves into the glass container, then add the grapes, whole. Combine the seasonings with the rice wine vinegar and pour into the glass container. Cap and allow to age for 4 to 5 days. Label.

HACKBERRY VINEGAR

$\frac{1}{2}$ cup ripe berries
$1\frac{1}{2}$ cups vinegar

6 peppercorns
1 tsp. lemon juice

Scald the ripe berries for a few seconds, then pour into a selected glass container. Combine the seasonings and the vinegar. Pour into glass container, and cap. Allow to sit for 3 to 5 days to age. Label.

HACKBERRY VINAIGRETTE

$\frac{1}{2}$ cup ripe berries
$1\frac{1}{2}$ cups vinegar
1 tsp. grated orange rind

pinch salt
pinch pepper
pinch dry mustard

Scald the ripe berries and place in a selected glass container. Combine the remaining ingredients, mix well, and pour into the glass container. Cap and allow to sit for 3 to 5 days to age properly. Label.

HAZELNUT DRESSING

$\frac{1}{2}$ cup ground hazelnuts
$\frac{1}{3}$ cup minced celery leaves
1 tbsp. minced onion

$\frac{1}{2}$ cup melted butter
1 clove garlic, minced
nutmeg to season

Combine all the ingredients except the nutmeg. Allow to warm gently over a very low heat for 20 to 30 minutes. Sprinkle with nutmeg and serve with fish or beef. Serves 4 to 5 folks. Store in a selected glass container in the refrigerator.

HICKORY NUT DRESSING

½ cup ground hickory nut meats	salt and pepper to taste
	1 minced garlic clove
1¼ cups oil	2 tbsp. vinegar
2 tbsp. lemon juice	2 tbsp. white wine

Mix together all the ingredients and serve as a dressing for vegetable salad. Yields about 1½ cups. Store in a selected glass container, in the refrigerator.

HOBBLEBUSH VINEGAR

½ cup ripe berries	pinch salt
1½ cups cider vinegar	pinch garlic salt

Scald the ripe berries and mix with the vinegar, salt, and garlic salt. Mix thoroughly. Pour into selected glass container, cap, and allow to sit for 8 to 10 days to age. Label.

HOBBLEBUSH VINAIGRETTE

½ cup ripe berries	1½ cups wine vinegar
1 tsp. grated lemon rind	1 tsp. sugar
½ tsp. Worcestershire sauce	

Scald the ripe berries and combine with the remaining ingredients. Mix thoroughly. Pour into a selected glass container, and cap. Allow to sit for 8 to 10 days to age. Label.

MANZANITA VINEGAR

½ cup ripe berries
1½ cups vinegar
1 tsp. lemon juice

Scald the ripe fruit for a few seconds, combine with the vinegar and lemon juice and mix thoroughly. Pour into a selected glass container, and cap. Allow to sit for 5 days to age. Label.

MANZANITA VINAIGRETTE

½ cup ripe berries
1 tbsp. oil
1 tsp. grated orange
  or lemon rind

pinch salt and pepper
1½ cups balsamic vinegar
1 tbsp. sugar

Scald the ripe berries and combine with the remaining ingredients. Mix well. Pour into selected glass container and cap. Store for 5 to 6 days to age. Label.

MUSTARD VINEGAR

⅓ cup mustard seed
1½ cups vinegar
1 tsp. oil

Place the mustard seed in the selected glass bottle. Add in the oil and vinegar of choice, and cap. Allow to sit for 1 to 2 days to age.

MUSTARD VINAIGRETTE

⅓ cup mustard seed	1 tbsp. oil
1½ cups white wine vinegar	1 tbsp. grated lemon rind
1 tsp. sugar	pinch salt and pepper

Combine the ingredients and pour into a selected glass container, and cap. Allow to sit for 3 to 4 days to age. Label.

MUSTARD DRESSING

1 tbsp. crushed seeds	2 tbsp. chicken bouillon broth
¼ cup cider vinegar	½ cup sesame oil

Combine the ingredients and mix thoroughly. Pour into a selected glass container, and cap. Allow to age for 3 to 4 days. Label.

ONION (WILD) VINEGAR

½ cup small onions	1½ cups white vinegar
small bundle green leaves	pinch salt

Place the small onions and a few green leaves in a selected glass·container and add in the vinegar and salt. Cap and allow to age for 2 to 3 days.

ONION (WILD) VINAIGRETTE

1 cup green onions with stems	pinch salt
⅓ cup of oil	pinch dry mustard
1 cup white wine vinegar	2 fresh sprigs dill

Place all the ingredients in a blender and combine. Place the mixture in a selected glass container, and cap. Allow to stand for 2 to 3 days to age. Label.

ONION (WILD) STIR-FRY

1 cup green onions
1½ cups rice wine
¼ cup peanut oil
pinch tarragon

pinch salt and pepper
pinch dry mustard
1 tsp. sugar

Mix in a blender. Pour into a selected glass container, and cap. Allow to age 1 to 2 days. Label.

ONION (WILD) SAUCE

10 fresh onion stems
1 tsp. Worcestershire sauce
ground pepper to taste
1 cup olive oil

½ tsp. dry mustard
½ tsp. salt
⅓ cup rice wine

Combine and blend. Pour into a selected glass container, and cap. Allow to age for 1 to 2 days. Label.

OREGON GRAPE VINEGAR

½ cup ripe berries
½ tsp. sugar
1½ cups vinegar

Place the ripe berries in a selected glass container. Add in the vinegar and sugar. Cap and allow to age for 1 day. Label.

OREGON GRAPE VINAIGRETTE

½ cup ripe berries	pinch salt
1½ cups white vinegar	1 tsp. sugar
1 tsp. lemon juice	3 tbsp. oil

Place the berries in the selected glass container. Add in the remaining ingredients, and cap. Allow to age for 1 day. Label.

PEPPERMINT VINEGAR

3 to 4 sprigs fresh mint
pinch salt
2 cups white wine vinegar

Place in a blender and combine. Run the mix through a sieve and strain out the pulp. Place three fresh sprigs of peppermint in a selected glass bottle. Add in the juicy sauce, and cap. Allow to age for 1 to 2 days. Label.

PEPPERMINT VINAIGRETTE

3 to 4 sprigs fresh mint	pinch salt
2 cups white wine vinegar	1 tsp. sugar
2 tbsp. oil	1 to 2 drops food coloring

Place all the ingredients except the food coloring in a blender and mix. Strain the mixture through a sieve. Place 3 to 4 four fresh mint sprigs in the selected glass bottle and add in the juicy pulp. Cap and allow to age for 1 to 2 days.

RASPBERRY VINEGAR

1/2 cup ripe fruit
2 to 3 fresh raspberry leaves
1 1/2 cups white vinegar

Place the fruit into selected glass container. Add in the vinegar and then carefully place in the fresh leaves. Cap and allow to age for 1 to 2 days.

RASPBERRY VINAIGRETTE

1/2 cup ripe berries
1 1/2 cups red wine vinegar
1 tbsp. lemon juice

pinch salt and pepper
1 tsp. corn syrup
1 tbsp. soybean oil

Place the ingredients in a blender and mix. Strain through a sieve to remove the pulp. Pour into a selected glass container. Add in a few ripe berries, and cap. Allow to age for 1 to 2 days. Label.

SALAL VINEGAR

1/2 cup ripe berries
1 1/2 cups cider vinegar
pinch salt

Place the berries in a selected glass container. Add in the salt and vinegar. Cap and allow to age for 1 to 2 days.

SALAL VINAIGRETTE

½ cup ripe berries
1½ cups cider vinegar
1 tbsp. oil
pinch tumeric

pinch salt
pinch dry mustard
1 tsp. ground lemon rind

Place the ripe berries in a selected glass container. Add in the remaining ingredients, and cap. Allow to age for 1 to 2 days. Label.

STRAWBERRY VINEGAR

½ cup fresh berries
2 to 3 fresh leaves
1½ cups cider vinegar or red wine vinegar

Combine the fresh strawberries and vinegar and blend. Strain through a sieve and keep the juice. Place in a selected glass container. Add in several strawberries, then the juice and 2 to 3 fresh picked strawberry leaves. Cap and allow to age for 2 to 3 days.

SWEET BAY VINEGAR

12 fresh leaves
1½ cups red wine vinegar

Place the fresh picked bay leaves in a selected glass container and cover with vinegar. A red wine vinegar is best for flavor. Cap and allow to age for 3 to 5 days. Label.

SWEET BAY VINAIGRETTE

12 fresh leaves   **pinch salt**
red wine vinegar   **pinch parsley**

Place the fresh picked sweet bay leaves in a selected glass container. Add in the spices and then the red wine vinegar, and cap. Allow to age for 3 to 5 days.

FLAVORED OILS

I N THESE RECIPES, YOU MAY USE WHATEVER OIL YOU WISH. THE choice depends upon the use. If you are using the flavored oil for frying or stir-fry purposes, you may want to use peanut oil or soybean oil. Olive oil is another dependable option. The decision is yours to make.

BARBERRY

½ cup ripe berries
½ tsp. sugar
1½ cups olive oil

Scald the ripe berries and pour into a selected glass container. Add in the choice of olive oil and sugar. Cap and allow to age for 2 to 3 weeks. Label.

CRANBERRY

½ cup ripe berries   ½ tsp. lemon juice
1½ cups oil   ½ tsp. sugar

Scald the ripe berries and pour into a selected glass container. Add in the lemon juice and sugar, then cover with olive oil. Allow to age for 2 to 3 weeks.

CURRANTS

½ cup ripe currants
½ tsp. sugar
1½ cups oil
pinch mace

Put the ripe berries in a selected container and add in the sugar. Cover with selected oil, and cap. Allow to age for 2 to 3 weeks. Label.

FENNEL

3 sprigs fresh stem/leaves   ½ tsp. sugar
1½ cups oil   10 peppercorns

Place the sprigs of fresh fennel in a selected glass container. Add in the peppercorns, sugar, and oil to cover. Cap and allow to age for 2 to 3 weeks.

MANZANITA

½ cup ripe berries   ½ tsp. sugar
1½ cups oil   pinch nutmeg

Scald the ripe berries and place in a selected glass container. Add in the sugar and cover with oil of your choice. Cap and allow to age for 2 to 3 weeks. Label.

MULBERRY

½ cup ripe berries   ½ tsp. sugar
1½ cups oil   2 whole cloves

Place the ripe fruit in a selected glass container. Add in the sugar, whole cloves and cover with oil of your choice. Cap and allow to age for 2 to 3 weeks. Label.

MUSTARD

1 tsp. whole mustard seed   ½ tsp. sugar
1½ cups peanut oil   pinch salt

Add the ripe berries to the selected glass container. Separately combine the oil, sugar, and salt. Mix well. Pour into a glass container and cover the berries. Cap and allow to age for 3 to 4 weeks.

ONION

1 tbsp. minced onions   ½ tsp. sugar
pinch rosemary   1½ cups oil

You may use fresh onions or dried onion flakes. Place the onion in a selected glass container and add in the sugar, rosemary, and oil. Cap and allow to age for 2 to 3 weeks. Label.

SWEET BAY

12 fresh sweet bay leaves
oil to fill container

Place the fresh leaves in a selected glass container and cover with oil to the top of the jar. Cap and allow to age for 2 to 3 weeks. Label.